Whoop - Up Country

Whoop-Up Country

The Canadian-American West, 1865–1885

by Paul F. Sharp

with drawings by CHARLES M. RUSSELL

UNIVERSITY OF OKLAHOMA PRESS : NORMAN

Library of Congress Cataloging in Publication Data

Sharp, Paul Frederick, 1918–
  Whoop-up country.

  Bibliography: p.
  1. Frontier and pioneer life—Northwestern States.
  2. Frontier and pioneer life—Northwest, Canadian.
  3. United States—Relations (General) with Canada.
  4. Canada—Relations (General) with the United States.
  I. Title.
  F597.S53   1973   978   73–3166

TO MY MOTHER AND FATHER
WHO SHARED THEIR LOVE FOR THE WEST
WITH THEIR CHILDREN

Three thousand miles of borderline,—
nor fort nor armed host
On all this frontier neighbor-ground
from east to western coast . . .

Our Borderline
AUTHOR UNKNOWN

Acknowledgments

THIS book has benefited greatly from the generosity of numerous scholars, librarians, and archivists. Visits to the Historical Society of Montana library in Helena were always a pleasure and a profit due to the western hospitality and enthusiastic cooperation of Director K. Ross Toole. Miss Marguerita McDonald and Miss Virginia Walton of the society's staff were especially helpful in finding fugitive materials, while Mr. Michael Kennedy's wit and wisdom smoothed over many rough spots.

I am also grateful for the unfailing courtesy and assistance of the staffs of the Provincial Library of Alberta, the Minnesota Historical Society, the libraries of the Universities of Alberta and Saskatchewan, the Wisconsin Historical Society, the Public Archives of Canada, and the National Archives in Washington. Miss Lucile Kane of the Minnesota Historical Society and Mr. Wilfred Smith of the Public Archives of Canada deserve particular mention for their interest in this study.

To Commissioner L. H. Nicholson, M.B.E., of the Royal Canadian Mounted Police I am indebted for permission to use the files of the police, and to Staff Sergeant D. G. Kells of Central Registry I am particularly grateful for valuable assistance.

Professional colleagues have been extremely helpful in their reading of the manuscript. Their assistance has enabled me to make this book somewhat less imperfect than it would otherwise have been. To Professor Earl S. Pomeroy of the University of Oregon and to Professors Alice Felt Tyler and Rodney C. Loehr of the University of Minnesota who read the entire manuscript I owe many useful suggestions. To my colleagues of the University of Wisconsin Professors Merle Curti and Vernon Carstensen I am also in debt for assistance in portions which they read. Above all, I gratefully acknowledge a deep obligation to Mrs. Anne Mac-Donnell, for many years librarian of the Historical Society of Montana, whose extensive knowledge of northern plains history saved me from many pitfalls and whose keen insights opened many understandings.

Two grants-in-aid from the Social Science Research Council made possible the extensive travel required to gather the scattered materials for this international study. Substantial assistance from the University of Wisconsin Research Committee hastened the completion of the book.

P. F. S.

Introduction

THIS is a fascinating book of regional American history. It is authentic, poetic and sympathetic, skillfully researched, beautifully written; a rare combination, indeed, whether in historiographic discipline or literature. It proves that facts may be more fascinating than fiction — a sometime cliché that generally holds unerringly true as regards Western Americana.

Almost a century ago this region's fabled Whoop-Up Country was an isolated, many-thousand-square-mile empire thinly spread over huge chunks of what today comprises much of Montana, U.S.A., and the great Canadian provinces of Alberta and Saskatchewan. The tenuous lifeline of this bilingual, international frontier was the always dangerous, often terrifying 240 miles of Whoop-Up Trail north from historic Fort Benton, Montana Territory. Despite sparse population and only a fleeting life-span, the Whoop-Up Trail and Whoop-Up Country produced more drama, human and animal conflict, and "story" than most regions ever attain. This vast buffalo land, it so happened, was fascinatingly peopled by the broadest assortment of Old West frontier characters imaginable: whiskey-traders, wolfers, robe hunters, painted ladies, renegades, bull-whackers, do-gooders, breeds, missionaries, hurdy-gurdy gals, red coats, U.S. marshals, merchant princes, cowboys and cowmen, plus a huge mélange of both savage and peaceable Red Men. Paul Sharp does justice to every facet of this all-encompassing portrait; the frontiersmen and their deeds synthesize into one of the most stimulating and colorful episodes in the annals of western history.

When one adds to this Dr. K. Ross Toole's edict: "This is a brilliantly written study which covers an immense field, yet never loses itself in generalizations; which contributes more to Montana history and the history of the Northern Great Plains than anything we've read in a long, long time . . ." it would seem that ample justification for keeping this book in the mainstream of Americana had already been established. Yet there is more to it than this.

First off, the unimpeachable talents of Charles M. Russell, who knew and loved Whoop-Up Country, lend themselves so harmoniously to the text that one might feel that C.M.R. had Paul Sharp's book in mind when he did the illustrations — some of them more than half a century ago — which appear here.

Personally, I respectfully call your attention to another dimension. Along with many Americans I have long been a devotee of Stephen Vincent Benét and his productive fascination with poetic and peculiar American names. What a field day Benét would have had with this. For example:

Forts: Not only named Whoop-Up, but Robbers' Roost, Spitzee, Standoff, Whiskey Gap, Slideout and Piegan Post. Such stark as well as euphonious landmarks and place names as: Belly River, Medicine Hat, Cow Island, York Factory, Wood Mountain, Cypress Hills, Eighteen Mile Coulee, Camp Disappointment, Bear's Paw Mountains, Big Alkali Flat, Sweetgrass and Pilgrim Creeks. Saloons called "Extradition," "Jungle," and "Medicine Lodge."

Indians (to mention a few): Pretty Bear, Crazy Horse, White Bird, Sitting Bull, Red Tomahawk, Four Horns, Medicine Bear, White Dog, Man-who-crawls, Crazy Bull, Flying Bird, Mountain Chief, Little Dog, Long Dog and Star Child.

But best of all, the names of the others — the big and the little, the bad and the good characters — who populated this fantastic rawhide frontier: every race, every color, every creed. No fiction writer could do better than simply pick characters from this splendid potpourri: Waxey Weatherwax, Guido Ilges, Major Martin Maginnis, Lt. Col. Acheson Irvine, J. Vital Turcotte, Adams Archibald, Kamoose Taylor, Moses Solomon, Crazy Vielle, Abel Farwell, Nat Banks, Lt. Gov. Dewdney, Winfield Scott Stocking, X. Biedler, Col. Patrick Robertson-Ross, Bedrock Jim, Philander Vogel, The 4th Earl of Carnavon H. H. Molyneaux-Herbert, Jerry Potts, Trevanian Hale, Johnnie Healy, Isaac G. Baker, Alexis Lebompard, Jos. Laverdure, Marquis R.A.T. Gascoyne-Cecil, and such men of the cloth as Brother Van and Fr. Martin Marty. These are the actual names of some of the real life people who give a storybook impact to Paul Sharp's scholarly treatise.

MICHAEL KENNEDY

Helena, Montana

Contents

xv

Illustrations

BETWEEN PAGES 44 AND 45

Fort Benton in 1862 was not yet the "Chicago of the Plains"

In 1874 Fort Macleod was an "atom of settlement in a wilderness"

Front Street, photographed in 1871, was for a time the town's only thoroughfare

To Benton's mile-long levee came supplies for an inland empire

Merchant princes of Benton — Isaac G. Baker, Thomas C. Power, William G. Conrad

The Diamond R muletrain winds through Prickly Pear Canyon, Montana

Wagonmaster Pres Lewis hoists "one for the road"

Wagontrains carried the commerce of the plains from Benton to distant points

The Concord coach, a "marvel of nineteenth-century craftsmanship"

"From sunrise until evening the caravan of wagons rolled on"

This interior of Sawtell's ranch was typical of the period

Ranching in the shadows of the Rockies

CONTENTS

xvii

The Illustrative Art of Charles M. Russell

Single Handed, famous 1912 oil painting by C. M. Russell depicting the Royal Canadian Mounted Police, the original of which is in the William Wadsworth Memorial Collection, Findlay Galleries, 320 S. Michigan Avenue, Chicago. Permission granted by Walstein C. Findlay, Jr. All rights reserved. Dust jacket

All others are from the originals, Charles M. Russell Room, Historical Society of Montana; and from the photographic files, State Historical Library, Historical Society of Montana, Helena.

CONTENTS

Whoop-Up Country

1

Trail to the North

TODAY'S tourists traveling northward on U.S. Highway 91 from Great Falls, Montana, to visit the Calgary Stampede or Banff and Lake Louise speed through a vast plain of wheat and grass. Though little remains to remind them of its past, they are passing through a region that pioneers called the Whoop-Up country and their modern hard-surfaced highway parallels the Whoop-Up Trail, a colorful and useful avenue of commerce and a high road of adventure in the years before the railways crossed the western plains.

Despite its rowdy name, this half-forgotten highway once brought trade and culture into a great interior market stretching northward from the Missouri River to the Bow River valley. From Fort Benton on the Great Muddy to Fort Macleod on the Oldman, it reached into the north, writing its history in whisky, guns, furs, freight, and pioneer enterprise.

This trail commands attention, for it was an international highway, neatly bisected by the Canadian-American boundary that marches steadily westward along the forty-ninth parallel with the precision of the surveyor's chain. But to the first settlers on both sides of this man-made boundary, the trail symbolized the economic, social, and cultural ties that for many years defied a politically inspired division of the northern plains. C. E. D. Wood, editor of the Fort Macleod *Gazette*, expressed this sentiment in the first issue of his little newspaper: "And to our American cousins in Montana; to our brother frontiersmen over the way, whose boundary touches our own, and whose in-

3

terests are so similar and allied to ours, to them we shall look for the patronage which they always extend to a new enterprise, trusting that the *Gazette* may make one more of the many bonds and ties already joining the two greatest countries in the world." [1]

Local historians in the United States have painstakingly searched out the stories of less important and less colorful thoroughfares and highway commissions have proudly and expensively marked their routes. The Whoop-Up Trail, however, faded into obscurity as grass healed the deeply rutted wounds on the plains and as time dimmed the recollections of those who remembered.

The story of this northern trail disappeared beyond an international boundary where for many years it was only a chapter in western Canadian history. Yet for a quarter of a century it was a main artery into the western plains, carrying thousands of tons of freight to government installations, Northwest Mounted Police posts, United States Army camps, cattle ranches, and Indian reservations. Along its dusty tracks rode Indians searching for game or plunder, scarlet-jacketed Mounties seeking enemies of the Queen, blue-coated United States cavalrymen preserving order, greedy whisky traders violating laws of God and man in their lust for profits, and ambitious traders seeking likely sites for their short-lived trading posts. In its boom years between 1874 and 1885, this trail carried one third of all the freight handled through Fort Benton and enriched Montana merchants with profits drained from Canada.[2]

The Whoop-Up Trail thus represented an economic intrusion and a "peaceful penetration" of cultural influence from the south that colored Canadian-American relations during these years. Many Americans hopefully viewed this development as a prelude to economic absorption and political annexation, while patriotic Canadians feared and resented it as a menace to their economic and political expansion. To them the trail symbolized a Manifest Destiny quietly penetrating the outer edge of the Empire, binding it with firm economic ties to the ambitious American republic.

TRAIL TO THE NORTH

Fort Benton in the post-Civil War years was the hub of an overland transportation network radiating as spokes in a giant wheel to the busy gold fields along the circumference of North American civilization. Through the treeless, dusty streets of this frontier village moved the commerce of the continental heartland.

To supply freight for these trails, toylike, shallow-draft sternwheelers fought their way up the Great Muddy, as capricious a watercourse as commerce ever forced to do its will. Senator Ingalls' famous description, "a little too thick for a beverage and a little too thin for cultivation," paid tribute to its dirty waters. The upper river was especially dangerous, for treachery lay under the shallow, murky waters in shifting sand bars, constantly changing channels, and the countless snags on which the fragile "Mountain" boats might be "stove in" without warning.

Perched at the head of navigation, Fort Benton was an unusual frontier town. "Chicago of the Plains" the village proudly called itself — "the door through which the country to the east, west and north of it was entered." [3] Eastern pilgrims always watched with mingled emotions the motley crowds that greeted their boat as it nosed into the wharf, for there stood merchants in high-collared broadcloth coats, French-Canadian and Creole rivermen wearing bright-colored sashes, tough trappers and traders heavily armed and wearing buckskin, bullwhackers and muleskinners in coarse, rough denim, and, in the background, red savages wearing leggings and blankets.

This diverse collection of humanity was eloquent testimony that Fort Benton was the most cosmopolitan city on the plains. Through this inland port passed pious missionaries and hunted desperadoes, merchants and gamblers, American soldiers and British policemen, hopeful land-seekers and speculators, miners, roustabouts, muleskinners, bullwhackers, and cowboys. Immigrants from nearly every nation of Europe visited it, as well as wanderers from China and Negroes from the Deep South.

The human stream pouring through Fort Benton was a con-

Whoop-Up country

stant reminder that the northern plains were the commercial hinterland of the proud little river town. With justifiable enthusiasm, the local editor could claim that his little village "commands the traffic of the country, holds the key to the business houses of the Territory . . . [is the] transportation centre of Montana." [4] With the opening of the Canadian plains, the country to the north was regarded as an addition to Fort Benton's territory — "a vast expanse of country . . . extending into Her Majesty's dominions, its natural and permanent tributary." [5]

Two hundred and forty miles northwest of Fort Benton lay Fort Macleod, northern terminus of the Whoop-Up Trail. Snakelike, the trail crawled out of Benton along the banks of the Teton River to the Whoop-Up crossing on Captain Nelse's ranch; then it struck out across the plains, passing Pen d'Oreille Spring and Yeast Powder Flat, to cross the Marias River near old Fort Conrad. Northward the trail swept past Rocky Springs in northern Montana to enter Canada near present-day Sweetgrass. In Canadian territory the trail forded the Milk River and split into three routes: the eastern branch to Nicholas Sheran's coal banks at modern Lethbridge, the central route to Fort Hamilton or Fort Whoop-Up, and the western route across the St. Mary River at Slideout to Fort Macleod.

Fort Macleod was even less pretentious than Fort Benton, for it was but an atom of settlement in an empty grassland wilderness. Smothered under great clouds of dust from the wheels of busy wagon trains in the summer and buried in seas of mud in spring and autumn, the tiny village seemed the end of civilization to those who ventured up the Whoop-Up Trail to its extremity.

The island site originally selected for Fort Macleod was an unfortunate one, for the community annually faced destruction as high waters from the mountains threatened to wash everything down stream. "Each succeeding Springtime," dryly observed the *Gazette*, "the betting is almost even that the whole concern, Fort, town and inhabitants will form a stately procession on the watery road to Winnipeg." [6]

Despite these unpropitious surroundings, the little Canadian village was an important economic and political center. Here the Mounted Police made their first headquarters in the West and through its streets moved supplies for police, ranchers, and Indians of the Canadian plains. Up the trail from Fort Benton flowed the lifeblood of this western community.

III

Just as the Whoop-Up Trail symbolized the unity of this northern grassland empire, its history demonstrates a centuries-long period of economic, cultural, and political interdependence imposed by geographic integrity. Here on the northern plains, the two great streams of Anglo-Saxon pioneering that had pushed across the continent finally reached their last west in the same environment.

But similarity does not imply identity. Environment never shapes advanced human societies entirely to its will. Other forces are equally important, and often more important. Certainly, significant differences marked the two national communities that developed along the Whoop-Up Trail. Though poured into the same plains environment, the two societies centered at Fort Benton and Fort Macleod retained their separate political and cultural identities.

Many extraregional relationships and many heritages from older societies were far too powerful to be affected by environment. Nationalism, the most pervasive force in our modern world, was unaffected by its movement into this semiarid and treeless plains country. It created Canadian plainsmen to the north and American plainsmen to the south. Each possessed loyalties reaching outside the region that prevented a complete identification of common problems. Thus nationalism achieved in the generation following the American Civil War what nature could not accomplish in millenniums; it gave reality to a political line that bisected a region of geographic unity.

Nature created a grassland region possessing a unity and integrity that its aboriginal inhabitants respected. The white man's politics rent it asunder to create highly complex societies whose orientation was changed from a north-south to an east-west axis. The decades during which these great changes were in the making were the years of the Whoop-Up Trail. Its story is the exciting one of creating Canadian and American institutions cheek by jowl in the West. Two societies so similar, yet so different that only a most cautious judgment can calculate the parallels or measure the differences. Society on these northern plains, Canadian and American, was the heir of many cultures, the image and transcript of none.

2

The Timeless Land

THIS was a land of grass, grass that rolled away like a carpet as far as the eye could see and stretched out to the limits of the imagination. The Whoop-Up country lay at the northern extremity of the Great Plains, one of earth's most extensive grassland regions.

This northern Great Plains region comprises an area of 300,000 square miles, of which roughly one half lies in Canada. With its base resting on the Pine Ridge escarpment near the Nebraska–South Dakota boundary and its apex reaching the forested Park Belt of mid-Alberta and Saskatchewan, the region includes most of six western states and much of three prairie provinces. Its eastern boundary is that indefinite zone of transition in which the hundredth meridian has become the symbol of the changing characteristics distinguishing it from the prairies of the Middle West, while to the west the foothills of the Rockies form a major physiographical boundary.[1]

The region is sometimes identified with the southern High Plains. But its rolling terrain, grotesquely eroded badlands, wind-scarred buttes, deeply trenched river valleys, numerous mountain groups, and glacially created surfaces contrast markedly with the level topography of the southern plains. Differences in soils, mean temperatures, rainfall, rates of evaporation, and plant and animal life further emphasize the dissimilarity. "The higher latitudes certainly differ widely from the plains which stretch from the Platte southward to the Llano Estacado of Texas . . ." observed Professor John Macoun as early as 1882.[2]

THE TIMELESS LAND

For centuries explorers sought an ocean passage across North America to the wealth of the Indies. Limited geographic knowledge, faulty logic, and everlasting hope led them on. "Geographers of that period erred only in the description of the ocean which they placed in the central continent," wrote the British explorer Captain William F. Butler, "for an ocean there is . . . But the ocean is one of grass." [3]

Captain Meriwether Lewis, first American to describe this northern region, fell naturally into the use of nautical language as he recorded his journey across the plains between the Teton and Marias rivers. In his famous journal he wrote on July 17, 1806: "I steered my course through the wide and level plains which have somewhat the appearance of an ocean, not a tree nor a shrub to be seen." [4]

The ocean figure of speech became a favorite cliché, repeated endlessly by those who visited the plains. The undulating swells rolling away to distant horizons like restless waves, the vast solitudes resembling the ocean wastes, the unlimited vision of the daylight hours and the myriads of bright stars during the night watches suggested the ocean environment, even to unimaginative travelers.

II

This was the timeless land. The first explorers from forested North America found its unbroken solitudes depressing, while its vast emptiness filled them with a sense of timelessness. Later travelers, armed with scientific techniques denied their predecessors, read the signs of age and change more precisely. Nature had taken her time in fashioning this region, and had left her processes clearly marked in geological formations.

A hundred million years ago the Whoop-Up country was a shallow sea. Gradually an uplifting movement raised the nearby Belt Mountains above the surrounding waters and elevated the sea floor sufficiently to create great stretches of low-lying lands and marshes.

Stability was not a geological feature of this northern region. A gradual depression of the area covered it with another shallow sea. Later, during the Cretaceous period, the floor re-emerged to form lowlands pocketed with shallow lakes and swamps. In these, semitropical ferns and rushes grew luxuriantly. Ages later, these plants furnished materials for the coal beds so common along the streams of the Whoop-Up country from the Missouri River to the South Saskatchewan.

Along the shores of these ancient lakes roamed huge, armored reptiles, saber-toothed tigers, and the last of the dinosaurs. Flying reptiles, three-toed horses, and other primitive fauna competed for survival in these lush surroundings. But they could not adjust to the great climatic and environmental changes of later geological periods and perished.

These vast oscillations alternately submerging and elevating the land in the shallow seas ended with a final uplifting movement that drained the entire region. Well-preserved fossils, sharks' teeth, and numerous shells remain to attest the region's long life under the seas, while similar rock formations along the Missouri and Belly rivers confirm the geological unity of the region.

To the west, subterranean fires and deep unrest disturbed the area. Volcanic action, architect of towering mountains and of deep valley troughs, now fractured the earth's crust. Masses of rock formed high ridges, wrinkles in the earth's surface comprising a cordillera for the continent. On the southern edge of the Whoop-Up country, but east of the Rockies, lie the Highwood Mountains. These extinct volcanoes, dissected by wind and water, stand as picket lines thrown out by the massive formations farther west.

Only yesterday, as geologists reckon time, the region received its last great face lifting. In the Pleistocene age, less than one hundred thousand years ago, the continental icecap moved south. Huge ice sheets covered the region to the Missouri River. Grinding, pushing, leveling as they moved, the ice masses acted like giant bulldozers, filling the depressions and covering the entire area with a mantle of glacial debris.

Their actions, however, were uneven. Forward thrusts were followed by retreats. Along these edges of advance the glaciers left mounds of debris, or moraines. At the farthest edge of advance, reached thirty thousand years ago somewhat south of the Missouri River, lies a well-defined frontal moraine. Here, large quartzite and limestone boulders, identical with Canadian rocks two hundred miles north, eloquently testify to the glaciers' force and action.

Early explorers were hard pressed to explain the prehistoric disturbance that had accomplished this earth-moving task. The Whoop-Up country's first great explorer, the brilliant surveyor David Thompson of the Hudson's Bay Company, realized that the soils had been deposited by an outside force. But he believed this powerful agent was "a great flood of water from the gulph of Mexico." This flood poured northward denuding the southern plains to leave only "sand and rounded gravel for a soil" and depositing its rich load on the northern plains.[5] Thompson's hypothesis, of course, not only replaced ice with water, but reversed the direction of the movement. It was nevertheless a shrewd guess.

The Whoop-Up country was a glacially created plain. Chestnut and brown soils, underlain by loosely consolidated sandstones and clay shales, comprise the earth carpet from which grew the universal grass cover. To Canadians this is part of the third prairie steppe; to Americans it is the short grass plains.[6]

Two great river systems, the Missouri and the South Saskatchewan, drain this high border country. To the north, the Bow River flows southeast from the Columbia ice fields, gathering mountain-born streams as it hurries along. These modest streams, the Highwood, Little Bow, Belly, Oldman, and St. Mary, unite to form the South Saskatchewan and flow eastward eventually to reach Hudson Bay.

Far to the south at Three Forks, Montana, the Missouri begins its tortuous 2462-mile journey to the Father of Waters. Turning eastward after clearing the mountains through Captain Lewis' famous "Gates of the Mountains," the river parallels the course of its northern rival. Fast-flowing streams, fed by melting snows in nearby mountains, reinforce the Missouri on its passage through the northern plains. The Sun, Teton, Marias, and Milk rivers lace the Whoop-Up country with a network of eastward flowing rivers.

These northern streams, unlike those of the southern plains, cut deep valleys into the soft, unconsolidated subsoil of the glacial drifts. Often those canyons are four to six hundred feet deep, with steep walls so sharply cut that the breaks in the plains are recognizable only within a short distance from the rivers. Lateral ravines, etched into the plains by smaller streams, form rounded buttes or terraced ridges, so familiar to western travelers as "badlands."

Erosion along the river banks created formations that excited imaginative explorers to visualize massive castles, equipped with buttresses, towers, domes, and parapets. Captain Lewis, one of the first to describe the beauty of these creations, set a literary pattern unconsciously copied by scores of later travelers.

"The hills and river Clifts which we passed today," wrote Lewis in his journals, "exhibit a most romantic appearance. The bluffs of the river rise to the hight of from 2 to 300 feet and in most places nearly perpendicular . . . The water in the course of time . . . has trickled down the soft sand clifts and woarn it into a thousand grotesque figures, which with the help of a little imagination and an oblique view, at a distance are made to represent eligant ranges of lofty freestone buildings, having their parapets well stocked with statuary; collumns of various sculpture both grooved and plain, are also seen supporting long galleries in front of these buildings . . ."[7]

More important than these scenic erosions were the rich alluvial flood plains deposited along the shores of the rivers. Fine silts, transported by high waters during spring floods, formed the rich "bottom lands" in which grew thickets of willows and groves of stately cottonwood trees. On these flood plains the region's first farmers cultivated hay and forage crops as well as vegetables and small grains.

Soils on the surrounding plains and benchlands, however, do not match these bottom lands. Though generally brown soils of unquestioned fertility, frequent stretches of sandy or gravelly soils occur. Moreover, the low rainfall of the region permits "alkali lands" to develop as ground waters fail to carry off the soluble mineral matter. These accumulate because of the rapid evaporation of surface moisture, which leaves white coatings of sodium or potassium as a crust or a powder in the "alkali flats."

Scarcity of rainfall gave an inescapable unity to the region. From earliest explorations onward this fact dominated travelers' reports, whether Canadian or American. The first accurate measurements of rainfall in the region were kept by the United States Army engineers. Their records revealed a mean annual rainfall from 1870 to 1874 of 11.42 inches, while between 1875 and 1878 the mean rose to 17.61 inches. By 1880 the chief engineer of the Department of Dakota concluded: "The mean average of this region is very small, probably not over 15 inches, this small amount in spite of many fertile valleys and rich prairie lands, will I fear, always condemn it to the comparative sterility of the Great American Desert." [8]

Great American Desert! Few terms in American history have caused so much confusion. Explorers used the term loosely, some implying only that the region was uninhabited or deserted, others that it lacked forest cover, while a minority regarded it a barren wasteland similar to the Sahara.

American experience on the southern and central plains fixed the desert name to the entire country from Mexico to mid-Alberta. Reports from army officers, railroad surveyors, and scientists confirmed fur traders' observations that the region was a desert — that is, treeless, or unoccupied, or uninhabitable, or barren, or simply different from the well-watered forest areas from which they came. The railroad surveys conducted between 1853 and 1856, in particular, confirmed the Great American Desert concept by emphasizing the difficulties of constructing and maintaining a transcontinental line through these desert portions of the continent that would never be occupied by settlers. [9]

This imprecision of terms was matched by British and Canadian explorers north of the international boundary. Captain John Palliser, more than any other explorer, fixed the desert concept in Canadian thinking. His journals frequently spoke of "arid prairies" along the forty-ninth parallel where his party was "in great want of water, and the heat was very great while travelling through burning sand." [10]

Palliser concluded that the Great American Desert reached into Canada to form a giant triangle. For years, succeeding writers cited "Palliser's Triangle" as a desert stretching from the international boundary to the fifty-second parallel between the hundredth meridian and the mountains. Many Canadians accepted the view that this region would be "forever comparatively useless." [11]

Captain Palliser's judgments were influenced by earlier American observations. He quoted frequently from the railway surveys, approving the statement that "in the central part of the continent there is a region, desert or semi-desert in character, which can never be expected to become occupied by settlers."

Canadian and British writers, in general, followed earlier American judgments. Henry Youle Hind, for example, quoted Dr. Joseph Henry of the Smithsonian Institution to prove that the entire region between the ninety-eighth meridian and the mountains "is a barren waste, over which the eye may roam to the extent of the visible horizon with scarcely an object to break the monotony." [12]

On both sides of the boundary the desert concept received support from those who opposed the rapid settlement of the region. Professor James C. Malin's observation that opponents of settlement welcomed hostile definitions of the plains environment [13] is amply borne out by the vigorous efforts of the fur trading companies, especially the Hudson's Bay Company, to picture the Whoop-Up country a barren land, incapable of supporting farmers or of agricultural development.

The myth of the desert was never universally accepted. Some explorers, rejecting it completely, used language creating an opposite myth, that of the Western Garden. Captain Lewis grew lyrical as he described the Whoop-Up country when he saw it in June 1805 along the Marias River. This "noble river," wrote the great explorer, "passes through a rich fertile and one of the most beautifully picturesque countries that I ever beheld, through the wide expanse of which, innumerable herds of living animals are seen, its borders garnished with one continued garden of roses . . ." [14]

Other climatic features contributed to the geographic unity of the region. This was the land of the chinooks, those warm, dry winds that pour down from the mountains during the winter. Unlike any phenomenon of the southern plains, they transform the coldest winter days with springlike temperatures in a few hours.

Western explorers expressed astonishment at the suddenness of temperature changes effected by these winds. Captain Palliser experienced a chinook in the Bow River valley early in December 1858; the snow vanished so quickly that his dog sleds were immobilized. Army officers at Fort Benton recorded chinooks that lasted as long as twenty days with winds reaching gale velocities.

Chinooks influenced the life of the region almost as much as aridity. Warm winds in winter cleared the plains of ice-encrusted snow, keeping the grass exposed for grazing buffalo and, later, for cattle and sheep. Temperature elevations of sixty degrees in a few hours "licked up the snow" and made raging torrents of rivers only recently covered with ice.

The severity of northern winters was considerably modified by these foehnlike winds, and mean annual temperatures were more equable than those in comparable latitudes farther east. Fort Benton's mean temperature of 45° F. compared favorably with Fort Snelling's (St. Paul, Minnesota) 39° F. Isotherms bend northward as they move west; thus the January normal temperature isotherm that passes through southern Iowa and central Illinois swings through the Whoop-Up country.

Army engineers reported in 1880 that comparative mean temperatures along the forty-seventh and forty-ninth parallels were several degrees higher in the northern plains than in the Middle West. Spring at Fort Edmonton, nearly four hundred miles north of the international boundary, came several days earlier than at the forty-ninth parallel in the Red River valley. With these findings, the chief engineer of the Department of Dakota concluded that temperatures in this region were "more equable and, therefore, the climate more desirable." [15]

But these statistics do not reveal the range of temperatures. In this the northern plains demonstrate extreme fluctuations. Summer readings of 104° F. to 110° F. are reached, while winter readings of −30° F. are not uncommon.

Extremes in temperatures are matched by violent storms of wind and hail in summer and blizzards with driving sleet and snow in winter. "Nowhere have I encountered one in such perfection as on the plains," wrote the distinguished British geographer William A. Bell in describing a Whoop-Up storm. "Nowhere do the elements appear so frantic with rage. The fight seemed to us almost endless . . ." [16]

High winds and fierce hail plagued the Lewis and Clark expedition in this region. During the three weeks' camp at the Great Falls of the Missouri, storms often delayed their work. On June 29, Captain Clark, Charbonneau, and Sacajewea took refuge from a sudden storm in a deep ravine. But the rain "fell like one volley of water falling from the heavens," and nearly trapped them in their improvised shelter. Though they escaped, Clark lost his large compass — a loss he thought serious, "as we have no other large one."

Later, when the captain returned to the main camp, he discovered considerable damage. The hail and wind had knocked some of the men to the ground, while others "without hats or anything on their heads [were] bloody and complained very much." He restored their spirits with an issue of grog. [17]

A phenomenon that excited universal admiration was the beauty of the aurora borealis. Some explorers found that the brilliant, dancing colors of the northern lights defied their powers of description. Others, like the Earl of Southesk, obviously enjoyed the challenge of describing them to their readers.

"After nightfall [August 24, 1859] there was a most beautiful aurora," wrote the Earl. "Sometimes like a tent with streams proceeding earthwards and in every direction from a fixed central point, sometimes like a very grand arch stretching from east to west through Arcturus, Vega, Cygnus and the neighboring stars. Then it became a mass of glowing red, spreading over the eastern side of the heavens and gradually passing to the south." [18]

No two displays seemed alike. To Professor Henry Youle Hind they "impart a solemnity and charm to the still night, which must ever remain one of its most delightful characteristics in the region." [19] Perhaps this was because, as the Indians believed, these lights were the spirits of departed men dancing in the sky.

III

Accustomed to the forests of the humid East, explorers described the Whoop-Up country as a treeless region. Indeed, of the more than two hundred species in the humid prairies and forestlands, only twenty cross the hundredth meridian onto the plains.[20] Few characteristics of the area affected explorers as much as the absence of familiar trees. This experience often prompted their use of the word desert.

But the Whoop-Up country was not entirely treeless. Along the numerous river bottoms grew cottonwoods, as well as trees of the slender, graceful willow family. Even on the plains, explorers found occasional clumps, or bluffs as Canadians called them, of coyote willows that defied aridity and fires to survive. Once these weedlike shrubs established themselves along a sand bar or in a bottom land, other species frequently followed.

Cottonwood trees played an important role in Indian life. Leaf buds yielded a yellow dye, leaves provided forage for horses, and bark served as a remedy against alkali-tainted drinking water or as a native tea. Groves of cottonwoods provided shelters in which they pitched their lodges during the winter.

Trees also covered some of the low-lying mountains throughout the Whoop-Up country. The Cypress Hills, named by half-breeds after pines they called "Cypre," were thickly covered with willows as well.

But this was a grassland with short grass the dominant vegetation. Bunch grasses (needlegrass and wildrye), wheat grasses, and gramas covered the plains. Buffalo grass, the typical short grass of the southern and central plains, was not common in this northern region. Professor Macoun, in a detailed description of the flora of the Whoop-Up country, argued that "the true buffalo grass is unknown on our prairies, but is common in Kansas and Colorado." [21] In general, this observation was correct, though isolated patches of buffalo grass did grow on the Whoop-Up plains. Most of the grasses called "buffalo grass" by travelers were not the true buffalo grass (*buchloe dactyloides*) but were one of the gramas.

These northern grasses were winter-hardy plants possessing great drought-resistant capacities. They were mostly perennials whose deep-rooted, vigorous underground stems protected the soil from wind and water erosion. And they possessed the economically important quality of curing when they matured, thus providing good forage for grazing animals during the autumn and winter months.[22]

Why was this a grassland, lacking the extensive forest cover of eastern North America? This question challenged the region's explorers, even as it has later ecologists. Most believed that prairie fires killed the trees and pushed the grasslands deeper into the forest fringes. Others thought that poor soils and insufficient rainfall prevented tree growth. Some argued that the vast herds of buffalo destroyed the tender shoots or pulled down mature trees during their shedding period in the spring.

Most of the early explorers sought a single explanation. Few of them realized that a complex of ecological factors, including semiaridity, an uneven distribution of rainfall throughout the year, the dry, hot winds of summer, and the character of the soils, determined that grass, not trees, was the natural climax vegetation.

Typical plains fauna inhabited this grassland region. Prairie dogs, badgers, foxes, and gophers found safety in their burrowing habits. Coyotes, wolves, deer, antelope, and buffalo escaped their enemies through their speed or found security in their great numbers. The region's numerous bears, as Lewis and Clark learned to their frequent alarm, required neither speed nor burrowing habits to protect them.

Above all, this was the home of the buffalo. On the northern grasses these huge beasts flourished in numbers that amazed explorers. Efforts to estimate accurately the buffalo population before the white man seem futile; indeed, those that have been made often appear ludicrous. Explorers used vague and poetic language as they witnessed the passage of the great herds. "Far as the eye could reach," wrote the Earl of Southesk in 1859, "these plains were covered with troops of buffalo; thousands and thousands were constantly in sight." [23]

Captain Meriwether Lewis' descriptions were equally imprecise. Along the Missouri River in 1806 he wrote that "we could hear them for many miles and there are such numbers of them that there is one continual roar." Later in the Marias River valley his party passed through "immence herds of buffaloe on our way in short for about 12 miles it appeared as one herd only the whole plains and vally of this creek being covered with them . . ." [24]

One judgment about numbers seems important. There were as many buffalo in the northern as in the central or southern regions. The species did not find the northern winters unduly severe.

Europeans found it difficult to describe these "Indian cattle." Some wrote of them as "crooked back oxen," or as "humped back cattle," while others compared them to the more familiar musk ox. "What curious freaks of nature these North American buffalo are," wrote one traveler. "The small hindquarters look out of all proportion to the massive strength of the shoulders and chest; smooth, and apparently shaven, like the back of a French poodle, they do not seem to belong to the same animal . . . Thick hair, for the most part, conceals the hump from sight, but both add immensely to the massive effect of the forepart of the body: the little corkscrew tail ends in a tuft." [25]

Millions of buffalo roamed these plains, despite the destruction of many of their kind by accident, disease, or predator. Death in fast-moving grass fires, drownings in treacherous rivers swollen by spring floods or on the "rotten ice" after a chinook, and mass destruction in quicksands reduced their numbers. Indians drove the animals over cliffs, killed them in "surrounds," or captured them in "pounds." Disease took a further toll of the animals. But it remained for the white man's technology to exterminate them in the eighties.

Contrary to widespread belief, the buffalo did not make regular or long migrations from the northern to the southern plains. F. G. Roe's recent and thorough study demonstrates conclusively that the animals made only irregular and limited migrations in their search for forage and shelter.[26] The northern herds did not move south in the autumn, nor did they return with the spring flights of migratory birds.

IV

Whoop-Up country was Blackfoot country. Three tribes, the Piegans, Bloods, and Blackfeet, comprised the confederacy that was the most numerous and powerful on the northwestern plains. When first reached by explorers in the late eighteenth century, they ranged over a vast domain from the North Saskatchewan to the Missouri River. However, their expansion over this sizable territory was comparatively recent, probably dating back no farther than 1720.[27]

Of their origins, these Indians had few legends. David Thompson, who lived with the Piegans during the winter of 1787–88, sought the story of Blackfoot origins in vain. All the elder tribesmen could do to satisfy his questions was to point to the northeast as the place from which they had come.[28]

Many years later, however, Walter McClintock found traditions among the Blackfeet telling of migrations from the far north. These migrations came down the Old North Trail, the prehistoric antecedent of the Whoop-Up Trail.[29] Modern anthropological research confirms these ancient legends. Their dialect, one of the Algonkian family, reveals this background.

When the white men first reached the Blackfeet they were stone-age nomads, fashioning their material culture from stone and following the buffalo. They were truly "buffalo Indians," hunting the animals on foot, stalking them with numerous ruses, capturing them in "pounds," or driving them over steep cliffs or cutbanks.

The Blackfeet were completely reliant upon the buffalo for their subsistence. For the Indians, the huge beasts were "general stores" providing food, clothing, shelter, and equipment. One of the best descriptions of this dependence upon the buffalo was written by the missionary John McDougall, who lived with them briefly as an involuntary guest.

"These men," wrote the missionary, "were thoroughly buffalo Indians. Without buffalo they would be helpless, and yet the whole nation did not own one. To look at them and to hear them, one would feel as if they were the most independent of all men; yet the fact was they were the most dependent among men. Moccasins, mittens, leggings, shirts, and robes — all buffalo. With the sinews of the buffalo they stitched and sewed these. Their lariats, bridle, lines, stirrup-straps and saddles were manufactured out of buffalo hide. Their women made scrapers out of the legbone for fleshing hides. The men fashioned knife handles out of the bones, and the children made toboggans out of the same. The horns served for spoons and powder flasks. In short, they lived and had their physical being in the buffalo . . ."[30] He might have added that the Indians subsisted on buffalo flesh and lived in lodges made of buffalo hides.

Before the white man's intrusion into the Blackfoot world, these northern Indians were self-sufficient. There was some trading with their primitive neighbors and occasional conflicts occurred, but they lived in small, self-contained family or village groups. Social and political organization was rather more democratic than most white men imagined, though many early explorers sensed the limited authority of Blackfoot chiefs.

The Piegans, with whom David Thompson lived, had two chiefs, one for war and another for civil affairs. "The chiefs," he wrote, ". . . have no power beyond their influence, which would immediately cease by any act of authority and they are all careful not to arrogate any superiority over others." [31] Captain Palliser later found that among the Blackfeet, "the greatest chief, in his daily intercourse with his people, commands no respect beyond that which all younger Indians pay their elders." [32]

Failure to recognize this limitation on the chieftains and to understand Indian social organization led to bitter conflicts with white governments. Canadian and American authorities often acted as if the chiefs were Oriental potentates, capable of dictatorial actions and unlimited control over their people.

Indian society rested upon a community control of many essential properties. Indians lacked the highly developed sense of property ownership of European civilization. Rigid customs ruled the buffalo hunts, for example, so that families lacking hunters shared the kill equally with those possessing skilled hunters. When food grew scarce the entire band suffered, not just those who were unfortunate in food gathering. "This wild man who first welcomed the newcomer is the only perfect socialist or communist in the world," observed Captain Butler. "He holds all things in common with his tribe — the land, the bison, the river, and the moose." [33]

Religion formed the basis upon which Blackfoot life rested. The Indians worshiped the forces of nature — the sun, stars, and powerful or cunning animals. To the Blackfeet, the physical world around them was a projection of human experience and human qualities. This anthropocentric view of the physical world ascribed human qualities to inanimate as well as animate objects. Thus, the sun, rain, buffalo, coyote, or bird possessed certain powers that were the realities in the Indian's life. These powers, presided over by the Great Spirit, could be made to serve the faithful Indian through the magic of his "medicine."

Each Indian carried a medicine bag containing sacred objects. These were his magic, peculiar to his own experience and uniquely personal. Tribal religion centered around the "dreamers," whose divinations foretold coming events of importance to the band. Their warnings of enemy intentions or prophecies of favorable sites for buffalo hunts conferred upon them a significant role. Advice in matters of marriage, exchange of goods, and personal affairs further enhanced the successful prophet's standing.

Rituals, ceremonies, and dances to the accompaniment of drums, rattles, and shrill whistles expressed the religious fervor of the group. Two dances, to the buffalo and to the sun, were particularly important. Each brought the individual into harmony with his environment, cemented his ties to the tribe, and confirmed his status in the community. Through symbol and sacrament, the Indian paid tribute to the Great Spirit, that invisible power made manifest in the physical world.

Smoking the calumet was another custom of universal importance. Explorers often spoke of this as "smoking the peace pipe," but the ritual held a religious meaning of greater importance. "Smoking was the Indian Angelus and whenever its smoke ascended, men, women, and children acknowledged the sacred presence of their Big Holy." [34]

For this ceremony, the Blackfeet grew their own tobacco. This was the only plant they cultivated, but they had no record of when or how they obtained the seed. When the white man brought in the superior tobacco leaf of the Atlantic seaboard, the cultivation of the native plant fell into disuse.

v

Western civilization transformed Blackfoot society. These changes began many years before white men reached the Indians through missionaries or traders. The gun and the horse revolutionized Indian life, making hunters more effective and warriors more deadly, while at the same time enlarging the scope of their nomadic wanderings.

Horses came to the Blackfeet from their Shoshone enemies to

the south and west. Through theft and trade the descendants of Spanish horses gradually moved northward to the Shoshones at the beginning of the eighteenth century. This gave the Shoshones a decisive advantage over their neighbors and the Blackfeet retreated before their newly acquired power.

News that the Shoshones possessed the horse spread quickly across the northern plains. "Young Man," a Piegan warrior, related to David Thompson in 1787 that when he was a youth about fifty years earlier, his people had eagerly looked for the Big Dogs. "We were anxious to see a horse of which we had heard so much. At last, as the leaves were falling, we heard that one was killed by an arrow shot into his belly, but the Snake [Shoshone] Indian that rode him got away; numbers of us went to see him, and we all admired him, he put us in mind of a Stag that had lost his horns: and we did not know what name to give him. But as he was a slave to Man, like the dog, which carried our things; he was named Big Dog." [35]

To halt the advancing Shoshones, the Blackfeet turned to the Crees for help. The Crees, armed with guns obtained from Hudson's Bay Company traders at York factory, joined the Blackfeet to turn back the Shoshones about 1730. Then, mounted on horses stolen from their enemies and armed with guns secured through their friends, the Blackfeet launched an expansion that carried them deep into the territory south of the forty-ninth parallel.[36]

Smallpox also reached the Blackfeet through neighboring tribes. Ironically, they first met this dread disease while raiding their Shoshone enemies who got the infection from other Indians trading with the French. David Thompson's *Narrative* pictures vividly the desolation of the stricken Shoshone camp when the Piegans reached it. "Next morning at the dawn of day, we attacked the tents, and with our sharp flat daggers and knives, cut through the tents and entered for the fight; but our war whoop instantly stopt, our eyes were appalled with terror; there was no one to fight with but the dead and dying, each a mass of corruption. We did not touch them but left the tents, and held a council on what was to be done." [37] Greed overcame fear, however, and the Piegans plundered the camp. Within a short time, the Blackfeet were themselves victims of the disease.

Periodic outbreaks of smallpox substantially reduced their population. As many as half their number may have died during these plagues. Indian power was greatly weakened so that when the traders finally arrived about fifty years later, they faced a far less formidable confederacy. The great epidemics of 1837 and 1869 broke Blackfoot power more effectively than any weapons later used against them by white men.

Blackfoot tradition blamed the malevolence of the white traders for their tragic suffering. To their neolithic minds, these deadly epidemics were controlled by the traders. Blackfoot stories blamed the plague of 1869 upon the evil genius of an American trader who swore revenge for the loss of his horses to a raiding party. He allegedly purchased several bales of infected blankets in St. Louis and placed them on the banks of the Missouri River where innocent Indians filched them.

Indians always denounced the reappearance of the disease as a deliberate act of wicked white men. Captain Palliser, however, found in 1857 that smallpox epidemics regularly ravaged the northern Indians. Not the "malevolence of a single white man" but the normal course of the disease continued to weaken Blackfoot power. [38]

Knowledge of the Blackfoot country grew steadily during the eighteenth century. Intense international rivalry for the Indian trade and the search for the Northwest Passage forced traders and explorers into the Whoop-Up country.

From the north, Hudson's Bay Company traders pushed into the region. Anthony Henday may have reached the Blackfeet in 1754 and Matthew Cocking may also have lived with them in 1772, though in both cases their journals are vague. They could have been with the Gros Ventre rather than the Blackfeet. David Thompson lived with the Piegans in 1787 and left in his *Narrative* a sympathetic description of Blackfoot life. Even at this early date, however, Thompson found the Blackfeet were feared by their neighbors as a warlike and powerful people living "a more precarious and watchful life than other tribes, and from their boyhood are taught the use of arms, and to be good warriors." [39] Five years later, the company's Peter Fidler also lived among the Piegans along the forty-ninth parallel near the foothills of the Rockies.

From the east, resourceful French traders moved out onto the plains along the South Saskatchewan. Loss of the great war for empire in 1763 eliminated them, but Montreal merchants continued the rivalry with the Hudson's Bay Company by forming the North West Company.

To complete the triangular approach to the Whoop-Up country, the Spanish moved up the Missouri River toward the mountains. In St. Louis ambitious Spanish officials dreamed of finding the water passage to the Shining Sea in the muddy stream that reached northwest along the borders of Louisiana. Fearfully they watched their British rivals moving south onto the plains to threaten the borders of their vast province. To protect their claims and to wrest the Indian trade of the upper Missouri region from the British, they organized the Missouri Company in 1793, offering a 3000-pesos reward to the first Spaniard who reached the Russian settlements on the Pacific.[40] Three expeditions failed, but their efforts were continued by American authorities who took up the search for the water passage when Louisiana fell into their hands through Napoleon's withdrawal from North America.

VI

American concern for the Whoop-Up country preceded the Louisiana Purchase by many years. Thomas Jefferson, whose inquiring mind combined qualities of scientific curiosity with shrewd geopolitical scheming, planned the exploration of the upper Missouri country years before Louisiana became American territory. The Lewis and Clark expedition was the successful culmination of these years of planning.

In 1783, Jefferson proposed an expedition to George Rogers

Clark and in 1786 he advanced the impractical plan to send John Ledyard across Europe to North America. From Paris, Ledyard was to pass eastward across Siberia to the North American coast; then across the continent to the American settlements. Ten years after his first proposal to George Rogers Clark, the Virginian demonstrated his continuing interest in the project by planning the explorations of André Michaux on behalf of the American Philosophical Society. These plans failed, but the dream that a transcontinental route could be found to link American commerce to the China trade did not fade. Nor did his curiosity to learn what lay beyond the Father of Waters die out.

In 1801 Thomas Jefferson became President of the United States. In November 1802 he discreetly inquired of the Spanish minister if his government would approve a "small expedition" to explore the upper Missouri. Two months later he submitted his famous secret message to Congress proposing an expedition across northern Louisiana "in the interests of commerce." Incidentally, he said, the expedition would also "advance the geographical knowledge of our continent."

Political motives prompted Jefferson's keen interest in a transcontinental expedition. American westward expansion moved inexorably forward and it required no flights of fancy to foresee the day when the region would no longer be Spanish. Moreover, the region possessed an economic value in the rich furs of its animals. British expansion gave a sense of urgency to Jefferson's schemes. Already Alexander Mackenzie, dynamic personality in the Canadian fur trade and great explorer, had written in his *Voyages from Montreal* that the entire region must be British to the forty-fifth parallel.

The great prize of this Anglo-American rivalry was control of the maritime bases on the Pacific coast and the interior water passages that men still hoped drained through the cordillera into them. "The object of your mission," wrote the President in his famous instructions to Lewis and Clark, "is to explore the Missouri river, and such principal stream of it, as, by its course and communication with the waters of the Pacific Ocean, may offer the most direct and practicable water communication across this continent for purposes of commerce."

But the northern plains were more than a zone of transit. They held out the promise of a valuable trade with the natives that led Jefferson to order the expedition to gather accurate information concerning "the articles of commerce they may need or furnish, and to what extent." Cordial relations with the Indians must be cultivated so that they might know of the "peaceable and commercial dispositions of the U. S. [and] of our wish to be neighborly, friendly, and useful to them, and of our dispositions to a commercial intercourse with them."

Jefferson obviously hoped to break the British monopoly on the northern plains. His design looked to the diversion of the fur trade to the Missouri River system, which he thought shorter and more convenient.

That Lewis and Clark understood the economic and political implications of their expedition is clearly evident in their actions in the Whoop-Up country. Captain Lewis searched carefully for a northern branch of the great river that might lead into the heart of the British trading country. Significantly, he thought the river he named Marias in honor of Miss Maria Wood was destined "to become . . . an object of contention between the two great powers of America and Great Britain with respect to the adjustment of the Northwestwardly boundary of the former." To these political prophecies he added hopefully, "it will become one of the most interesting branc[h]es of the Missouri in a commercial point of view . . . and most probably furnishes a safe and direct communication to that productive country of valuable furs exclusively enjoyed at present by the subjects of his Britannic Majesty." [41]

To confirm this hope, Lewis turned northward on the return journey in 1806. With great enthusiasm he sought a river draining the region north of the fiftieth parallel and he crossed the Marias still hopeful. On Cut Bank Creek, however, he realized that this river would not take him that far north. He remained optimistic that the Milk River might serve as the avenue for

American trade from the northern fur country. Even this hope proved futile. On July 26, 1806, fearing that he might not reach the lower Missouri before winter closed in, he broke camp and headed down the Marias. His last camp he dubbed Camp Disappointment.

But greater disappointment lay ahead. Throughout its transcontinental journey, the expedition had carefully avoided trouble with the Indians. Except with the Snakes, they had carried out Jefferson's instructions to conciliate the natives. Friendly Indians warned Lewis of the hostility of the Blackfeet. Frequently, in his journals, the captain expressed thankfulness that he had avoided these aggressive Indians, and hoped that he could by-pass them. But his hopes were dashed on July 26 when he sighted a small party of Piegans along the Marias River.

Lewis did everything within his power to avoid trouble, but his luck ran out. He conferred medals upon the Indians and gave them presents from the Great White Father in Washington. Patiently he convinced them of the friendly intent of his expedition, even inviting the Indians to camp overnight with his party.

All went well around the campfire. The eight Piegans talked freely, giving Lewis information of the northern plains he eagerly sought. Conviviality between white and red seemed complete and the diplomatic captain "plyed them with the pipe untill late at night." But here Lewis made a mistake that cost the expedition dearly. When the men retired he failed to warn them properly of their danger and permitted a careless watch.

On the following morning the white men awoke to find the Indians virtually in command of the camp. While they slept, the Piegans had seized most of their guns and gave every appearance of making off with their horses. A brief fight broke out during which Reuben Fields stabbed one of the Indians and Captain Lewis shot another. The quick action of the party saved it from destruction, but the death of the two Piegans created a hatred for white men among the Blackfeet that virtually closed the Whoop-Up country to traders for thirty years.

This small fight on the Marias upset Jefferson's scheme to

open the northern plains to American commerce. If anything, it gave a further advantage to the Hudson's Bay Company, though British traders also suffered from Blackfoot hostility. Not until the 1840s were the Blackfeet conciliated sufficiently to tolerate the construction of Fort Benton by the American Fur Company.

During these decades the Blackfeet were the terror of the northern plains. Party after party of American traders suffered defeat and loss at their hands. Even after trade relations were restored they retained their reputation as troublesome and aggressive Indians. As late as 1859 Captain John Palliser's expedition nearly mutinied when his men learned of the approach of a Blackfoot band. Only the sternest actions by the British explorer kept his men from deserting.[42]

Despite this continued Blackfoot hostility, knowledge of the Whoop-Up country grew rapidly during the fifties. Railroad survey expeditions under Isaac I. Stevens gathered detailed information of the region between the forty-seventh and forty-ninth parallels, while numerous parties of gold-seekers, especially those under Captain James L. Fisk, crossed the Whoop-Up country on their way to the gold fields. Captain John Palliser's expedition collected data concerning the region north of the unmarked international boundary.

Far more was known of the American portion of the region than of the Canadian. Until the international boundary survey party of 1874 and the occupation of the Canadian West by the Northwest Mounted Police during the same year, much of the region was a blank space on Canadian maps.

Along the Missouri River a restless population of gold-seekers and free traders gathered to invade this last frontier. Their activities removed any remaining blank spots from the map of the Whoop-Up country. Fort Benton boasted many men in the sixties who knew every river and stream, every coulee and alkali flat between the Missouri River and the South Saskatchewan. But their intimate knowledge of the country was folk learning, not yet transcribed onto maps in Ottawa or Washington.

3

Invasion of the Free Traders

WITH gin, gimcracks, and gunpowder the empire builders civilized aboriginals on all the world's frontiers. The northern Great Plains were no exception to this formula of expansion so successfully applied throughout the Americas, Africa, Asia, and Australia. In common with all frontiers of European settlement since the sixteenth century, traders on this last frontier exchanged liquor for whatever of value the aboriginals possessed, whether land, gold, animals, or furs. By the time the white men carried their culture to the Indians of the Whoop-Up country, however, traders lubricated their exchange with cheap whisky or watered rum rather than gin.

In the years before the American Civil War, two great companies contended for mastery of the fur trade in the high border country. Slowly, inexorably, the Hudson's Bay Company fought its way into the Far West, led by servants who explored half a continent for their London masters — Peter Pond, Alexander Mackenzie, Henry Kelsey, David Thompson, Peter Skene Ogden, and scores of others. The irresistible lure of beaver led hard and resourceful men into bitter and violent struggles as the company fought its rivals, the North West Company and the XY Company, for the wealth of an empire. In 1821, merger ended the conflict between Canadian rivals, and the honorable company ruled supreme north of the forty-ninth parallel.

Up from the south came the lusty American Fur Company. With equal vigor and ruthlessness the American company crushed its rivals, sending its posts farther and farther up the Missouri River toward that heaven of beaver, the Rocky Mountains.

Violent collision between the British and American companies seemed imminent in the 1830s. Southward the Hudson's Bay Company thrust its power into the Missouri and Columbia river basins. Northward the Americans sent their agents into river valleys drained by the South Saskatchewan to challenge the great monopoly on the threshold of its vast domain.

But the threatened conflict never materialized. Ugly rumors swept the ranks of both companies and hard feelings prompted recriminations from both sides of the unmarked international boundary, but the northern plains, naked of beaver and home of the implacable power of the Blackfeet, became a neutral ground, a barrier behind which the two rivals reached an uneasy truce. By 1833, men spoke of a "gentlemen's agreement" born of necessity, not of respect.

Both companies tried to occupy the region but failed. When the Hudson's Bay Company made its peace with the Nor'Westers in 1821, it took over two posts built by its rivals in the Whoop-Up country. Chesterfield House on the South Saskatchewan River near present-day Empress, Alberta, and Piegan Post, or Old Bow Fort as it was later called, near modern Calgary, were outposts in the Blackfoot country. Frequent depredations, however, made them too costly to maintain, forcing the company to withdraw to the north. Thus, to trade for English goods, Blackfeet had to travel far to the north to Rocky Mountain House or Fort Edmonton.

Similarly, the American Fur Company thrust its posts into the Blackfoot country. From its strategic base at Fort Union at the junction of the Yellowstone and Missouri rivers, Kenneth McKenzie established for a short time a foothold at the mouth of the Marias River in 1830. Then, under the driving leadership of James Kipp, Andrew Dawson, and Alexander Culbertson, the company built in rapid succession Forts Brule, Lewis, and Benton. These took the American Fur Company far up the river, but always on the periphery of Blackfoot power; for over fifty years after Lewis and Clark, the plains country of the Blackfeet remained unoccupied by British or American adventurers.

Trade tactics of the two companies were much the same. Money values remained unknown to the unsophisticated Indians for whom values continued to be measured in beaver skins. A gun, or fuke in Hudson's Bay trading, might be worth fifteen skins while a blanket would fetch ten.

Fear of surprise attacks during the trading by enraged or drunken Indians forced both companies to take extensive precautions. Captain Butler thought Rocky Mountain House "the most singular specimen of an Indian trading post to be found" with its "bars and bolts and places to fire down at the Indians who are trading." [1]

Even more impressive was the method of exchanging the goods. Through a narrow wooden grate, too small for an irate Indian to reach the trader, the goods appeared in exchange for furs. But this description fitted nearly all the trading posts established along the edge of the Blackfoot country. From Fort Union westward, these little trading posts resembled military bastions and were universally called forts, though this title suggested a strength that few of them possessed.

Necessity dictated these warlike measures since both companies used liquor to lure their savage guests to the exchange. With an eye to economy, the honorable company served imported rum while the American company dispensed a domestic whisky from Chicago or St. Louis. Years later, W. S. Gladestone, former employee of the Hudson's Bay Company, recalled the whisky trading of the great corporations. "We all traded whisky. Well, the Hudson's Bay Company traded rum up to the year 1860. I have seen as maney indans Drunk at Edmonton and Rocky Mountain House as ever i seen aney where else and when they got drunk we have put them to bed and treated them a good deal better than some of our civilized Bartenders . . ." [2]

Time must have softened the harsh realities in Gladestone's memory. Rather than peaceful slumbers as an aftermath of the whisky trading, Indians often turned on the traders or upon each other in wild scenes of brutality, violence, and destruction. This despite the fact that the rum or whisky was greatly weakened with water. Though Indians grew increasingly sophisticated, demanding more potent whisky with each trading season, they remained terribly susceptible to its effects, often becoming helplessly intoxicated after but a few drinks.

Friends of the companies often repudiated charges of whisky trading. Others, unable to conceal entirely the character of the fur trade, found logical arguments to support the practice. As is so often true in international politics, each company charged the other was the greater sinner, while both claimed that established customs left no alternative if the Indian trade was to be held.

After visiting Hudson's Bay posts in 1859 the Earl of Southesk advanced yet another telling argument. "Morally," thought the Earl, "this custom must be injurious to them; physically, it is harmless, nay beneficial, for the sickness following their intemperance relieves them of the bile caused by their excessive consumption of fat meat when buffalo are plentiful." [3]

Gradually the Hudson's Bay Company weakened its hold on the region south of the Red Deer River. Fort Edmonton and Rocky Mountain House were too far for Blackfoot bands to reach easily, particularly in view of the danger of attacks from the Crees, bitter enemies who blocked their passage.

Company policy unwittingly encouraged the advance of American traders into the region. Rocky Mountain House was often too poorly equipped to handle the Blackfoot trade, thus forcing the Indians to take their robes and pelts to the Yankee traders. Captain Palliser discovered during 1857 and 1858 that Mr. Brazeau, unusually able and talented as he was, could not hold the Blackfoot trade at Rocky Mountain House and "seemed to be most wretchedly supplied with goods for the trade, and latterly had to send away bands of Blackfeet, 80 to 100 strong, well laden with buffalo robes, bearskins, wolfskins and other less valuable furs." [4]

While company rule in the northern regions remained unchallenged, in the southern districts whites as well as Indians moved unchecked and uncontrolled. Year after year, the company sustained losses in its South Saskatchewan fur trading, though these were substantially offset by the importance of buffalo meat, secured on the plains and processed as pemmican.

Securing pemmican was a major interest of the company. Thousands of buffalo were killed annually, their meat dried and placed in large troughs, where wild berries were added for flavor. Then melted grease was poured over the meat and the two were thoroughly mixed with a wooden shovel. Once the mixture was completed, the meat was pounded into rawhide bags, which were then sewed shut. With these the company solved its problem of transporting in small bulk over great distances a highly nutritious food for the men of its inland transport system. Pemmican from the plains kept the western organization functioning.

Legally, the company was responsible for policing its domains. Practically, however, the possession of magisterial powers was of little consequence since there existed no means of enforcing this authority. Thus, the region was a territory without effective law, a derelict area without even the shadow of authority to control those who entered it.

At the same time, the American Fur Company fell upon evil days. Pressed by financial reverses and hard hit by the decline of the fur trade, the company sold its interests in 1864 to the Northwest Fur Company. Almost at once the iron-willed dominion of the old days collapsed and the era of the free trader was at hand.

II

With surprising speed the buffer zone ceased to be neutral. Gold-seekers rushed into the region as rumors swept Montana of fabulous strikes along the Teton, Marias, Milk, Oldman, and Bow rivers. By 1859 numerous parties passed through the region searching for colors in the fast flowing streams which tumbled out onto the plains from their mountain sources. Even Captain James Fisk's expedition of 1866, though headed for the established fields, turned aside long enough to explore a number of rivers in the Whoop-Up country. For nearly a month, eighty of the party searched every creek and stream of the Teton and Marias valleys. But all efforts failed and the prospectors soon departed for more promising diggings.[5]

The region lost forever its isolated character, for hard on their heels came robe hunters and wolfers. Eastern industry learned that buffalo hides made excellent belts for power machinery. This discovery created an insatiable demand for hides that sent thousands of hunters onto the plains after the buffalo. Use of hides for coats and robes further increased their value.

Great herds suddenly vanished before the relentless guns of the buffalo hunters. This mass destruction provoked a sentimental outcry from easterners and prompted Horace Greeley, who had earlier seen the magnificent spectacle of the plains black with moving masses of the shaggy animals, to protest. "Nowhere is the blind, senseless human appetite for carnage, for destruction, more strikingly, more lamentably, evinced than in the rapidly proceeding extermination of the buffalo." [6]

But Greeley and the eastern critics missed the point. The destruction of the buffalo was only one phase of a national policy that consumed natural resources without taking thought of tomorrow, a Gargantuan prodigality born of the faith that America's resources were inexhaustible. Not until the buffalo were nearly gone did men take notice, and then only to regret their passing, not the shortsightedness and mass greed that had exterminated them.

Free traders fundamentally altered the character of the Indian trade in the Whoop-Up country. Though half-breed "winterers" had comprised a type of free traders under the Hudson's Bay Company's rule, now independent traders poured into the region from the south. Unlike the wintering "freemen" who sold most of their furs to the company or to buyers in the Red River settlements in Manitoba, the invading traders from the Missouri reoriented the trade to divert the flow of robes and pelts to American markets. This was a grievous blow to the company, and it aroused an anger which could still command politicians and call governments to its assistance.

INVASION OF THE FREE TRADERS

John J. Healy and Alfred B. Hamilton, Indian traders and jack-of-all-trades plainsmen from Sun River, spearheaded the invasion when they moved their trade across the boundary in 1869. News of their success in the Blackfoot country quickly spread throughout the territory. When the Helena *Daily Herald* announced to its readers that the two traders had netted $50,000 in their season's traffic, the editor added the obvious comment that this was "not very bad for a six months cruise among the Lo Family across the border." [7] Scores of independent traders agreed with him to the point of gathering up their traps, laying in a fresh supply of whisky, and heading north to share in the new bonanza.

By 1870, Indians visiting Rocky Mountain House from the plains carried rapid-firing weapons of the latest design. Company officials were chagrined to discover the formidable character of the opposition while other tribes envied the great power placed in the hands of their hated enemies, the Blackfeet. The following year, plains Indians failed to appear at the Hudson's Bay post for the annual trading.

Free traders launched a new era in this region, though one entirely familiar along the American frontier since enterprising Englishmen started it all in 1607. Their brief period of power in the Whoop-Up country was based on the time-honored policy of grabbing the robes while they lasted, meanwhile debauching the Indians with whisky to secure their properties quickly and cheaply. The region north of Fort Benton became one of the most lawless areas on the frontier, a rendezvous for tough and restless men from every part of North America and Europe. In an anarchy that recalled the bloody conflict between the Nor'-Westers and the Hudson's Bay men or the ruthless struggles of the American Fur Company with the Rocky Mountain Fur Company in an earlier age, the free traders fought each other, resisted the monopoly of the honorable company, and tricked the Indians as they freely violated the laws of both countries in their greed for profits.

With the low cunning of their kind, they callously stripped

the proud Blackfeet of every possession. Robes, pelts, horses, weapons, even squaws, were bought and sold for a few cups of Whoop-Up bug juice, with the trader enjoying a quick profit and the Indian speedily reduced to miserable poverty.

The great corporations, of course, sold whisky in the years of their power. But they viewed the Indian trade from a different perspective. With corporate strength sustaining them, and the perpetuity of corporate existence stretching out ahead of them, they could look to the future. Their planning was often slight and inconsequential, but it recognized that any program which took all the Indian possessed and reduced him to poverty invited disaster. To destroy the Indian was to ruin the trade, which was precisely what the free traders accomplished in a remarkably short time.

Captain Butler viewed with alarm the activities of the free trader. His reports compared the trader's philosophy to that of a "man who takes his shooting for the term of a year or two and wishes to destroy all he can." Moreover, argued the explorer, he has only two objects in view: "First, to get the furs himself; second, to prevent the other trader from getting them. From Texas to Saskatchewan there has been but one result, and that result has been the destruction of the wild animals and the extinction, partial or total, of the Indian race."[8] His fears were fully confirmed.

III

Free traders were the picket line of American commerce deployed against the Hudson's Bay Company. Through their energy, courage, and resourcefulness, eastern industries prospered and eastern capital flourished. They were only the advance agents of a commercial empire reaching back to St. Louis, Chicago, and New York. Eastern humanitarians, though shocked by the traders' treatment of the Indians, gladly clipped coupons made valuable through their enterprise.

Most of the traders secured financial support from the leading merchants of Fort Benton. I. G. Baker and T. C. Power backed many of the Whoop-Up traders, furnishing them credit in the form of trade goods and sometimes actually joining the venture as partners. By 1870 these two ambitious merchants controlled the lion's share of the trade flowing northward from Fort Benton to the Blackfeet, Piegans, and Bloods. Their extensive interests also included permits to trade with Crows, Gros Ventres, and Assiniboins.

From modest origins in the fur trade, the two merchants built great fortunes. By the 1880s, they headed the largest and richest firms in the region, and furnished the Hudson's Bay Company formidable competition.[9] Many British and Canadian observers regretted the great influence of these companies in the Whoop-Up country. "Oh, my Hudson's Bay company," lamented A. Staveley Hill, British financier and member of Parliament, "all this might have been yours, if you had not sat by with folded arms and allowed your own legitimate business to have been grabbed by some Montana adventurers."[10]

Fort Benton was the center for the trade into the northern plains; through it passed goods destined for Indian consumers as well as the robes for eastern markets. By 1875, over 100,000 robes and pelts were shipped annually to eastern markets by Benton brokers. Sir Cecil Denny recalled seeing 20,000 robes ready for shipment the following spring. Most of the profits, moreover, stayed with Benton merchants who ventured their capital, not with the traders who risked their lives in the Indian country.

Indian traders played a curiously anachronistic role in American society during these years. They were engaged in a trade condemned by most Americans as brutal and disreputable, but approved by their own social groups as beneficial. Thus, most of them were on the defensive, sharing with Johnny Healy the view that eastern opinion regarded them as "monsters of hideous form and revolting aspect."[11] Indeed, public opinion denounced the traders for debauching Indians with whisky and for killing them with smallpox and syphilis. Even fellow westerners sometimes grew bitter about their trade in rapid-firing weapons which armed the Indians with more modern rifles than those the army troops carried against them.

To these charges, the traders turned deaf ears. With the aggressiveness characteristic of those under constant attack, they launched a "positive good" argument of their own. "Traders have done more towards subduing the evil propensities of the Indians than all the soldiers and agents of the government," boasted Healy. Traders thought of themselves as allies of the Indians, taking them the good things of life produced by the factories and looms of eastern industry.

Few westerners really disapproved of the whisky trade to the Indians, at least while there were still Indians to be victimized. Since whisky tended to weaken Indian power, many regarded it as a powerful weapon in reducing the Indians to a sedentary life on reservations from which they could not impede the white man's plans. To these, it was a civilizing agent in disguise, for it helped prepare the way for a "higher culture."

Most of the traders were young men, and many were only recently out of uniform from the Union or Confederate armies. They comprised a polyglot group representing every nationality, with Negroes frequently serving as runners to smuggle the whisky across the boundary into Canada. By frontier standards most of them were "decent" men, abiding by the strict customs of their social group and living by the code of the community. Most of them avoided violence and resorted to it only in extreme situations, despite the folklore reputation they enjoy for quick triggers and gunsmoke.

Outsiders, except the missionaries whose judgments condemned them on every count, usually modified their strictures once they came to know these frontiersmen. Sir Cecil Denny testified that the Northwest Mounted Police found them "a very decent lot of men in spite of all we had heard against them." [12] The Earl of Dunraven admitted that he found some rough characters among them, men who occasionally shot each other in gambling quarrels and drunken sprees. But most he found to be agreeable young men, civil and obliging. Moreover, they possessed a keen sense of independence and self-respect, qualities which Dunraven regarded highly and praised as universal western traits.[13]

IV

Whatever the character of the traders, the nature of their commerce is clear. Furs no longer comprised the major item of barter; Indians now brought buffalo hides and wolf pelts to the posts. Buffalo robes were of two kinds, the highly prized "head and tail" robes which were complete hides, uncut and unsewed. Such hides frequently brought as much as twelve dollars in trade goods to the Indians fortunate enough to possess them. Far more common were the "split robes," cut down the middle and sewed with sinew. Indians also brought their ponies to the traders. These were frequently the source of considerable profit to the Indians, especially if they returned to steal the horses for a later exchange with another trader.

Well-equipped traders offered a wide range of cheap goods to the Indians. Tobacco, salt, sugar, flour, and tea quickly became standard commodities in the exchange and reduced the red men to complete dependence upon the trader for subsistence. Similarly, the traders' axes, knives, hatchets, fire steel, and weapons replaced stone-age tools so thoroughly that without them the natives starved. Blankets, calico, colorful cotton fabrics, and innumerable trinkets, such as brass wire, beads, silver ornaments, and wide leather belts, completed the traders' stock.

Whisky, however, brought the greatest profits. Many traders, lacking both capital and scruples, turned to liquor as their chief reliance. Profits could be stretched to incredible limits as untutored Indians, lacking the white man's sense of values, became the trader's victims when liquor addled their brains. Traders also resorted to the old trick of diluting the whisky as the trading progressed so that many intoxicated braves received little more than colored water for their labors.

On top of this, the traders seldom used good whisky. Usually they adopted a formula that placed a fiery, but cheap, concoction into the Indians' hands. One such formula called for a quart of whisky, a pound of chewing tobacco, a handful of red pepper, a bottle of Jamaica ginger, and a quart of molasses. This potent mixture was then thoroughly diluted with water and heated to bring out its full powers.

Other formulas seem equally stimulating. Most traders simply mixed high wine with water, added tea leaves and tobacco, and presented their customers with a drink that gratified unsophisticated palates with its breathtaking satisfactions. A few traders, possessing greater imagination or more capital, mixed Perry's Famous Painkiller, Hostetter's Bitters, tobacco, and molasses with the alcohol. Often they added a dash of red ink, since the savage, like many patrons of the modern bar, found pleasure in a colorful mixed drink.

Whatever the ingredients, the potions were hot. Frequently they touched off wild frenzies in which savage reprisals were levied against the traders. If they could not be reached, the Indians often turned on each other in terrible scenes of violence. Colonel S. C. Ashby later recalled one frenzied brave who rode into a Baker trading camp shouting, "You miserable, dirty white dog. You are here with your cattle eating our grass, drinking our water, and cutting our wood. We want you to get out of here, or we will wipe you out." [14]

Undoubtedly, the whisky trading story has suffered gross exaggeration. Tall tales, wild yarns, and pure myths soon colored the events as lively imaginations and a desire to tell a good story distorted and altered the truth. Sometimes vested interests sought to discredit the free traders by portraying their activities in the worst possible light. Hudson's Bay Company officials encouraged rumors in eastern Canada that more than five hundred well-armed, carefully drilled, and disciplined American desperadoes roamed the Whoop-Up country, killing and plundering at will. Here is yet another example of that complex amalgam of local and international politics which conceals so much of the evidence and challenges cautious judgment.

Information regarding the Whoop-Up traders is confused and fragmentary at best. Old timers often confessed to exploits that

COURTESY HISTORICAL SOCIETY OF MONTANA

Fort Benton in 1862 was not yet the "Chicago of the Plains"

The Whoop-Up Trail extended from Fort Benton on the south to Fort Macleod on the north

In 1874 Fort Macleod was an "atom of settlement in a wilderness"

COURTESY HISTORICAL SOCIETY OF MONTANA

Front Street, photographed in 1871, was for a time
the town's only thoroughfare

"Pioneer Benton was bleak and unattractive"

To Benton's mile-long levee came supplies for an inland empire

Merchant princes of Benton

Isaac G. Baker

Thomas C. Power

William G. Conrad

The Diamond R muletrain winds through
Prickly Pear Canyon, Montana

Wagonmaster Pres Lewis hoists "one for the road"

Transportation was the key to western empire

Wagontrains carried the commerce of the plains
from Benton to distant points

The Concord coach, a "marvel of nineteenth-century craftsmanship"

"In the Whoop-Up country the wheel ruled supreme"

"From sunrise until evening the caravan of wagons rolled on"

This interior of Sawtell's ranch was typical of the period

Graziers and grangers early moved into the Whoop-Up country

Ranching in the shadows of the Rockies

Few of the Montana cowboys
resembled the now legendary
"knights of the plains"

Branding cattle on a Whoop-Up ranch in 1888

they exaggerated or even created from whole cloth. Numerous examples of this exist, but one of the most famous concerns the alleged "Snookum Jim" letter. William Pearce apparently began the yarn in his reminiscences:

"To show the utter lawlessness of the country at that period, it is only necessary to produce a letter written by a resident of 'Whoop-Up' to a friend in Fort Benton, the fall of 1873:

Dear friend:
My partner Will Geary got to putting on airs and I shot him and he is dead — the potatoes are looking well.

Yours truly,
Snookum Jim"

Here, indeed, is evidence proving beyond doubt the brutality of the American traders. But Pearce produced no such letter, while both internal and external evidence indicate strongly that the incident is pure fabrication. Despite this, some historians have repeated the story as sober truth.[15]

Other stories combined fact with fiction so adroitly that to winnow the grains of truth from the chaff of exaggeration is virtually impossible. Typical of this type are the accounts, in many versions, of intrepid whisky runners avoiding United States marshals to deliver their illicit product to northern Indians. These yarns usually picture the diligent marshal carefully watching the trader's activities as he purchases his supply of whisky from obliging wholesalers in Helena or Fort Benton. Then, at the proper moment, the marshal's attention is distracted, sometimes by invitations to dances or parties, more often with false rumors of crime at other points. While the marshal's back is turned, the wily trader loads his goods on fast wagons and heads for the international boundary. Once more, the marshal is outwitted and the determined frontiersman reaches his goal unmolested by the law.

Such tales furnish unlimited grist for the storyteller's mill, and old-timers obligingly produce more when the supply threatens to fail. These accounts usually prove to be worthless under the careful scrutiny of historical research; but most have sufficient truth in them to provide atmosphere. Captain Denny correctly estimated their value when he cautioned, "the whisky trade was equally exaggerated, for although it was bad enough it could not come up to the tales told of it."[16] But most of us want our western adventure stories with villains whose crimes match the majesty of the plains and mountains in which they rode.

During the early years of free trading north of the Missouri River, many traders simply entered the Indian camps to conduct their exchange. While this direct method saved the costs of constructing a trading post, it quickly revealed a fatal weakness. When Indians became excited through fiery whisky or over unfair treatment, the trader often lost his entire stock of goods and sometimes his life. This encouraged the building of trading posts, most of which were quickly dubbed "whisky forts."

To call the roll of these little trading posts north of the forty-ninth parallel is to recapture the spirit of the era. Forts Whoop-Up, Slideout, Standoff, Robbers Roost, and Whisky Gap indicate by their names the character of the trade. Forts Hamilton, Kipp, Conrad, and Spitzee carried less sensational titles, but their careers were similar.

It is virtually impossible today to write an accurate history of these colorful little forts. Local historians cannot agree on the simplest facts. No fewer than five men, for example, claimed in their memoirs the dubious credit for building Fort Standoff. Best evidence points to James Kipp's half-breed son, Joseph, and his partner, Charles Thomas.

This post, built near the confluence of the Waterton and Belly rivers, got its name in typical fashion. United States Marshal Charles D. Hard, an able and conscientious peace officer, launched a one-man campaign in the early 1870s to make hard the way of the transgressor. His efforts forced whisky runners to adopt innumerable ruses, particularly in smuggling their goods across the Indian reservation lying between Fort Benton and the international boundary.

On one occasion, Marshal Hard pursued a group of traders with unusual vigor. Mile after mile, the determined officer pushed the whisky traders. Finally, in the vicinity of the unmarked international boundary, he overtook them.[17] James W. Schultz, from oral as well as written reminiscences, reconstructed the tense scene.

" 'It is the Marshal all right and we might as well stop right here and stand him off,' said Joseph Kipp, leader of the band.

" 'Well, Joe, I've got you at last. Just turn around and head for Fort Benton,' shouted the irate Marshal.

" 'Hard, you're just twenty minutes too late. You should have overtaken us on the far side of the creek back there.'

" 'Oh, come. No joking. This is serious business. Turn your team,' insisted the Marshal.

" 'Hard, right here you are no more a Marshal of the United States than I am, for right here we are in Canada; the north fork of the Milk river is the line.' " [18]

It was not the boundary, but the argument convinced the outnumbered marshal who returned to Fort Benton empty-handed. The traders, meanwhile, christened their new post Standoff, in memory of their brush with the law.

Fort Slideout won its title under equally exciting conditions. During the course of trading at a little post on the Belly River, the Benton men received a warning from a friendly Indian boy that a band of Bloods was on the warpath. They had already wiped out one trader and now they planned to attack the post. W. S. Gladestone later recalled the incident:

"We went into the shack and had a few drinks of bug juice and got talking about what we should do. There was no use staying there for the Indians would not come any more to trade. A Dutchman in the gang said we had better slide out, so it has been called Slideout ever since." [19]

Yet another explanation exists for this curious title. Traders at Standoff speculated on a suitable site for another post. While they debated, two of their number quietly slipped away during the night to establish a second post on the Belly River. When the remaining traders discovered their absence the following morning, they roundly cursed their two companions for failing to take them in on the deal and derisively dubbed the new post Slideout. This version is perhaps less exciting than Gladestone's, but it is probably as accurate.

V

Fort Whoop-Up was the most famous of the whisky forts. Located at the junction of the St. Mary and the Oldman, it became the center of the Indian trade in the region between Fort Benton and Fort Edmonton. Built originally by John Healy and A. B. Hamilton in 1869 as Fort Hamilton, it was then merely a collection of log huts placed in a crude semicircle and connected by a picket fence.

Angry Indians burned this post to the ground shortly after its completion and the Benton partners were compelled to rebuild. The elaborate post which they constructed near modern Lethbridge soon gave its name to the trail joining it to Fort Benton as well as to the region around it.

Rather than a semicircle of shacks, this new Fort Whoop-Up boasted heavy squared timbers, built in the shape of a rectangle. Earth-covered roofs protected it from fire, while two formidable bastions at opposite corners, each mounting an ancient brass cannon, guarded the approaches. Loopholes in the mud-chinked walls guaranteed a stout defense in the unlikely event of an Indian attack.

This grim exterior contrasted strangely with the interior where large stone fireplaces and spacious quarters created an atmosphere of comfort in a rude wilderness. A blacksmith shop, commodious warehouses, cook rooms, and living quarters gave the fort an appearance of permanence foreign to other posts in the region. William Gladestone, former Hudson's Bay ship carpenter, directed the construction which required the labor of thirty men working nearly two years to complete. Healy later claimed that the Benton traders invested $25,000 in the post. Neither Healy nor Hamilton possessed sufficient capital for such a venture, but Hamilton was a nephew of Isaac G. Baker, from whom sufficient funds were readily available to underwrite so profitable an enterprise.

Three small wickets to the right of the sturdy oak gates served as openings for the trading. Through these, the Indians pushed their robes in exchange for goods. Red men seldom entered the fort, especially during the trading when arguments often touched off fights. Iron bars across windows and chimneys further guaranteed that uninvited savage guests would not drop in on the traders at an unguarded moment.

Around Fort Whoop-Up revolves much of the folklore of the whisky trading era. Here, Johnny Healy ruled with an iron hand, creating many of the legends that surround his name even to the present day. Here, too, François Vielle, "Crazy Vielle," functioned as half-witted court jester to the crude little community. While Healy feared neither God nor man, Crazy Vielle feared both, once leaving two Jesuit priests stranded on the plains when a distant dust cloud terrorized him into thinking a Blackfoot war party was on their trail. Despite urgent pleas by the priests to stay with them, to trust in the safety of their black robes and to have faith in God, the frightened French half-breed continued his flight, pausing only long enough to compose another Crazy Vielle aphorism. "You trust in God," shouted the departing guide, "I trust my horse."

No one really knows how Fort Whoop-Up got its unusual name. Some old-timers insist that the expression was first used in an interview between Benton merchant John Power and John Wye, just returned from across the boundary. When asked by Power how things were going, Pennsylvania Dutchman Wye replied, "Oh, we're just whoopen-on-em up," which struck public fancy to be quickly shortened to "whooping it up."

Others remember that the title came from traders whose fast, six-horse wagons "whooped it up" for the boundary to avoid both police and army patrols. A more likely explanation lies in the fact that "whoop you up" was a common Missouri River expression meaning to be rounded up. William Pearce recalls that

I. G. Baker shouted after departing friends, Healy and Hamilton, "Don't let the Indians whoop you up!"

However it came, the name stuck. Soon official government maps, both Canadian and American, marked the wagon road into Canada as the Whoop-Up Trail. This, in turn, led frontiersmen to refer to the entire region as the Whoop-Up country. Its name thus recalled the stirring days when ambitious men flouted the law and defied the power of the Hudson's Bay Company to organize a questionable trade.

VI

The men who opened the country never questioned the integrity of their enterprise or the reality of their good works. John Healy regarded the traders as "the best brand of prairie men that the world produced doing legitimate business scattered through the various posts. These men taught the Blackfeet, Piegans, Bloods, Sarcees and Crees to behave. They made the country safe and possible for people to travel the prairies in safety . . ." [20]

Reports from less biased observers emphasized a very different aspect of the trade. Explorers, missionaries, government officials, and army officers unanimously denounced it as completely demoralizing to the Blackfeet and their cousins, the Piegans and Bloods.

Disease and social disorganization as well as whisky came with the trader. Within a remarkably short time, the Blackfeet were reduced from one of the most powerful plains tribes to a poverty-stricken rabble. Father Scollen sadly reported to Lieutenant Governor Laird in Winnipeg, "In the summer of 1874, I was traveling amongst the Blackfeet. It was painful to me to see the state of poverty to which they had been reduced. Formerly, they had been the most opulent Indians in the country, now they were clothed in rags without horses and without guns." [21]

This destruction of material prosperity was more than matched by a tragic decay in social organization. A well-knit tribal community collapsed into small bands, fearful of each other and avoiding contact whenever possible. Only the timely arrival of the Mounted Police in 1874 prevented the complete destruction of these northern Indians.

Ironically, many of the traders urged complete destruction of the Indians as the answer to the Indian problem. Whisky, poison, firearms, and disease — these grim companions of civilization were effective allies in this extermination policy. "If we had only been allowed to carry on the business in our own way for another two years," complained one of the whisky traders, "there would have been no trouble now as to feeding the Indians, for there would have been none left to feed: whisky, pistols, strychnine, and other like processes would have effectively cleared away these wretched natives." [22]

Equally destructive to Indian welfare was the wave of wolfers who invaded the Whoop-Up country with the free traders. These men, who lived and slept on the plains like the wild animals, were universally despised by whites and reds alike.

Each autumn small parties of wolfers headed out onto the plains. With strychnine rather than bullets they accomplished their mission by sprinkling the poison into carcasses of dead buffalo. Hungry wolves devoured the meat, thus contributing their pelts to the wolfers' cache.

Westerners deplored this indiscriminate slaughter. Indians resented the wanton destruction of their dogs which unsuspectingly ate the poisoned buffalo meat. When the wolfers sprinkled strychnine in a buffalo carcass, they left a death trap on the plains which was an unmarked hazard. So many valuable Indian dogs fell victim to the poisoned bait that the Indians killed the wolfers whenever they could.

Wolfers feared the Indians and frequently protested to traders who supplied them with repeating rifles and ammunition. To end this arms traffic in the Whoop-Up country, they organized a band known as the Spitzee Cavalry. Led by John Evans and Harry "Kamoose" Taylor, the wolfers tried to drive the traders out of the region.[23]

Though the ostensible purpose was to stop the trade in repeating rifles, many merchants in Fort Benton believed the wolfers played a more devious game. In the river town, the wolfers' organization appeared to be an attempt by the I. G. Baker and Conrad interests to force the T. C. Power traders from the lucrative Whoop-Up trade. Power's traders were forced at gun's point to sign pledges not to sell arms or ammunition to the red men.

Johnny Healy at Fort Whoop-Up stubbornly refused to sign the Spitzee ultimatum. His successful defiance of the wolfers made him a legendary figure throughout the northern plains.

Healy's account of the clash with the Spitzee Cavalry, while somewhat different from the generally accepted version, seems to portray faithfully the tense situation. He later recalled that he was fully warned of the approaching wolfers and knew of their determination to put an end to his trading, even if it required force to achieve it. Calmly the trader loaded a small cannon, placed it in position to command the big room of the post and ordered his assistant, Jack Reese, to fire it when he heard the sentence, "Gentlemen, since you will not listen to reason, you must take the consequences."

By the time Evans and his Belly River wolfers stormed into Fort Whoop-Up, Healy was ready for them. Despite the obvious hostility of the Spitzee men, the trader invited them to dinner and to a conference after the meal. In all surviving accounts, the the parley which followed the dinner was one which its participants never forgot.

"Mr. Healy," said Evans, "there is a serious charge preferred against you of selling guns and ammunition to Indians and we have come down to see about it."

Then followed the reading of an indictment that the wolfers had drawn up against Healy. Secretary "Kamoose" Taylor only had time to complete the final sentence, "guilty or not guilty," when the Whoop-Up trader turned on him.

"Guilty, and you be damned," roared the infuriated Irishman. "What right have you to come down here and try me? What are you? A renegade from justice? You! You! You're a mad dog among a pack of decent hounds . . ."

This outburst brought Bedrock Jim to his feet and into the verbal battle. "I suppose I am one of the hounds?" he challenged.

"Who are you?" calmly asked the trader. "Who do you represent?"

"I represent Mr. Conrad," replied Bedrock Jim, thus revealing to Healy that the I. G. Baker people were deeply involved.

With this admission as a weapon, Healy charged that the wolfers played the Baker game and pleaded with them not to destroy T. C. Power's extensive stock in his charge. An eloquent ten-minute speech convinced the wolfers they had made a mistake.

"Gentlemen," said Mike Walsh, one of the wolfers, "I move that we all go down to the river and wash some of the wool out of our eyes!"

That was the end of the Spitzee Cavalry. But the feuds and animosities created by the affair at Fort Whoop-Up poisoned relations in Fort Benton's trading community. For several years, T. C. Power, John Healy, and others remained bitter.[24]

Another version of the Spitzee affair presents an equally belligerent Healy. Rather than a loaded cannon, however, he is pictured as sitting behind the counter of the trading room quietly smoking a cigar. As the argument with the wolfers grew acrimonious and violence threatened, Healy suddenly poised his lighted cigar over an open keg of gunpowder, threatening to blow them all to hell unless they cleared out without delay.[25]

However Healy accomplished it, his courage and stubbornness destroyed the Spitzee Cavalry. Never again was it a force in the Whoop-Up country.

VII

Fort Whoop-Up and the era it symbolized were short-lived. The exploitative character of the trade and its destructive effects upon the Indians determined that it could not survive long. It was only a passing incident in the development of the region.

Competition from the free traders bit deeply into the Hudson's Bay Company's trade on the plains. Protests from the company's friends in Ottawa stirred the Dominion government to action. But Ottawa officials never accepted uncritically or at face value the lurid accounts of the Whoop-Up trade reported by company officials and their advocates. While sympathetic, members of the Macdonald government were well aware of the uneasiness prevailing among company men in the face of costly competition from Fort Benton. They understood the bias that distorted Whoop-Up events into strident pleas for government intervention with a military expedition into the west.[26]

Canadian resentment against the free traders mounted each passing year. By 1872, Canadian newspapers called for the occupation of Fort Whoop-Up by government forces and public opinion, shocked by the reported brutality of the traders and aroused by an offended national spirit, demanded an end to the invasion from the south.

The reign of the whisky traders was nearing its end. When scarlet-clad troopers of the Northwest Mounted Police reached the Whoop-Up country in the autumn of 1874, the trade was doomed. Its collapse concluded a colorful but tragic chapter in the Whoop-Up story.

4

Massacre at Cypress Hills

FREQUENT massacres darkly stain the pages of
western history. But few of them challenge the historian as much
as the skirmish between whites and Indians in the low-lying
Cypress Hills of southern Saskatchewan. Here, in May 1873, a
fight between a party of hunters and traders from Fort Benton
and a band of North Assiniboins touched off an international
incident. It heightened the tension already existing between
Britain and the United States and fanned the smoldering embers
of national spirit into flame on both sides of the international
boundary in North America.

In such an atmosphere, national bias quickly distorted fact
into fiction to create as vigorous a set of legends and myths as
surround any similar incident in American history. To the south,
American historians pieced together a story of valiant frontiersmen bravely fighting for their lives against fearful odds as savages sought to "wipe them out." To the north, Canadian historians painted a picture of American border ruffians, drunk with
whisky and greed, brutally slaughtering innocent and defenseless
Indians without purpose or justification.

Neither interpretation seems defensible in view of the available evidence. And neither does credit to the objectivity or schol-
arship of those who, by reason of inadequate research or national
bias, have perpetuated legend as history or myth as truth.

Tragedy at Cypress Hills began with a commonplace frontier
incident. A small party of wolfers, returning from a winter of

hunting in the northern reaches of the Whoop-Up country, camped on the Teton River only five miles from Fort Benton. Since they were so close to the river town and were surrounded by ranches, the men relaxed the vigil so carefully maintained during the long trip down the Whoop-Up Trail. But they were betrayed by this false sense of security, and while their night herders slept, a band of thieving Indians made off with their horses. The men awoke to find themselves the victims of an honorable but dangerous Indian sport.[1]

Here was another of the conflicts between the white man's highly developed sense of property ownership and the Indian's different set of values. To the plains Indians, horse stealing was a highly regarded achievement, bringing to the successful thief much of the same honor and recognition that modern American society confers upon the baseball player who steals home base.

But the wolfers did not regard it a game. To be left on the plains without their horses was a serious matter, and they broke camp aroused by the audacity as well as by the success of the raiders. After ascertaining that their horses were indeed stolen and not estrayed, they moved down the trail into Fort Benton, a party of angry and determined men.

In Fort Benton, their pleas for assistance in apprehending the culprits and in recovering their stolen property fell on deaf ears. There, the military commander refused their request, arguing that his force was too small to provide an escort for such a mission. Left to their own devices, the wolfers organized an expedition, one fated to violence through the absence of authorized law enforcement.

With surprising speed the expedition outfitted itself for the trek across the plains. There is no evidence that the men lingered in Benton finding strength or courage in the many saloons facing the busy river front. Despite this lack of evidence, several writers have made much of the party's fondness for "Montana Redeye," and one writer, claiming information directly from an Indian participant, describes the manner in which they spent the winter in the river town nursing their wrath: "In many a barroom session the wolfers boasted of the dreadful vengeance they would heap on the red men when the poplars were in leaf again." [2] But this is entirely fictitious, for they remained in Benton only long enough to outfit the expedition.

The men who rode north from Benton that day were typical hunters, trappers, and wolfers of the high border country, neither better nor worse than most. Experienced in Indian warfare and schooled in plains lore, they were capable of caring for themselves whatever the emergency. Heavily armed with the latest repeating rifles and revolvers, they thought themselves a match for any roaming band of hostile Indians they might encounter.

To establish the character of the men in the little party is a difficult exercise in historical evidence. Testimony varies widely, depending upon the bias of the witnesses. On the whole, it seems clear that thus far historians have too harshly judged the group. By the standards of eastern society, whether Canadian or American, they were vulgarians, whose occupations and environment had shaped them to a coarseness thought characteristic of the frontier. By contemporary western standards they were typical frontiersmen — "thirteen Kit Carsons" as one newspaper phrased it; "advanced guards of civilization" in the no less modest words of yet another. [3]

Only Thomas Hardwick had a "tough" reputation, one fully described by his sobriquet, "Green River Renegade." Most of the others, however, were veterans of previous conflicts with Indians, which had left them victims of the universal western view that violence and bloodshed were inevitable in their contacts with the red men. Some of them were also veterans of the Civil War with the experience of four years of conflict shaping their conduct. This was a dangerous combination, for it prepared them to regard violence against the Indians as natural and to praise the destruction of Indian power as promoting civilization. But the judgment that they were therefore capable of any crime, however depraved, is an unwarranted assumption based on the widely accepted exaggeration that western society comprised "desperadoes, murderers and degenerates; in short, a majority of the white population."[4] This picture of the western community may provide a proper atmosphere for a Hollywood thriller, but it does not accord with the facts of the social history of the region.

This was also an international brigade. Though denounced in contemporary Canadian newspapers as "American gangsters," "American scum," and "American frontiersmen," and stigmatized by later historians as "one of the Missouri River gangs," or as "American gunmen," it was actually an Anglo-American party with citizens of both nationalities well represented. Of those whose nationalities can be ascertained, Ed Grace, George Hammond, and Donald Graham were Anglo-Canadians while Jeff Devereaux, S. Vincent, and Alexis Lebompard were among the several French-Canadians.

With all possible speed and without particular caution, the Benton party pushed hard on the trail of the stolen horses. Natural leadership quickly asserted itself so that without an election or any formal balloting, John Evans took command. This large, well-built, good-natured frontiersman was dubbed the "Chief" by his companions in recognition of their confidence in his ability to direct them on their mission.

Evans had demonstrated this same quality of leadership during the previous season when he served as captain of the Spitzee Cavalry. George Hammond, who was soon to join Evans in the fight at Cypress Hills, had openly challenged Johnny Healy in the days of the Spitzee Cavalry. The two traders came to blows over the Spitzee affair, accusing each other of "dirty cowardice" and "thieving deceit." Thus, several of the chief figures in the struggle for control of the Whoop-Up trade the previous year were now involved in the fight at Cypress Hills.

When I. G. Baker's allies, Evans and Hammond in particular, became involved in the affair at Cypress Hills, the Power traders found an unexpected opportunity for revenge and a chance to reverse the pressure of the previous year. Now they hoped to exclude the Baker traders from the field. But their maneuvers were far more subtle than the crude threats of the Spitzee Cav-

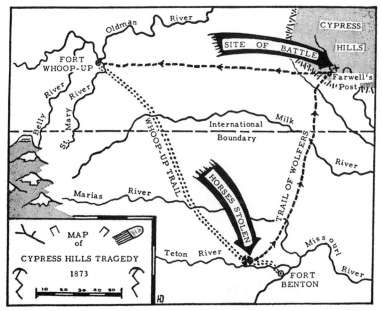

COURTESY HISTORICAL SOCIETY OF MONTANA

alry, for they used the American and Canadian governments to eliminate their rivals and to advance the firm's monopolistic goals. The affair of the Spitzee Cavalry, which has always been treated as an isolated incident, is then of great importance in understanding the hue and cry which accompanied the Cypress Hills melee.

II

Such thoughts were far from their minds as the Benton men hastened northward. Traveling night and day with but short rests they tenaciously followed a trail that led them into the Cypress Hills. In this rough and eroded region with its deep ravines and thick stands of coyote willows, the trail became too faint to follow and they were forced to give up their search. This was disappointing, but Abel Farwell's trading post on Battle Creek was only a few miles distant and there they hoped to rest their horses and gather information about the stolen property.

When about five miles from Fort Farwell, as the little trading post was called, the men halted to make camp. Here they decided to send two of their number into the trading area to reconnoiter. It fell to John Evans and Thomas Hardwick to announce their presence to Farwell and to secure what information he might have about their mission.

Farwell greeted his old friends cordially, urging them to bring in the rest of the party to join his men for dinner and to spend the night at his post. Evans, however, was too concerned about the lost trail for social amenities and pressed Farwell for information. He was particularly anxious about the nearby camp of Little Soldier's North Assiniboins, where some of his men believed they would find the stolen horses. He bluntly came to the point; were they the thieves? "No," said the trader, "the camp has only five or six horses, and they have not got yours." [5]

This was disappointing news and Evans hurried back to his companions to share it with them. It was a blow to their hopes of finding the horses on the morrow and of returning at once to Fort Benton. Evans later recalled his frustration: "sick and disappointed at not having obtained our horses and tired after a long day's ride, we lay down to sleep after exchanging news." [6] Hardwick, however, remained with Farwell to enjoy the comforts of the little fort, including its well-stocked liquor chest.

The Benton party reached Fort Farwell at a most unfortunate time. For weeks, the surrounding district had been feverish with excitement as Indians, half-breeds, and traders lived under an armed truce. The very evening of their arrival witnessed the climax of an incident dating back to the previous month when a band of seventeen Indians abused Farwell's hospitality and slipped away with thirty of his horses while his guards slept. Among these horses was one owned by the Canadian George Hammond. On the night the Benton men arrived at the fort, this horse was returned to Hammond who generously paid the Indian bringing it in. Unhappily, the disappearance of this same horse the following day touched off the fight which became known to history as the Cypress Hills massacre.

Fort Farwell was only one of four trading posts built in this district in the autumn of 1872. After the winter's trading, however, I. G. Baker's bulltrains collected the furs and two of the posts were abandoned. Abel Farwell, assisted by his interpreter, Alexis Lebompard, continued to trade as a representative of T. C. Power Company of Benton. Less than two hundred yards away, but across the creek, another post remained open under the management of Moses Solomon. In this post, as assistants or as hunters, lived three other white men soon to be involved in the fracas, John McFarland, George Bell, and Philander Vogle.

So tense were conditions around these two posts that several Indian skirmishes had already served as grim harbingers of the approaching tragedy. Fort Solomon was the particular target of Indian resentment, for Solomon and his traders had treated the Indians badly. By May, hatred for the white traders had reached fever pitch among the Indians and plans for a showdown with the traders were already underway when the Benton party arrived.

Not far from the two trading posts a large settlement of half-breeds watched this guerrilla warfare with growing apprehension. A wave of fear swept the community of freighters and hunters when a band of Indians killed a white trader named Paul Rivers.

Frequent Indian threats to wipe out Fort Solomon reached the unhappy métis community during the month of April. On one occasion, the Indians bluntly warned Joseph Laverdure, a half-breed freighter in Abel Farwell's employ, that despite the close ties between their people and his, the métis would be hurt if they got in the way when "a hundred guns go off." [7]

Sometime later, and only two days before the fight, a badly frightened Assiniboin appeared in the half-breed winterers' camp. His story of an impending attack upon Fort Solomon confirmed the métis' fears and gave added emphasis to the repeated warnings already current in their camp.

On top of this, the half-breeds received a direct warning less than two hours before the fight, when another Indian from Little Soldier's camp added his testimony. "It is a pity you half-breeds are here, for we have determined to clean out the whites and take all their stock, as soon as the Americans come out of the fort we intend to take all they have and if they make any resistance we will fight them." [8]

To make disaster a certainty on that Sunday in early May, whites and red men alike spent much of the morning drinking. Moses Solomon's whisky trade with the Indians had already caused great difficulties; now Abel Farwell joined in the traffic by providing drinks from the supplies he had purchased earlier from William Rowe when that trader departed for Fort Benton. Farwell later denied that he ever traded in spirits, arguing that he bought out Rowe's stock only "to keep him out of the business." [9] While Farwell's sentiments appear entirely commendable, there is adequate evidence to indict him along with Solomon. [10]

Shortly after noon the Sabbath calm was broken by George Hammond's shout that the Indians had again stolen his horse. Quickly the Benton traders crowded around the excited man demanding to know what had happened.

"Why they have stolen my horse again, let's go over and take theirs in return," said the aroused Hammond. To the métis he told a similar story in French, ending his recital with the threat, "For that horse I'll have two." Gun in hand, he started angrily for the Indian camp closely followed by several of the Benton party who were willing to assist him in recovering the missing animal.

What really happened from that moment onward is shrouded in a haze of confused testimony. There is no thoroughly reliable account of the massacre and most of the witnesses contradicted their own testimony at one time or other. To reconstruct with complete accuracy the detailed events at Cypress Hills is impossible, but the main events can be pieced together from the maze of evidence.

Abel Farwell testified later that he sought vainly to restrain Hammond, urging caution with the plea that the Indians did not have his horse. When this failed to appease the Canadian, Farwell volunteered to go into the Indian camp alone to speak to Little Soldier.

Immediately, he turned toward the Indian camp, hurrying through the coulee and across the remaining distance to Little Soldier's tent. There, he quizzed the Indian chief about the missing horse, which Little Soldier insisted had not been stolen but was even then grazing on a slight hill some distance beyond Farwell's post. Unhappily, Little Soldier was too drunk to act decisively or to hold his young warriors in check. They at once showed resentment at the provocative manner in which the white men approached their camp and began abusing the traders with taunts and insults. Farwell used every possible device to quiet the Indians and get them to listen to reason. Little Soldier readily acquiesced, going so far as to offer two of his own horses as hostages to Hammond until the missing horse could be recovered.

Meanwhile, the seeming hostility by the young braves frightened the Benton men. Their apprehension quickly became alarm as they discerned the women hurrying away and the men casting off their garments in apparent preparation for combat. To protect themselves, the men crowded into the coulee, which was three to eight feet deep and ran within fifty yards of the Indian camp. This movement, in turn, prompted Little Soldier and his Indians to ask why the white men took such menacing positions.

At this point, Farwell later claimed, he heard Thomas Hardwick calling from the coulee and ordering him to get out of the way or get shot. With a warning to the Indians to scatter, Farwell returned to the men in the coulee to plead for sanity. "Would you shoot at a party of Indians when there was a white man among them?" he asked.

"If you had come out when you were first told we would have had a good shot," answered the sullen Hardwick.

Farwell then explained Little Soldier's proposition, but the men refused to believe his story. They feared his duplicity or, at best, his inability to understand the Indian's speech. To play for time, Farwell said he would get Alexis Lebompard to confirm his story and turned to call his interpreter from the fort. Before he could move more than a few steps, he saw George Hammond fire into the Indians and a fight immediately broke out.

Protected by their cutbank fortress, the whites poured volley after volley into the exposed Indians with deadly effect. In spite of this, the warriors charged the coulee, only to be repulsed with heavy losses. Years later, time had not dimmed John Duval's memory of the courage and tenacity of Little Soldier's braves: "Three times those plucky warriors returned to almost certain death." [11]

After their third costly attack, the Indians withdrew to a coulee behind their camp from which they kept up a vigorous fire against the whites. To dislodge them from this position, Evans and Hardwick mounted their horses and rode to a hill overlooking the Indian stronghold. From this vantage point, the two men raked the Indian ranks.

Instead of fleeing, the Assiniboins executed a flanking movement of their own through a thicket of willows and small trees. This maneuver was so effective that Hardwick and Evans were immediately in danger and several of the white men rushed to their aid. At the head of this rescue party rode Ed Grace, "a Canadian of great bravery." His rashness cost him his life, for the moment he entered the woods, a concealed Indian sent a bullet through his heart.

Grace's death sobered the Benton party. Soon they withdrew to the fort which commanded a view of the Indian camp and from which they laid down a field of fire so effective that it prevented the Indians from returning to their lodges. At nightfall, they scattered, giving up their camp and leaving their dead on the field.

From this point onward, Farwell's account is of a saturnalia of unrestrained bloodlust and brutality. Little Soldier, too drunk to flee, was found hiding in a lodge where he was killed by S. Vincent; his head was cut off and mounted on a pole as a grisly trophy of victory. Farwell also charged that Indian squaws left in the camp were abused and children slain along with adults.

At dawn, a melancholy scene of death greeted the Benton men at the Indian camp. Scattered about by the capricious whims of combat lay the pitifully few possessions of the Indians. After burying some of the dead, the while men pulled down the empty lodges and burned the abandoned clothing in a great pyre.[12]

Next, they faced the task of burying their own dead. After some debate, they decided to place Grace's body under the floor of Solomon's fort. Then, to prevent the Indians from later mutilating it, they soaked the green logs with coal oil and burned the post to the ground.

That afternoon they resumed their search for the missing horses. This time they rode almost straight west into the Whoop-Up country, where they hoped to find a party of Bloods alleged to be the thieves. Then, too, the Cypress Hills district had suddenly become very unhealthy for white men, for only twenty miles north lay a large camp of Crees, friends and allies of the Assiniboins.

Some days later they reached Fort Whoop-Up where they learned of a camp of Bloods farther west which might shelter their stolen property. With more rashness than wisdom they rode on to what was nearly a second disaster, for this camp turned out to have one-hundred and fifty lodges of well-armed and mounted Indians.

They were greeted with open hostility. Donald Graham's account of the affair, the only detailed record of this incident, is tense with suppressed excitement. With their weapons ready for instant use the Indians sullenly welcomed their uninvited guests. One young boy rode beside the white men, flexing his bow and arrow and repeating again and again, "I know I can kill a white man."

With a courage more apparent than real, the men rode directly to the head chief's tent. Here they found an ancient chief, clad in the blue coat of an American soldier but wearing a King George medal on his breast. To him they told their story, but were much relieved to learn that their horses were not in that camp. Had trouble started, Graham and his companions "knew that not one of us would get away."[13]

Without further ceremony or argument, the worried men left the camp. Out of sight of the Indians, they spurred their horses and rode hard until nightfall, putting as much distance between them and the Bloods as possible. Even then, they mounted a strong guard during the night to prevent a surprise attack from their late hosts.

Meanwhile, Farwell and several of the Cypress traders hurried to Benton as rapidly as possible. There, they broke the news of the fight and were acclaimed noble frontiersmen who had taught the Indians a costly but necessary lesson.

III

In the years that followed, Abel Farwell's account of these events was accepted without qualification as an accurate eyewitness report. However, his story of the decapitation of Little Soldier appears to be a fabrication, and other serious problems challenge the accuracy and reliability of his testimony.

Basic to his story is the claim that he honestly played the role of peacemaker, seeking to hold in check the passion of murderers. But this is open to question, for it was widely known among the traders that Farwell could not speak the Indians' language, except for the simplest terms used in trading. Lebompard, his interpreter, later testified, "I knew from my relation with Farwell and the Indians that he could not understand them." [14]

Far more important is the question of Farwell's disinterestedness. His lack of prejudice is the foundation upon which his account rests; up to the present, historians have taken it for granted. From the beginning of the controversy, however, Farwell faced accusations such as "paid informer," "hired tool," and "biased witness."

These always appeared to be the false charges of men facing justice through the testimony of a witness who sacrificed friendship and social status to tell the hard truth, and accounts by active participants who testified with a noose about their necks are properly suspect. But there is a set of important records ignored by historians.

These are the eyewitness reports of men not involved in the actual fighting, but who watched safely from a distance. Their testimony sheds considerable light on the entire affair, especially on such moot questions as to which side fired first. Joseph Laverdure, for example, testified that "the Assiniboines fired first, but not at the Americans; they fired at random giving out cries of contempt or provocation." [15] The Benton men then replied to the challenge, thus touching off the fight.

Another métis witness, Joseph Vital Turcotte, testified in a similar vein. "I saw them cross the river to go to the Indian camp; they went forward near the coulee; four Indians came towards them naked apparently challenging them; the Benton party were on foot, as they were going towards the coulee four shots were fired by the Indians; almost at the same moment the Americans fired." [16]

Even more damaging to Farwell's reliability is the obvious manner in which he altered his story after consulting with his employer in Fort Benton. Fellow-trader John Wells reported to Ottawa officials shortly after the melee that Farwell "rode to my camp to trade and to hire fifty carts to take his goods to Ft. Benton. He told me that the Assiniboines had commenced the affair, that they had stolen three of their horses and two days after this brought back one horse for which they asked to be paid in liquor and Farwell said they gave them two gallons." [17]

Whatever the truth about the Cypress Hills incident, its aftermath is clear. News of the fight aroused indignation throughout Canada. It came as a climax to a decade of lawlessness in the Whoop-Up country and offended the sense of law and order of the eastern provinces. The story from Battle Creek, gaining in exaggeration and distortion as it spread, hastened the formation of a police force to patrol the unoccupied plains north of the forty-ninth parallel. Though the Macdonald government had already introduced a bill in Parliament to organize the Northwest Mounted Police, the news from the West reinforced the need for immediate action. Public clamor to end the whisky trade from Fort Benton and resentment over this invasion of Canadian sovereignty by freebooters and whisky traders strengthened the sinews of Canadian nationalism and touched the raw nerves of anti-Americanism, always close to the surface.

Reports of the affair filtered back to Ottawa by late summer, but official investigation of the incident began in Washington. In August 1873, letters protesting the outrage reached the Department of Interior from its Indian agents.[18] Since the affair had occurred on British soil, the department immediately transferred the case to Secretary of State Hamilton Fish for action. Two days later, Fish dispatched a note with all the available evidence to Sir Edward Thornton, British minister in Washington.[19]

For the next two years, Canadian officials sought the men responsible for the Cypress Hills fight. Sir John A. Macdonald launched the inquiry by instructing Gilbert McMicken, commissioner of Dominion police in Winnipeg, to investigate the case. McMicken failed to reach Bismarck before the river season closed, and his orders were canceled. By the following year, the Northwest Mounted Police were organized and took over the investigations.[20]

Not until the spring of 1875 were the police able to take action on information in their possession. In May, Lieutenant Colonel Acheson G. Irvine was commissioned to continue the investigation by going to Fort Benton to prepare extradition warrants for the alleged murderers. Irvine's trip to Fort Benton, up the river from Bismarck on the little steamer *Fontanelle* and then across the Indian-infested prairie, opened his eyes to the problems of law enforcement in the American West. Good fortune also led him to find Alexis Lebompard at a little post on the Missouri River. Without revealing his real purpose, Irvine employed the aging plainsman as a guide and from him secured considerable valuable information. Lebompard later proved to be an important witness in the trials at Helena and Winnipeg.

Fort Benton merchants greeted the Canadian officer cordially and assisted him in his mission. Irvine found the Conrad brothers, Charles and William, valuable sources of information. These partners of I. G. Baker, along with the rest of the business community in Fort Benton, were weary of the costly and wasteful conflicts disturbing their trade in the Whoop-Up country. They had earlier welcomed the arrival of the Mounties as a guarantee of peace in that troubled region; now they were determined to assist in ridding their community of men who persisted in regarding Fort Benton as a frontier fur trading post rather than a commercial and financial center.

Meanwhile, Colonel James F. Macleod, an assistant commissioner in the force, entered Montana from Fort Macleod on a similar mission. The two officers were so successful in completing their case against Evans and his men that on May 7 the British minister in Washington requested warrants for their arrest and extradition on charges of murdering the Assiniboin Indians two years earlier. Warrants were issued for the arrest of John Evans, Thomas Hardwick, Trevanian Hale, John Duval, George Bell, Jeff Devereaux, Philander Vogle, George Hammond, John McFarland, James Hughes, James Marshall, Charles Smith, Charles Harper, and Moses Solomon.

Federal machinery was set in motion at once to apprehend the alleged murderers. Officials in Washington instructed Montana's territorial governor, B. F. Potts, to cooperate with Canadian officers, and United States Marshals Charles D. Hard and John X. Beidler were sent the same instructions.

On June 21, 1875, seven of the wanted men were arrested in Fort Benton. Local officers, including Sheriff Hale of Chouteau County, refused to assist Canadian and federal officials. Fears of an aroused public opinion cooled their enthusiasm for cooperation and hopes for continued public favor paralyzed their will to act. So the arrests were made by federal marshals assisted by army troops stationed at Fort Benton. This unpopular action by federal officers increased the tension between local and federal officials and clearly revealed one of the difficulties of enforcing laws on the American side of the frontier. Under federal guard, the men were then transferred to Helena for an extradition hearing before United States Commissioner W. E. Cullen.

Public reaction throughout Montana was immediate. The arrests aroused intense opposition and touched off demonstrations throughout the territory. Causes for this reaction are not difficult to find, for the arrests violated the accepted view in the American West that white men could take the law into their own hands against the Indians. Many Montanans also objected to the arrests as a use of governmental power to assist the Hudson's Bay Company in its efforts to eliminate American competition from the Whoop-Up country. Independent traders in Fort Benton felt keenly on this issue and refused to believe that the Canadian government acted in good faith. For many years the belief persisted that the Northwest Mounted Police only served the interests of the company "in their attempt to monopolize the trade of the Northwest." [21]

Deep-seated prejudices came to the surface in this controversy. Petitions circulated widely denouncing "British invasion" of American rights and picturing the Benton men as innocent victims of the "Anglo-Canadian Indian pacification policy." Anglophobia had its brief day in Montana as a result of the arrests.

Always in the foreground of this agitation was a small but highly articulate group of Irish Fenians in Fort Benton. "Colonel" John J. Donnelly, lawyer, justice of the peace, and professional agitator, led the Fenians in their attempt to make a *cause célèbre* of the arrests. Donnelly's long record as a Fenian spokesman recommended him for this role. The Colonel had already led two abortive invasions of Canada, one from Vermont and another from Dakota Territory. Now he occupied the stage of public clamor for a last moment of glory, preaching hatred of neighboring Canada and of her British institutions.

More important in arousing public fears was the universal sentiment that Indian power could only be held in restraint by such incidents as that at Cypress Hills. Citizens in the Bozeman district, for example, protested the arrest of Evans and his friends with the argument that "there is but one way to punish and bring to account these savage perpetrators — that is, *to pursue and punish according to their own method of warfare.*" [22]

Many Montana editors and spokesmen openly defended the

massacre. They argued that it was a positive good, insisting that it was not a crime but offered a salutary lesson to the red men. The editor of the Fort Benton *Record* summarized this argument with a pointed question: "if the whites are to be punished for protecting their lives against Indians, will they not at once renew the hostilities of former years, under the impression that no matter what depredations they commit, their victims alone will be the sufferers?" [23] If the Cypress Hills incident did nothing else, it exposed the failure of American Indian policy and revealed the weakness of a frontier philosophy that argued for the rule of law for one segment of the community, while allowing the anarchy of violence for another.

On July 7, 1875, Commissioner Cullen began the hearings. Though excited miners pressed into the crowded courthouse and exuberant demonstrations broke out in neighboring saloons and filled Helena's streets, Cullen kept his head and refused to be stampeded by local prejudice and clamor.

Much of the best legal talent in the territory matched skills in the heat of the packed courtroom. Colonel Wilbur F. Sanders presented the Canadian case with vigor and enthusiasm, though Merritt C. Page, district attorney and chief prosecutor, appeared extremely reluctant to defy the public agitation swirling about the court.

To defend the prisoners, Joseph K. Toole directed a formidable battery of lawyers from the firms of Johnston and Toole, Chumasero and Chadwick, and Shober and Lowry. Though Canadian officials appear not to have known it, this selection of lawyers revealed the political implications of the extradition case, for Sanders spoke for a Republican group bitterly opposed to the Irish Democrats of Joseph K. Toole.

Canadian officers applauded Sanders' courage when he denounced the Benton men as "Belly River wolfers, outlaws, smugglers, cutthroats, horse thieves and squaw-men." They gave no indication, if indeed they ever knew, that much of this was inspired by the political motive of discrediting the strong Irish Democrats of Fort Benton. Sanders' attack was so effective that five years later in the general elections of 1880, the Benton Democrats were still popularly called the "Belly River wolfers" and the "Whoop-Up Democrats." They never forgave Sanders for his role in the Helena trial and the whiplash of his tongue remained an unpleasant memory for many years.

Evidence presented in the hearings proved contradictory and inconclusive. Abel Farwell, chief witness for the prosecution, told a confused story. Evidence from fellow traders implicated Farwell in the whisky trading and weakened his testimony by challenging his character. Commissioner Cullen discharged the prisoners on the ground that the Canadian government had not presented sufficient proof of an assault with intent to commit murder. "It is difficult to believe," said Cullen, "that an impartial jury, whether in the United States or Dominion of Canada, would find these defendants guilty upon this testimony of either offenses charged against them . . ." [24]

Jubilant crowds greeted the news of Cullen's decision. A torchlight parade through Helena's main streets expressed their enthusiasm, and liquor flowed freely as Montanans celebrated the return to freedom of their wolfer heroes.

The Helena trial reached an unexpected anticlimax when local officers arrested Colonel James F. Macleod. This farcical turn of events came as a result of Jeff Devereaux's charge of false arrest against the Canadian officer. Chief Justice D. S. Wade speedily dismissed the charge, for Macleod had acted "strictly under orders of his own government and with the approval of the Government of the United States." [25]

Helena's celebration seemed colorless in contrast to the welcome Fort Benton lavished upon its returning heroes. "With flags flying, band playing and horses prancing," the little frontier town devoted an entire day to greeting its ex-prisoners.

That evening, a mass meeting gathered in Solomon's hall to express its enthusiastic pleasure. A carefully selected civic committee staged the event in a hall "tastefully decorated" with a large American flag on which appeared the fighting slogans, "Home Once More," and "Didn't Extradite." Beneath Old Glory a crayon drawing of the British lion in full retreat with an American eagle twisting his tail completed the patriotic motif.

After a few preliminary formalities, Colonel Donnelly harangued the audience with an impassioned speech. The happy purpose of greeting Fort Benton's heroes quickly disappeared in a welter of denunciations, particularly against the federal and Canadian authorities arranging the arrests. "But for the official clothed in a little brief authority, who would thus trample upon the rights of American citizens for the gratification of a Canadian policeman," roared the Fenian, "I have no language sufficiently strong to express my contempt." [26]

Feeling ran high in the river town for many months. Many citizens treated Farwell with "silent contempt" as an informer and a "hired witness." On at least one occasion, the trader received a letter threatening physical violence. Soon he moved north of the border where employment with the Canadian government relieved much of the tension of life in Fort Benton. John Evans, on the other hand, quickly capitalized on his unexpected popularity. With an eye for business opportunity, the "Chief" opened his own establishment in Fort Benton, the "Extradition Saloon."

IV

Fort Benton's enthusiasm quickly turned to dismay as news reached the town that three more of the Cypress Hills participants faced trial in Canada. There, the Mounted Police arrested Philander Vogle, George M. Bell, and James Hughes for the "wanton and atrocious slaughter of peaceable and inoffensive people."

At once, the Fort Benton *Record* seized upon the arrests to launch a new crusade. With little restraint the editor denounced the Canadian government for its "secret hearings" followed by the quiet removal of the men to Fort Garry, "away from their witnesses and all intercourse with their friends." This treatment, he charged, was a "modern star chamber" and an insult to the American people who were told by the Canadians that "the evidence upon which a conscientious American juror refused to commit, was more than sufficient to convict an American in Canada." [27]

The atmosphere in Winnipeg argued for a judicial treatment of the evidence. Far removed from the excitements and tensions of the frontier the Queen's court administered justice without the pressure of public clamor. On October 13, 1875, with Chief Justice C. J. Wood presiding, the court presented bills of indictment against the prisoners and committed them to trial.

The Fort Benton men, however, faced a discouraging situation in Winnipeg. Over a thousand miles from their homes and without a penny to finance their defense, they turned to James Wickes Taylor, the American consul, for advice. Taylor's attitude, though formally correct, did little to encourage them to hope for strong support. Soon they sought aid from their distant friends in Montana. Through published pleas and in private correspondence they told of their plight and implored financial assistance.

Wisely, they directed most of their pleas to John Evans. Nor did the Benton saloonkeeper disappoint them. He wrote assurances that their old friends would assist them and, good as his word, he soon collected nearly four hundred dollars for the defense. Since the lawyer's fees alone promised to exceed five hundred dollars, this was far from adequate, but the resourceful Evans promised that further aid was on the way.

Behind the scenes, moreover, events conspired to assist the prisoners. Taylor, whose first reaction was one of cool formality, now became convinced that the men actually had a strong case which justice demanded must be presented as effectively as possible. The Benton men could hardly have found a more able or influential advocate. Judicial in temperament, scholarly in tastes, and universally respected throughout Canada, Taylor was in a splendid position to organize their defense.

To argue their case, the American consul immediately secured the services of S. C. Biggs, a prominent Winnipeg barrister. Then he turned his energies to unearthing every scrap of evidence for his superiors in Washington. From these investigations, Taylor soon decided that the "massacre" was in reality a "frontier fight" in which the Indians, as well as the whites, shared the guilt. "It ought not be called a massacre," concluded the consul. Moreover, he became increasingly alarmed that "serious international complications" would arise from the trial.[28]

In Washington, State Department officials shared Taylor's concern. Though the department "made every effort to relieve the prisoners by application through the British Minister," it quickly realized that the key to their defense rested with the eyewitnesses in Fort Benton. Unfortunately, these witnesses were also under indictment for the same crime and refused to testify in Winnipeg unless granted assurances of "safe conduct" and immunity from arrest while in Canada. These the Canadian government, for obvious reasons, could not grant.[29]

Taylor despaired of organizing a case without these vital witnesses. The State Department strongly supported the Winnipeg consul, arguing to the British government that a fair trial for these American citizens was impossible without them.[30] Because of the representations of the department and the arguments of Taylor, the chief justice postponed the trial until the following June while their efforts continued to secure evidence for the defense. Ungraciously and quite falsely, the Fort Benton *Record* greeted the news of the postponement as another proof of British injustice in which the men were to be held in prison yet another year before coming to trial.

Taylor's worries grew as he sought to prepare the defense. He suggested a commission appointed by the Canadian government to secure depositions from the absent witnesses. His hopes soared when J. H. Cameron introduced a bill into the Canadian House of Commons authorizing such a commission. The Cameron bill had its first reading on February 23 and its second reading on March 23; then it was referred to the committee on private bills where it quietly died.

The consul now feared that the Canadian government would demand a conviction because its Indian policy in the West required a token punishment to impress its Indian wards. "I am full of apprehension," he wrote Washington, "The authorities propose holding a treaty with the Indians in the vicinity of Cypress Hills this summer and hope for a favorable result of their negotiations, if the prisoners are condemned to death . . . Their danger is that they may be sacrificed from considerations of government policy." [31]

By early June, Taylor confessed to Hamilton Fish by telegram that he despaired, "waiting from day to day for a favorable turn of events." This shift in fortune came in an unexpected fashion when James McKay, prominent Scotch half-breed and a member of the provincial government, volunteered to assist the defense. Moreover, when the case came to trial, McKay testified that he knew Little Soldier and his band of Assiniboins as "Indians who would rob, pillage and murder if they had the opportunity." [32]

When the trial convened on June 20, 1876, Taylor's hopes had revived. Within three days these hopes were fully justified by a turn of events that undermined the Crown case and led to the acquittal of the prisoners.

Along with Farwell, the government brought eight witnesses to the trial, four métis and four Indians. These witnesses, everyone believed, were brought to support Farwell's testimony. Before their appearance, however, they visited a priest who cautioned them to tell the truth under their sacred oath. The surprising result of these interviews was that only one métis and one Indian testified for the prosecution while three of the witnesses, though brought to Winnipeg at great government expense, testified for the defense.

On June 23, Taylor telegraphed Washington, "Bell, Hughes and Vogle acquitted . . . Testimony of informer Farwell not fully supported by other witnesses for prosecution. Please inform governor of Montana." [33]

Chief Justice Wood concluded the trial with a charge to the jury which comprised the most thoughtful summary of the Cypress Hills affair. While there was no evidence that the men had participated in murder, said the judge, there was no justification for the fight in the conduct of the Indians. Whisky was the real culprit and this fight was another of its fearful effects upon the western Indians.

Though the chief justice did not emphasize it, more than the guilt or innocence of three individual frontiersmen was on trial in the Winnipeg court. Under indictment was a frontier society which tolerated the sale of whisky to the Indians and encouraged violence against them when disagreements arose.

James Wickes Taylor suggested other interesting aspects of the affair in his analysis for State Department officials. He was convinced by the evidence that T. C. Power and Company had imposed upon the Canadian government and that their employee, Abel Farwell, was the "instrument of a scheme which proved entirely successful," a scheme "to misrepresent what was an ordinary Indian fight, as an outrage by the whites, and by criminal prosecutions, to exclude competition from the Cypress Hills in the trade for buffalo robes." [34] "His testimony in the extradition proceedings at Helena was impeached and I have no doubt that he perjured himself." [35]

As important as the trial itself was its aftermath. The tradition quickly developed in the Canadian West that the men received "very strict sentences." [36] Thus, the police won the esteem and friendship of the Indians, who were convinced that the Queen's justice fell equally upon the red and white. Curiously, not only is this tradition of severe punishment false, but the men actually considered demanding indemnities from the Canadian government for their long incarceration.

Not until 1882 did the Cypress Hills case reach its legal end. In March of that year, the Canadian government dismissed the indictments against all the Fort Benton wolfers. "It seems a long time to have waited," Taylor wrote Evans, "but I have had to overcome a great amount of prejudice in this case, but 'all's well that ends well'." [37]

5

Law in Scarlet Tunics

IN 1869 the ancient and honorable Hudson's Bay Company transferred to the government of Canada its title to the vast preserve granted in its charter of 1670 and known as Rupert's Land. This real estate transaction of nearly 2,300,000 square miles, exceeding in size and rivaling in importance the more famous Louisiana Purchase, deeply stirred Canadians with its promise of greatness for their homeland. An Imperial proclamation transformed the infant Dominion from a struggling state with only a tenuous foothold in the heartland to a continental power whose empire was soon to reach the Pacific.

But alarming reports poured into Ottawa from the newly acquired region. Indians were restless and half-breeds fearful of their future under the new administration. For more than two centuries the paternalistic Hudson's Bay Company had looked after their interests. What would be their fate now that Canadian politicians were in control?

Lurid stories of American free traders, dealing in whisky and guns, shocked eastern Canadians. Powerful armies of freebooters ensconced in heavily armed forts were invading Canadian territory and making a mockery of its recent transfer to Canadian sovereignty. These armed invaders were already within her gates; what if Fenian armies, trained and armed in a tolerant United States, joined them? In the face of such apparent threats, could Canada ignore any longer her new West without risking her dream of a continental empire?

Patriotism, humanitarianism, and economic interest demanded that these free-trading invaders be brought to heel. Hudson's Bay officials, worried by serious inroads into their Indian trade; missionaries, shocked by the brutality and wantonness of whisky traders; and explorers, disturbed by the knowledge that this vast region was in fact a derelict territory without law or symbol of authority — all urged immediate action by the Canadian government.

Anxious men pondered possible solutions. Captain Butler, newly returned from the West, confirmed reports of unrest and lawlessness and advised prompt action by the federal government to make real its legal title to the land. Civil government similar to that in India should be created and a "well equipped force of from 100 to 150, one-third to be mounted" must be sent out at once, he warned Ottawa officials.[1]

Colonel Patrick Robertson-Ross returned from the Whoop-Up country with similar conclusions. Reporting faithfully information gleaned at Hudson's Bay trading posts, Robertson-Ross informed the government that life and property were not safe on the western plains. Unless a military force was at once dispatched to protect company posts, a disaster seemed imminent. Military posts must be stretched across the plains from Manitoba to the Rockies and 550 mounted riflemen were required to restore order.

Exaggeration marked many of these reports. Fears of Indian troubles, loss of trade by the Hudson's Bay Company, and misleading hearsay reports combined to paint a picture which was neither faithful to the facts nor credible to those who knew the contemporary West. When interviewed in Ottawa following his surveying trip through the Whoop-Up country in 1872, Sanford Fleming faced questions by Mennonite leaders regarding safety of persons on the plains. He answered them by claiming that the only weapon he had carried was a small pocketknife with a blade at one end and a corkscrew at the other. His only regret, he said, was that he had used only one end of this insignificant weapon, and that not often enough!

Nor were Ottawa officials stampeded into sending costly military expeditions into the West as many alarmists urged. "The Government," wrote Alexander Campbell to Lieutenant Governor Morris at Winnipeg, "after a full consideration believe that the state of affairs in the North West is not of so grave a character as to warrant them in incurring so heavy an expense as the measures you suggest would involve." [2]

Sir John A. Macdonald and his colleagues viewed this problem in its larger continental perspective. To send a considerable military force to the West would be unwise, not only because the Canadian government was too hard pressed financially to underwrite such an expedition, but also because the neighboring republic would view such an adventure with great suspicion. Anglo-American relations were at low ebb in the years following the Civil War and deep resentment still rankled in Washington over Britain's friendly policy toward the Southern Confederacy in spite of the recent treaty of Washington which did so much to clear the diplomatic atmosphere. It would hardly be politic, now that Anglo-American relations were on a steadier course, to make a show of force along that long, unguarded boundary passing through the Whoop-Up country. Americans, lacking the political sophistication to distinguish Canadian policy from British imperialism, were certain to object vigorously. Indeed, these fears were confirmed, for when news reached Washington that Ottawa proposed to send a corps of "Mounted Rifles" to the West, opposition quickly appeared. Discreetly, Macdonald changed the name of his force to Mounted Police.

On April 28, 1873, Sir John announced his government's intention to submit a bill "for the establishment of a Police Force in the North-West Territories." He gave no hint, nor could he have foreseen, that with this act, and the handful of scarlet-clad policemen it authorized, the Canadian government would successfully challenge two centuries of North American frontier tradition that lawlessness was an inevitable accompaniment of settlement and that Indians must always suffer despoliation, demoralization, and destruction at the hands of the civilization builders.

Hardly had the government announced its plans when news

of the bloody frontier fight at Cypress Hills broke with a fury in eastern newspapers. Storms of protest swept through Canada when exaggerated accounts described the fight as a bloodthirsty assault of whisky-sodden American frontiersmen upon innocent and defenseless Indians. No further argument was necessary; a police force must be sent west as quickly as possible.

An Order in Council on August 30, 1873, brought the Northwest Mounted Police force to life. Six divisions of fifty men, under the command of a commissioner, each with a superintendent, an inspector, and two sub-inspectors, made up the complement. This modest force was expected to carry out an assignment that many observers, sympathetic as well as hostile, believed would require an army of considerable size.

Stamping out the notorious whisky traffic was only one immediate purpose of the newly created force. Boundaries must be patrolled, customs collected, smuggling halted, and possible Fenian invasions checked. Beyond these immediate objectives, the police must gain the confidence and respect of savage plains Indians while guiding them through the painful transition from a nomadic way of life to a sedentary reservation existence. All this must be done without the bloodshed and tragedy that marked Indian policy south of the boundary. A great heartland empire must be conquered for law and order so that the steel of the Pacific Railway could push westward unmolested by hostile tribes and the way cleared for permanent settlers to move in without fear or danger.

In view of the magnitude of this assignment, there was considerable truth in the Honorable Frank Oliver's observation: "Ordinarily speaking, no more wildly impossible undertaking was ever staged than the establishment of Canadian authority and Canadian law throughout the western prairies by a handful of mounted police." [3]

II

To write a law was easy; to create the police force it authorized was another matter. Slowly, even painfully, the new organization took shape, recruiting its manpower and procuring its equipment. Numerous delays frustrated optimistic ambitions to field a force speedily as some men failed to measure up to the rigorous requirements and supplies sometimes proved faulty or inadequate.[4]

Not until October, moreover, did the members of the force learn the name of their first permanent commissioner. Then the government announced that the task of guiding the Mounties during their formative years was the heavy responsibility of Lieutenant Colonel George Arthur French, inspector of artillery and warlike stores. Possessed of a stern, even unyielding will and a driving energy, the new commissioner quickly revealed a single-minded devotion to the welfare of the infant organization. Unhappily, he also revealed an infinite capacity to irritate politicians with his unbending rectitude and undiplomatic disregard for political sensitivities. Within a year, policy decisions were made in Ottawa without French's knowledge and his reports were soon marked by caustic comments. "Being kept in entire ignorance of the policy of the Government, relative to the employment or distribution of the Force, I am quite at a loss to understand . . . I do not see how the intentions of the Government are to be carried out," complained the commissioner.[5]

With relentless energy, Commissioner French whipped his recruits into a police force. But not until July 8, 1874, were the six divisions sufficiently trained and equipped to depart from Fort Dufferin, Manitoba, for the Whoop-Up country.

Meanwhile, western Indians were prepared for their arrival by the Reverend John McDougall. Under instructions from the government, the missionary informed the Blackfeet that the Queen's police were soon to arrive to protect them from the rapacious American traders. He told the Indians, moreover, that the Mounted Police did not expect them to become military allies but only to greet them with a "friendly eye."

Far to the west of Fort Dufferin lay the lawless region the police were pledged to conquer. Eight hundred miles of virtually unknown land separated them from their goal and their ignorance of the country into which they rode matched its spacious distances. Years later Sir Cecil Denny recalled, "It is curious today to remember what a vague idea we really had of the long journey before us . . ."[6]

Policemen, both officers and men, were inexperienced in plains life and innocent of its simplest facts. With half-breed guides whose knowledge of the country ended at the Cypress Hills and with horses and equipment ill adapted to the plains, the force suffered great hardship and distress. In Fort Benton, westerners who followed their painful progress across the plains through reports brought in by Indians were appalled by the succession of blunders that marked their course. And they marveled at the raw courage which kept the column slowly moving westward along a trail strewn with broken carts and abandoned animals.

Never before in western history had such a force challenged the Great Plains. Shadowy, unseen Blackfoot scouts silently watched the strange cavalcade as it fought its way through an unknown and hostile land. Their reports puzzled old chiefs and stirred the hot blood of young warriors eager for the kill. Who were these red-coated invaders and what was their purpose? Gleaming lances and creaking artillery argued that this was a white man's war party, intent upon fighting. Were the Queen's "pony soldiers" then no different from the blue-coated "Long Knives"? If this was true, what was the meaning of the plows, mowing machines, and cattle? What were these men really up to? Who were these men who knew so little of the country that their horses starved while they were forced to make dry camps, unable to find water?

Indian misgivings were more than matched by the exaggerations and half-truths believed by the police. They were so inexperienced that their first sight of Indians, a roving band of Sioux, was exciting though disillusioning. "They were a very dirty lot, and did not give us a high opinion of western Indians," recalled Captain Denny.[7] This opinion of the noble savage was further strengthened after a few stops at abandoned Indian camp sites. Soon the police learned to avoid these spots, for the Indians always left lice, and lice were no respecters of persons, enjoying the pleasures of a scarlet-clad host as much as they had their former savage habitation.

Other surprises awaited the eastern tenderfeet. The guides proved so incompetent that the force wasted valuable time finding passages around sloughs and lakes and seeking suitable fords across rivers. Inadequate maps further plagued the expedition so that by mid-August there was real danger that they might not reach their destination before snowfall. If that happened, the whole expedition might be lost. Horses and oxen died for want of forage, violent thunderstorms caused stampedes, and prairie fires awed the men with the fury of their vast destruction as flames raced wildly ahead of roaring prairie winds.

This inexperience in western ways led to blunder after blunder, causing costly delays and unnecessary hardships for the men. Equally disturbing was their ignorance of the real character of the assignment which awaited them. Lurid stories of Indian massacres stimulated many fears as the men half expected each new rise of land to reveal hordes of savages ready to descend upon them. When a scout from Fort Benton joined the cavalcade on August 12, his stories of Blackfoot depredations and of the whisky traders' strength further misled them.

From the lowest ranking sub-constable to the commissioner himself, the police grossly overestimated the number and power of the whisky traders and their hold upon the Whoop-Up country. Most fully expected to fight pitched battles with the desperadoes to wrest from them the land which was properly Canada's. The picture of hordes of depraved men, armed to the teeth and determined to hold the country at all costs, had been accepted in the East as an accurate picture, and the police shared it. Much to the embarrassment of the Mounties, the image persisted in the East even after it proved to be false.

Commissioner French shared these miscalculations. He was so misled that he actually related as true a story that the traders at Fort Whoop-Up had captured their two cannon from the United States Army. He reported to Ottawa that these men were so powerful that they had assaulted an army column, looting it of military supplies and equipment. With the commissioner writing such stories to the government, it is not difficult to understand the atmosphere of rumor and suppressed excitement that settled upon the column as it approached the dreaded Whoop-Up country in early September.

By early September, the caravan was indeed in the Whoop-Up country, but where were the hundreds of whisky traders? And where were the rivers that flowed into the South Saskatchewan on their maps? But most of all, where was Fort Whoop-Up, their prime target?

III

The fact is, the police were lost. Worse still, grass was so poor that horses and oxen were starving and rations for the men were desperately low. Two expeditions were sent forward along the river to find Fort Whoop-Up, but both returned with no information. Colonel P. Robertson-Ross, whose report was filled with inaccuracies, had carelessly reported that the whisky fort lay at the junction of the Bow and Belly rivers, when he should have placed it at the Oldman and St. Mary rivers. Frustrated, hungry, cold, and lost, the force was in a serious situation, though they were less than seventy-five miles from Fort Whoop-Up and only a few miles from the heavily traveled Whoop-Up Trail.

Commissioner French was bitterly disappointed. With caustic irony he described the country around them: "And so we were at last at our journey's end, the Bow and Belly rivers, where there was supposed to be such luxuriant pasturage; according to most accounts, a perfect Garden of Eden, climate milder than Toronto etc. As far as our experience goes that vicinity for at least sixty or seventy miles in every direction is little better than a desert, not a tree to be seen anywhere, ground parched and poor, and wherever there was a little swamp it was destroyed by the buffalo." [8]

Now another concern suddenly appeared. Snow fell on September 9 as a grim warning of the approach of winter and ice formed on small ponds to remind French and his men that the northern Great Plains had other, and worse, hazards in store for them. Horses and oxen were in pitiable condition and only the high morale of the men kept them stubbornly moving on. A week's rest was what the men and animals sorely needed, reported French, but "in reality the Force had to leave there as quickly as possible to prevent their being actually starved to death . . ." [9] Misinformation, inexperience, and ignorance had nearly wrecked the expedition.

Painfully the weary column dropped down to Three Buttes along the international boundary. There they hoped to find shelter, grass, and food caches left by the boundary survey parties. But French needed help. His force required supplies and he sought accurate information. Accompanied by Assistant Commissioner James F. Macleod and a small party, he headed for Fort Benton for assistance.

Fort Benton warmly welcomed the Canadian police. Bentonites were curious to see these easterners whose passage across the plains they had followed through Indian eyes. Benton society always greeted eastern dignitaries eagerly and the Mounties now sampled for the first time the hospitality of wealthy merchant families of the river city.

At last, French and Macleod secured reliable information of the Whoop-Up country. From Benton merchants, particularly the Baker and Conrad families, they learned of the character of the whisky trade, the potentialities of the region, and the effect of their appearance upon the whisky traffic. They were surprised to discover that they were camped at West Butte, only a few miles from the great overland highway which led directly to Fort Whoop-Up.

More important for future planning was the memorandum prepared from information furnished by I. G. Baker, one of the best informed and most reliable members of the Fort Benton community. Carefully, and in considerable detail, the Benton trader briefed the policemen about their country north of the forty-ninth parallel.

With considerable surprise the officers learned that their expedition had already struck a deadly blow at the whisky traders, though they had yet to see one of the rascals. "The effect of the expedition," reported Baker, "was sudden and decisive: completely paralysing the trade . . ." The merchant also confirmed the demoralizing effect of the traffic upon the Indians, but added that the whisky smugglers had also ruined legitimate trade in the region.

Equally surprising was Baker's advice that only "fifty men would be sufficient to guard the Hoopup country. Six armed men could go anywhere." This revelation began the realistic education of the police as to the actual character of their problem. Fears of a series of military engagements gradually faded as the facts came into clearer focus. But Baker also warned that the force, though small, must remain. "If the Force is withdrawn from the Hoopup country, affairs there will be worse than ever. The U.S. Marshal has been active in trying to stop the whiskey traffic; but is unable to suppress it alone, owing to the facility of crossing the border."

Thus armed with accurate knowledge of the country, the officers completed their mission by securing supplies and competent guides. Purchasing food and equipment proved simple enough, for Benton merchants eagerly sought the police contracts. In fact, one enterprising Yankee trader had already packed his traps, headed north to Three Buttes, and was even then selling food, especially sugar and syrup, to the hungry troopers. His prices seemed outrageous to the policemen, and indeed they were, for John Glenn reaped a modest fortune from charging what the traffic would bear. In a few days, however, I. G. Baker's bulltrain was creaking northward heavily loaded with food and supplies for men and animals, and the crisis at Three Buttes was passed. Not until later did the police learn that they had also relieved a crisis in Benton, for their contracts lifted the river merchants from depression into prosperity.

Equal success marked their efforts to find competent guides. Again the police followed the advice of the I. G. Baker Company and hired the half-breed scout Jerry Potts, whose colorful career recommended him as a plainsman thoroughly versed in the ways of the West. No one then would have predicted that Potts was soon to become a legend with the force and a hero throughout Canada. To Bentonites, Potts was only one of many frontiersmen whose skills, courage, and toughness had pulled him through many a tight spot. To the police, unacquainted with this reckless breed of men, Jerry Potts came to symbolize infallible judgment on the trail and uncanny wisdom in plains lore. Accompanied by Potts and Charles Conrad of the Baker firm, the police returned northward to complete their assignment.

October 1 was an important day for the Mounties, for they met their first whisky traders. But if they expected to find heavily armed desperadoes, they were disappointed. The bulltrain moving down the trail to Fort Benton to bring in the year's harvest of robes and pelts was commanded by traders whose appearance was singularly normal. Moreover, careful search failed to reveal any liquor, though the police were rightly convinced that whisky had been the chief item used to secure the robes from the Indians.

Eight days later the police reached notorious Fort Whoop-Up, seat of the whisky trade and home of its infamous managers. Here at last was the major objective of their long trek across the plains and hearts beat faster as they scanned its wooden walls. Flying above its bastion was a homemade American flag, as if to defy these Canadian troopers. But a strange stillness prevailed. Perhaps it was only that scores of men were even then silently picking their scarlet-clad targets to begin the defense that rumor had said they would make against the police.

Methodically the police prepared for combat, giving their weapons a final check and wheeling their fieldpieces into position. But Jerry Potts, accompanied by Major Macleod, continued to ride toward the main gate in a casual manner which argued he either was rash to the point of lunacy or knew more than the police about Fort Whoop-Up.

The half-breed guide, of course, was right. Instead of a hail of bullets and stiff resistance, the police were greeted by a virtually abandoned post. Only Dave Akers and a few squaws comprised the garrison of this formidable bastion of lawlessness. D. W. Davis, in charge of the post for the Benton traders, was temporarily absent. Akers, with a hospitality that somewhat disconcerted the tense policemen, invited them to stay for dinner. And a good dinner it proved to be.

Thus Fort Whoop-Up was conquered. Without the firing of a shot, this infamous den of iniquity, this nest of villains and depraved wretches had fallen. The brave men who had expected a bitter fight were welcomed with a feast. What kind of a country was this?

IV

Quickly the news spread throughout North America. Law had come to Whoop-Up. Most of the whisky traders furtively poured their whisky into creeks and quietly returned to Fort Benton to take up other activities. Those few who ignored the warnings of their fellow traders were soon arrested and heavily fined. A new era had opened in the Canadian West while the old lingered south of the line.

In eastern states and provinces, meanwhile, newspapers circulated wild reports about the fate of the police. Rumors of death and destruction filtered back as the force marched westward. Some papers pictured the force as a shattered remnant of the proud cavalcade that had marched out for Fort Dufferin, now lying helpless in the heart of the Indian country and faced with disaster. Opposition papers in Canada, hoping to discredit this adventure of the Macdonald government, poured criticism upon the politicians and police officers responsible for a fiasco in which lives and money had been wasted. Unfair and untrue as these reports were, they hit the government where it hurt and made the police extremely sensitive to criticism.

Gradually, however, the true story was learned. With the growing knowledge of what had actually happened, a new version of the westward march appeared. This interpretation pictured the expedition as an unprecedented conquest of an unknown land, in which the Mounties had done what no one had ever attempted before. This view soon hardened into the tradition that the police were the true pioneers of the plains.

Sometimes versions appeared which added curious details. By 1883 one widely repeated story pictured the police as greeted by hordes of grateful Blackfeet who, with the Reverend John McDougall at their head, formed a cordon to welcome the scarlet-clad warriors and protect them from the enraged whisky traders.

The achievements of the westward march, like the epics of ancient Greece, suffered distortion by false legends and unbelievable exaggerations. The great accomplishment was not in blazing a trail across the plains. This had already been done by hundreds of men, women, and children, both whites and métis. Eastern Canadians were innocent of any knowledge of the plains and quickly ascribed uniqueness to events new to their national experience. Captain James L. Fisk had previously led four expeditions across the northern plains along routes lying only a few miles south of that followed by the police. Hundreds of gold-seekers had followed these northern overland routes while Boundary Commission parties, comprising both Canadians and Americans, had passed through the Whoop-Up country without suffering hardship or risking disaster.

Exaggerated estimates of police achievements on the western trail annoyed many westerners. The Reverend John McDougall, who was certainly a stout friend of the police, was finally moved to rebuke Colonel William D. Jarvis for misinterpreting the significance of the westward march. In his reminiscences the missionary recalls that on one occasion Colonel Jarvis regaled him with "a very fiery description" of the journey from the Red River into the West.

Finally, this western man of God could stand it no longer. "Colonel," said McDougall, "nine or ten miles north of Edmonton there dwells, when at home, a French half-breed who, when the spring comes, will load his carts with his winter's trade and catch of furs and pemmican, and, with his wife and children, will take the trail you came by, crossing all the streams you crossed. In due time he will reach Fort Garry; then he will sell his furs and robes, and purchase his fresh supply of goods and articles of trade, load these onto his carts, turn his face westward, recross all the streams, now at their highest, reach his home north of Edmonton, put up several stacks of hay, fix up his winter quarters, mend his carts and harness, and having carefully stored his goods, he and his family with the same horses and carts will cross the Saskatchewan and travel out from two to three hundred miles on the plains, make a big turn through the country, run buffalo etc. . . . And still it is not yet winter, and thus this native has travelled about three times the distance you and your party did, Colonel; and they had no government behind them, and what they have done is a common occurrence in this Western country."

"It is needless to say," concluded McDougall, "that the Colonel saw the point, and we heard no more about the greatness of the feat of crossing the plain on an old trail in a summer's time." [10]

The true glory of the expedition lay in its transformation from a force of inexperienced recruits into a hardened command, capable of continuing the march despite every hardship and discomfort. Here was the first great testing of the quality of the Northwest Mounted Police, and they passed it proudly. With this victory over themselves, they created an *esprit de corps* that became the hallmark of the force. And they securely laid the foundations of a tradition that still sustains the organization.

v

In the busy months that followed the capture of Fort Whoop-Up, the police established the rule of law throughout the entire region. Relentlessly, they cleaned out the remaining whisky posts and sent the traders hurrying south with the news that the free and easy days were over. By October, the construction of Fort Macleod was well along and out of this post, patrols ranged far and wide. From this strategic site on an island in the Oldman

River, the police controlled the trail north to the Bow River country and south to the boundary.

When Commissioner French departed for the new headquarters at Fort Pelly, he left Assistant Commissioner James Farquharson Macleod to command the police in the Whoop-Up country. Trained in law, Macleod possessed the legal knowledge and experience essential to his task. At the same time, he brought to his post the military experience so important to the success of a frontier commander.

On top of this, Macleod possessed tact, humor, and good judgment. These qualities assured his popularity and commanded respect, in Ottawa as in the West. Much of the initial success of the Mounties in their early years on the plains was the reflection of the energy, ability, and spirit of this popular officer.

During December and January, Macleod proudly claimed the "entire suppression of the liquor traffic" in his reports to French. Most of the traders simply vanished. The high profits were gone now that the scarlet riders enforced the laws. Many stayed in the country to enter legitimate enterprises and some became close friends of the police. "In spite of all we had heard against them," later wrote Captain Denny, "we found them a very decent lot of men." [11]

But disturbing reports began to reach Macleod from the Reverend John McDougall at Morleyville. Not all the traders had abandoned their business, for there remained a handful of desperate men whose careers in crime placed them irrevocably outside the law wherever they lived. And there were others who hoped the police would prove as inept and irresolute as their opposite numbers across the international boundary.

One such trader was J. D. Weatherwax of the firm of Wetzel and Weatherwax, a leading Benton business house. McDougall quietly informed Macleod that Weatherwax, through partners, continued to operate whisky posts on the Bow River. Confidential agents in Fort Benton confirmed this, though Weatherwax himself was conducting a legitimate trade near Fort Macleod. Here was a big catch and Macleod cursed the severe weather and the shortage of horses that prevented an immediate raid on the Bow River posts. But he promised his superior at Fort Pelly that as soon as bulltrains brought the illegally purchased robes down the trail to Fort Macleod, he would act.[12]

Before the policeman could secure direct evidence to confirm McDougall's charges, two wagons suddenly appeared with robes consigned to Weatherwax. The assistant commissioner decided to act anyway, hoping that direct evidence could be secured from the teamsters or from the Indian victims. He therefore issued a summons for Weatherwax and his partner Berry to appear. At the same time, he ordered Inspector Winder to confiscate all of Weatherwax's robes and equipment.

Weatherwax was furious. Vehemently, he denied any connection with the whisky trade, claiming he had sold trading goods to Berry in a legitimate business transaction. "Waxey," as his Benton friends called him, protested that his firm possessed no contraband whisky, though he suspected that the absent Berry might be guilty of an illicit trade with the Indians. Berry, however, could not be found and Macleod was forced to release Weatherwax for the moment.

Weatherwax's freedom was short-lived. In a few days a crestfallen Indian appeared before the assistant commissioner charging that he had been victimized by whisky traders on the Bow River. Bitterly, he complained that he had traded his robes for only three cups of whisky and his horse had fetched only eight. Like so many other Indians, he concluded once he was sober that he had been cheated, and hastened to the police to report his fate.

With this evidence in his hands, Macleod issued a warrant for "Waxey's" arrest. Again the trader angrily protested his innocence, claiming that Berry was the guilty man. When Macleod showed no disposition to be swayed by this argument, Weatherwax turned to threats. Though universally known for his genial disposition, the Benton merchant now stormed and raged, threatening to use his political influence in Washington to have Macleod dismissed. This threat failed to intimidate the officer and "Waxey" drew a stiff fine and a prison sentence.

Fort Benton was shocked by the news. Weatherwax, one of its leading merchants, languished in prison, and public opinion seethed with excitement. Quickly the Fort Benton *Record* came to the trader's defense, pouring columns of scorn upon the police and denouncing Macleod with unrestrained invective. Its editor was the same John J. Healy who had been deeply involved in the trade north of the boundary during its early years. Now he defended his friend in every issue of the little paper.

Soon his editorials took on a bitter anti-police and anti-British tone. "To the scarlet uniform belongs the fame — we will not mention the gain — of destroying the whiskey traffic" growled the *Record*'s editor in February.[13] By March, his Irish temper raged at full torrent and his Fenian sympathies led him to wild charges. "We knew from experience that wherever the English flag floats, might is right, but we had no idea that the persons and property of American citizens would be trifled with. We surmised, however, that on our frontier, within marching distance of our troops, almost within hearing distance of our gas-bagrights of American citizen legislators, the Bull-dogs would be properly chained and controlled."[14] All this was in the best Anglophobic tradition and offered the Fenians another opportunity to vent their spleen upon the hated redcoats across the boundary.

But Healy's passionate charges quickly spent their force. When he denounced the Mounted Police as "mounted grabbers of the spoil," he overreached himself and alienated the sober element of the community. In a short time the *Record* had a new editor. Ironically, Healy was soon sheriff in Chouteau County, cooperating with the very men he had so rashly attacked.

Healy's sound and fury failed to impress Benton's business community. They knew he had not drawn the proper conclusions, for "Waxey's" arrest made it painfully apparent that no one was too big for the law where it was administered by the Mounted Police. While Healy raged, I. G. Baker quietly wrote his friends in Ottawa, "The police you stationed north of here are certainly doing a great deal of good in suppressing the whisky trade and controlling the Indians at that point." [15] Baker was much too shrewd to miss the obvious lesson.

VI

Destroying the whisky trade was an important victory. But success in handling the western Indians quickly overshadowed it as a far more significant achievement. Against a background of continual violence, bloodshed, and hatred south of the boundary, the Northwest Mounted Police conceived and executed an orderly, well-planned, and honorable policy.

From the moment of their arrival in the West, the police regarded their mission to the Indians as paramount. To pacify and restrain the Indians and to prepare them for a sedentary life required all the patience, wisdom, and tact which Major Macleod and his tiny band possessed.

Their simplest decision, though it was also their most important, was to treat the Indians with honesty and respect. The tragic record of deceit and broken faith provoked by the forked tongues of the Long Knives had cost the American government millions of dollars and thousands of lives; yet the Indians remained untamed.

American experience served as guide and warning to Canadian officials. It convinced them that no policy could succeed, however humanitarian or enlightened it might be, unless it was based on consistency and integrity. Honest agents, incorruptible police, and unimpaired good faith — only these could avoid a repetition of the disasters across the boundary. "The experience of the United States," argued one Canadian official, "shows that it is of great importance that the confidence of the Indians in the good faith of the Government should not be shaken, and that Indian affairs should be honestly administered." [16] It seemed an obvious lesson, but American officials required more than a century to learn it.

Commissioner French was especially determined that the Mounted Police should escape the tragic consequences of corruption throughout their organization. With great emphasis he urged Ottawa officials to read carefully General Custer's book, *Life on the Plains*. This revealing document, thought French, clearly exposed the misery and death that followed from "rascally contractors, furnishing inferior stores, which when opened by the troops, when hundreds of miles from any source of supply, proved to be rotten and worthless." [17]

Police policy was further guided by the insight that plains Indians could not be expected to forget centuries of tribal customs to accept the white man's laws overnight. Major Macleod and his policemen often found it difficult to hold their tempers, but their fixed purpose to exercise tolerance and patience prevailed. Stone-age savages must be given time to adjust to the unfamiliar rules of the new society imposed upon them.

As settlers moved into the Whoop-Up country, this policy soon came under attack since Indians possessed but little understanding of the sanctity of private property, so important in North American society. To the south, an Indian was summarily hanged if he transgressed these provisions of the white man's code, but the Mounted Police believed that the Indians must be guided firmly yet patiently through this painful period of transition.

Irate ranchers deeply resented the tolerant policy of the police. "We have no protection from the police," complained a rancher to the Reverend Alexander Sutherland in 1879. "The Indians steal our cattle, as they often do, but we can get no redress. In that respect we would be better off if there were no police in the country at all." [18] This attitude had irrigated the West with blood, and Canadian police were resolved to avoid it at all costs.

Their greatest trials came during the starvation of 1879. With the disappearance of the buffalo, the Indians lost their food supply and turned to range cattle for sustenance. Sternly the Mounties restrained the ranchers from reprisals while patiently they sought to prevent the Indians from continuing their depredations. They were so successful that many a proud warrior hunted gophers to prevent his family from starving. Meanwhile, with desperate warnings the police urged Ottawa to increase the appropriations for rations to feed the starving Indians. The crisis was finally passed without a general Indian war, but it was close.

To change Indian practices of generations challenged every skill the police could muster. Macleod grimly warned the Indians time after time that they must abandon their "pinto buffalo" hunts in which raiding parties stole horses and counted coups among neighboring tribes. Despite confiscation of the stolen horses and frequent punishment, the practice continued. Not until late in the 1880s were officials on both sides of the international boundary able to restrain the Indians from these forays.

Equal justice for red and white was the lodestar by which the Mounted Police charted their course in the Indian country. Indians came to learn, though slowly, that they could depend upon the justice and integrity of the scarlet riders. Individual Indians, not whole tribes, were punished for crimes, for the police understood the folly of indicting whole peoples for the actions of the few. To the amazement of observers south of the forty-ninth parallel, the policy worked. Few American frontiersmen believed the Indians capable of returning faithfulness for faithfulness, or honor with honor.

To create confidence in red-coated justice became a passion with the Mounties. When the men involved in the Cypress Hills fight were arrested and sent to Winnipeg, the police used every possible device to secure convictions. This determination came as a reaction to the bitter criticisms of eastern newspapers during the march west. The threat of failure hung ominously over their efforts if these critics prevailed. Hughes, Bell, and Vogle were symbols in the East of the lawlessness that had taken the police into the country. Now the Mounties were determined that the image of these men as brutal butchers must be confirmed if they were to silence their critics with concrete evidence of their good works.

This determination also grew from a deep conviction that the Indians must see a striking demonstration of red-coated justice, speedy and inexorable. "These arrests," said Major Irvine, "will do more to establish confidence of the Indians in the Government, than any quantity of presents, promises or pow-wowing." [19]

For these reasons the arrests were widely publicized. Easterners were told that bloodthirsty wretches had been brought to justice. Indians were informed that the men were in jail and were punished for their attack on the Assiniboins. Even though the court released the men as innocent, the prestige of the police was kept high and western Indians were taught to look to the Mounties for advice and protection in every crisis.

In their relations with the Indians, the police sought to use persuasion rather than force. This was a policy of necessity, since the force was too small to overawe the savages. It was also a policy of wisdom, for the Indians responded to it with gratitude. Observers in Fort Benton were amazed by the success of the police, though they never tired of predicting that the tiny force would be wiped out by the Indians when the test finally came. Not until 1879, when Star Child ambushed Constable Graburn, was a policeman killed by hostile action, and the dire threats of Benton critics were never realized.

This policy rested upon the fact that the men of the force were not westerners who shared the frontier view that the only good Indian was a dead one. The police were imported easterners and Europeans whose attitudes closely resembled those of people in the American East.

Nowhere is this more clearly revealed than in the diary of Constable R. N. Wilson. While on guard duty one day, the constable allowed four Indians to escape. To save himself from reprimand, Wilson could have shot all four as they ran, "but I did not try to hit any of them, because a policeman has no orders that would justify him in killing an escaping prisoner." [20] No true frontiersman would have hesitated.

VII

No single factor adequately explains the striking success of the Mounted Police. Canadian administration of justice on the plains developed under institutions very different from those in the American West. Basically, it is clear that the socially approved patterns of behavior prevailing in the Canadian East were extended into the West, with the physical environment only slightly influencing the experience.

Mores of the relatively more stable and mature eastern provinces dominated Canadian policy decisions in the West, and a repetition of the troubles clouding the American story was avoided in Canada. Moreover, constitutional differences placed far greater powers in the hands of the central government under the Canadian confederation than in the American system.

With federal officials determining policy, the Mounted Police exercised powers to enforce laws never conferred upon local authorities in the United States. Indeed, to American westerners, this concentration of power seemed both misplaced and dangerous, as destructive of local autonomy and personal freedom. To many, the rule of the police appeared to be a military occupation in which the Mounties acted as both policeman and judge. "As justices of the peace they can hear and determine any charge manufactured by themselves, as policemen, and punish for any offense so charged," complained one American observer.[21]

Canadians expressed similar fears. One critic, writing in an eastern Canadian newspaper, described the system in this fashion: "The Salteaux chief in this case comes before Major Walsh, magistrate, to lay an information. Major Walsh, magistrate, issues a warrant which has to be executed by Major Walsh, policeman. Major Walsh, as a policeman, arrests the parties, and carries them before Major Walsh, the magistrate."[22]

Frontiersmen, whose social and political views were libertarian by eastern standards, were impressed by the effectiveness of the Mounties' power. But this concentration of authority was feasible only because the Whoop-Up country was virtually uninhabited by white settlers. A handful of traders comprised the region's population familiar with Anglo-American legal codes. Later, when settlers poured into the region, mounting criticism forced an end to the policeman's dual role.

Far more serious during the early years was the tragic problem of the métis. These half-breeds, most of whom lived to the north and east of the Whoop-Up country, expressed keen resentment at the government's apparent callousness to their plight. Louis Riel, who was soon to lead his unhappy people in their last desperate bid for justice, voiced this resentment in a confidential letter to James W. Taylor. "But law is administered in such a military style; and justice is virtually left at the discretion of the Mounted Police that it is a matter of doubt for me today whether the people will even be allowed to petition." [23] These were exaggerated fears, but they indicated an alarming reaction to government policy which Ottawa officials did little to moderate.

This concentration of authority, so essential to firm policy in the Indian country, was further assisted by the absence of the influences of a continuing frontier in Canada. Westward-moving pioneers in British North America moved southward into the American states of the Old Northwest when they reached the Pre-Cambrian Shield, that barren and rocky wilderness which shoves its thumb deep into the Upper Middle West. Thus the continuity of the frontier experience was broken, except in the fur trade, that most primitive of exploitative enterprises. Only in this phase of Canadian development did the excessive mobility of the frontier remain a vital force. The violent and bloody conflicts between the Hudson's Bay Company and the North West Company testify eloquently to these influences.

For the Canadian people, however, the Pre-Cambrian Shield comprised an obstacle. Yet it also served as a positive good, permitting Canadians to consolidate, to mature, and to build a stable base from which to project their institutions into the Far West. When they finally burst through the Shield onto the plains, therefore, they came as easterners, innocent of the influences of a continuous frontier environment. They established institutions possessing a sophistication unfamiliar to plainsmen south of the boundary. If the instability and crudity of the frontier were intolerable to Canadians as they viewed the West, so the concentration of power and emphasis upon orderly settlement were equally feared by American frontiersmen as intrusions upon traditional freedoms.

It has been popular to ascribe this social and political instability to the physical environment of the Great Plains. In such a view, the ninety-eighth meridian assumes an almost mystic symbolism, for beyond it "practically every institution . . . was either broken and remade or else greatly altered." [24] Measured against the straightedge of Canadian experience on the plains, this view seems too monolithic to be adequate; too primitive to explain subtle differences. Inherited institutions also underlay the contrasting experience of the two peoples in the same physical setting; neither society was bent to the will of environment in matters of law, either in its character or its enforcement.

Centralized control from Ottawa was never as rigid as the formal organization seemed to indicate. Slow communications as well as deliberate policy gave policemen in the West considerable latitude. Yet the fact that the Mounted Police represented the Crown helped solve many local problems. Western policy engaged the attention and energy of Canada's ranking statesmen. Sir John Macdonald himself, as well as able lieutenants such as Frederick White, devoted their abilities to the administration of the Mounted Police. To contrast the Macdonald government in Ottawa with the Grant administration in Washington is a measure of the difference in the quality of statesmanship directed to solving western problems in the two countries.

As a national police force, the Mounties recruited the finest men available for such duty. Undoubtedly, the romance and adventure, as well as the promise of a land grant at the end of service, attracted able recruits to the force. Few of the men lacked military experience, proudly reported the commissioner in 1874, since most of them were veterans of the Regular Service, the Royal Irish Constabulary, or the Militia.

Most observers were deeply impressed with the high caliber of the officers of the new organization. The Fort Benton *Record* argued that the success of the police was not due to any peculiar organization but to the energy and ability of its officers. Their success was due "above all, to the honesty of purpose with which they perform their arduous and sometimes very unpleasant duties." [25] Moreover, continued the American editor, "The military force of the United States would be equally good if controlled by the same ability and honesty of purpose." Certainly the officers of the Mounted Police possessed a sophistication and an urbanity few frontier peace officers could match. How would a plainsman have described an officer who could write: "The prairie was carpeted with wild roses, and for a time I tried to avoid stepping on them, but they were so plentiful that the avoidance of them became irksome and I hardened my heart and walked on." [26] These were the men who bravely marched alone into armed and hostile Indian camps to arrest offenders in the presence of irate friends and relatives!

The police, of course, had many problems. Both officers and men sometimes failed to measure up to the organization's standards and were dismissed. For a time desertion was a serious concern. Many of the men became dissatisfied with the strenuous duties required of them for a dollar a day. Wild yarns of Indian massacres and whisky-inspired tales weakened others to the point of desertion.[27] But the greatest stimulant came in the traders' glowing stories of quick fortunes waiting in the Montana gold fields. Prospects of wealth in the diggings proved so attractive that on one occasion twenty men deserted en masse for the "land of freedom."

Deserters from the police found shelter in Montana, just as deserters from the American army sought refuge in Canada. Both nations sought recovery of stolen equipment, but neither exerted itself to recapture the deserters, feeling that both services were improved by their departure. Curiously, officers in both organizations urged their recruiting agents in the East to seek men in rural areas rather than in the cities. Each discovered that the rate of desertion among men with rural backgrounds was significantly lower.

VIII

To their western assignment the Mounted Police brought courage, efficiency, and the devotion to law characteristic of the Canadian community. Plains Indians were impressed by the unbending dignity and calculated showmanship of the force, as well as by their discipline, pageantry, and military bearing.

The scarlet tunic, now tourist bait for wide-eyed American visitors, was carefully chosen and proudly worn. Indians feared and distrusted the dark uniforms of the Long Knives, but the red coats reminded them of the traditional friendship of the Great Mother for her children. Scarlet tunics, black breeches with yellow stripes, high leather boots — this was the uniform which became the distinctive symbol of the Mounted Police everywhere in the world.[28]

Mobility was a key concept in the strategy of the police. They avoided the folly of using infantrymen to control mounted nomads and quickly occupied strategic posts at Fort Macleod, Fort Walsh, Wood Mountain, and Calgary. These enabled the force to move without carrying extensive supply trains and freed them from reliance upon the exorbitant prices of sutlers and traders during periods of emergency.[29]

Great courage in the presence of danger quickly became an established tradition with the Mounties. When Major Walsh entered a camp of four hundred angry Assiniboins to arrest nineteen stubborn fugitives in 1877, the Fort Benton *Record* hailed the act as one of supreme courage and expressed the widely held western view that "Custer's charge was not a braver deed . . ."[30] No higher tribute could come from contemporary westerners, who had already canonized their Indian-fighting hero.

Unfortunately, these acts of heroism also became the basis for folklore exaggerations which embarrassed the police with their unreality. Typical of these stories was the often-repeated yarn describing the herding of Canadian Indians to the international boundary by an entire American army. There the blue-coated regiments were greeted by a handful of intrepid Mounties.

"Where's your escort for these Indians?" the anonymous American commander was alleged to have asked.

"We're here," answered the Canadian corporal.

"Yes, yes, I see. But where is your regiment?"

"I guess it's here all right," said the policeman. "The other fellow's looking after the breakfast things."

"But are there only *four* of you then?"

"That's so, Colonel, but you see we wear the Queen's scarlet." [31]

Such folklore as this soon disturbed the Mounties as much as it irritated their opposite numbers across the forty-ninth parallel. This superman role insulted men whose skills, sternly disciplined and imaginatively used, required no exaggeration to do them honor. The police themselves resented the Hollywood stereotype into which they were cast, for none knew better than they how often success had balanced precariously on the razor edge of fate.

Nor was their task as difficult as many admirers of the force have made out. Careful analysis suggests that their problem was actually quite a different one from that facing American officials. The destruction of Indian power on the American plains made easier the task of reducing the Indian in Canada. The disappearance of the buffalo which occurred with dramatic rapidity after the completion of the Union Pacific Railroad in 1869 was so complete on the northern plains by 1877 that Canadian officials were alarmed at the prospect of a "catastrophe." By 1881, police reports reveal that the Indians were starving and that they were compelled "to depend on the Government for assistance, being forced in so doing, to remain about the Police Posts, Indian Agencies or other settlements." [32]

Yet another factor, only slightly emphasized today, materially aided the police. During these years, many of the Canadian Indians actually stayed in the United States pursuing the buffalo and posing no problem to the Mounted Police. Lieutenant Governor Edgar B. Dewdney of the Northwest Territories confidentially reminded Sir John Macdonald of this fact some years later when he wrote, "As long as Col. J. Macleod held the position of Commissioner of Police, Indian matters appeared to have gone on pretty well in Treaty 7, but it must be recollected *that during this time the bulk of the Indians were South of the Line* and the duties of the Agent not heavy." [33]

On top of this, the region lacked the great population pressure of the frontier farther south, for the Canadian West was virtually uninhabited by white men save for a scattering of traders. Unlike the American experience, the law arrived before the rush of settlement onto the Canadian plains, giving the Indians time to adjust to the new sedentary life before white settlements engulfed them.

Canadian policy succeeded in the absence of gold-crazed miners or land-hungry farmers. These arrived after the Indians, as wards of the state, were on their reservations. Canadian officials at the time were immensely grateful for this difference. Assistant Commissioner A. G. Irvine summarized it in this manner: "The experience of our neighbors to the South of the International boundary cannot be without its lesson to us. In their case the military had had no trouble with Indians until settlers appeared on the scene. The settlers, unaccustomed to the Indian manner and habits, do not make due allowances and exhibit the tact and patience necessary to successfully deal with Indians, and which is showed by an organized force kept under control." [34]

Moreover, the Indians fully grasped the importance of police friendship. If they turned against the Mounted Police, they feared destruction between the upper stone of Canadian rejection and the nether stone of American power. And in a practical sense, against whom could they go on the warpath in these years before settlement? Police officer L. W. Herchmer authoritatively argued that "the Indians could only retaliate on the Police themselves and on a few traders, quite able and only too ready to take care of themselves." [35]

"To Maintain the Right" is the proud slogan of the Mounted Police. Their occupation of the lawless Whoop-Up country created a tradition giving vitality and significance to a phrase that was only a challenge before 1875. How complete was their success is clearly reflected in the tradition in Canada today that the Dominion never had a "Wild West" like the United States. So quickly and completely did the police crush the lawlessness in

Whoop-Up that most Canadians are now unaware of its existence in their history.

Whoop-Up country so changed its character with the entry of the police that the name itself fell into disuse. Ruthlessly the Mounties smashed the gangs of fly-by-night traders who had no investment except a wagon and a few barrels of liquor. Patiently they accomplished the more important task of pacifying the Indians. In the wake of these achievements, legitimate enterprises of commerce and agriculture came in to develop this last great frontier of the Canadian-American West.

While doing all this, the police established a reputation. One which the Fort Benton *Record* summed up in the terse phrase "they fetched their men every time." [36]

6

Law in Chouteau County

LAWLESSNESS, gun play, and mob violence are favorite western themes. With smoking six-shooters or knotted hemp, frontiersmen lived and died at the dictates of "Judge Colt" or "Judge Lynch."

These are exaggerated views. They caricature western society and distort the realities of crime and punishment along the frontier. Tall tales of garrulous old-timers and lively imaginations of colorful writers nourished the myth to formidable proportions. The "Wild West" exists chiefly in the paper pulps, on the silver screen, in Frontier Days celebrations, and in regional chauvinism.

No society could have survived under the conditions pictured in the legends. Social disintegration would have destroyed the growing western communities before they were firmly established. Had every westerner lived by the myth and defended his honor with Colt's "Great Equalizer" at the slightest provocation, only one honorable man would have survived in each community. The fact is, few men used these famous weapons, even when they carried them. "It is, after all but rare that business takes the serious turn of shooting," wrote William Shepherd after his experience in the West. "Most of the frays rise out of gambling and drunken quarrels, and shooting is relegated to the saloons and haunts of the most depraved." [1]

Yet law enforcement was a serious problem in the Whoop-Up country. South of the forty-ninth parallel, frontier conditions of excessive mobility, heterogeneous population, feverish speculation, social instability, and primitive political institutions encouraged a disregard for law and order.

The fringe of settlement traditionally served as a refuge for those who lived outside the law. The Civil War intensified this problem by creating a generation of border ruffians and bandits who found a safe and profitable haven in the sparsely settled West.

To some observers, the frontier was synonymous with lawlessness. Montague Davenport, a British visitor who traveled through the region in 1875, concluded that "the spirit of lawlessness increases as we go West. I think the American eagle should be portrayed with a six shooter in his claw: he is incomplete without it." [2]

Others disagreed with this harsh judgment. Charles E. D. Wood, editor of the neighboring Fort Macleod *Gazette*, ridiculed the picture of the "Wild West." "The general idea Eastern people have of these western places," he wrote, "is that everyone goes about with a pistol at his waist and a big knife in the other side . . . that two or three men are shot in the streets every day, and in fact that a man carries his life in his hands." Wood refused to endorse eastern views of Fort Benton as a lawless, degenerate frontier town but believed it "a busy little place and law and order are most thoroughly enforced there." [3]

Sensitive to eastern criticism, the editor of Fort Benton's *River Press* suggested a comparative analysis. While the region undoubtedly had its criminals and tough cases, he believed that Chicago's record of 176 murders with only two convictions during the years between 1875 and 1881 "beats the West all hollow." [4] Such comparisons did not diminish the magnitude of the problem on the frontier; but they did place it in a proper perspective.

Crime control was a national problem, not one peculiar to the West. Decentralization of authority in local governments was the heart of the matter, for through them law enforcement and judicial administration functioned. Many counties and municipalities were too poor or too easily victimized by gangsters to support adequate programs.

Traditionally, Americans have cherished their local units of government as essential to their democratic institutions. Few would deny that they have served as schools for citizenship, encouraging incentive and rewarding initiative while providing the balance between individual liberty and governmental authority. They have kept government close to the people in an atmosphere of friendliness and personal concern.

All this has cost the American people a considerable price in inefficient, even corrupt law enforcement. At times, in fact, this decentralization has paralyzed law enforcement, leaving the community at the mercy of its predatory citizens. Combined with the traditional American tolerance for crimes that do not touch the citizen directly, it has opened opportunities for criminal careers usually denied citizens of other nations possessing similar legal codes.

Americans launched their assault upon the Great Plains West with more than two centuries of frontier experience behind them. Yet the institutional structures within which this last frontier was conquered differed only slightly from those of the first colonists who pushed their way up the river valleys of Connecticut or into the Piedmont regions of Virginia.

Legal responsibility came only with settlement. Whole communities along the frontier remained without formal legal institutions until territorial organization made possible the creation of county units of government. But these were often so sparsely settled, so tax poor, and so corruptly governed that law-abiding citizens sometimes took the law in their own hands to restore peace and order through vigilante societies and through extra-legal courts.

Westerners have been regarded by some historians as great innovators. Yet they stumbled along with anachronistic pre-Revolutionary legal machinery that provided neither peace nor security, preferring to leave unchanged the granite-like political forms comprising their inheritance.

The federal government remained powerless to restrain lawlessness in the vast western wilderness. As Bernard DeVoto has pointed out, federal officials could hardly dispatch a company of dragoons to pursue a murderer across the plains or through the mountains.[5]

All this, as we have seen, is in striking contrast to the solution contrived across the international boundary. There the Imperial experience of a constabulary force, such as those organized in Ireland and India, was applied to the sparsely settled West. It took no troop of cavalry to pursue a solitary murderer across the plains. A single policeman, armed with Dominion authority, accomplished the task.

Many thoughtful Americans urged a similar system in their West as they learned of the successes of the Northwest Mounted Police. But western communities, intensely jealous of their traditional powers in the administration of justice, refused to accept such a system. It appeared to be synonymous with a military rule that undermined local government and abandoned traditional guarantees of personal freedom. Few Americans approved a system that gave the police the power, as Colonel James F. Macleod privately admitted, "to try any case and have only to wait for a *wink* from *Ottawa* to hang our man." [6]

II

Other factors also complicated the problem of law enforcement on the Whoop-Up frontier. Lenient jurors often refused, despite the evidence, to indict or punish offenders. Pleas of "self-defense" so often saved the guilty from punishment that outraged citizens acted illegally to ensure justice.

A surprising overemphasis upon legal formalities and upon "due processes" impeded the cause of justice. "Innocent until proved guilty" frequently meant that the guilty were always innocent.

Provoked by these perversions of justice, irate citizens occasionally turned to lynch law to enforce a rough but speedy justice. There was great reluctance to use this dangerous weapon. The Fort Benton *Record* in 1877 argued that "one half of the persons lynched are innocent of the crimes for which they suffer, and not infrequently the ends of private malice are gratified under the pretence of punishing wrong-doers."[7] Still, a few lynchings did occur in the Whoop-Up country, on both sides of the boundary. In April 1875 Benton citizens seized two manacled and helpless Indians from the sheriff's custody and shot them for the unproved murder of a white man. Army officers who were sent to Benton with troops to protect the town from Indian retaliation denounced the act as "wanton" and "brutal." And Benton's little newspaper forthrightly condemned it as filling "every God fearing citizen with horror, disgust and contempt." This fearful deed, announced the editor, "is a wretched reminder that Benton is not yet free from that barbarous class of society so common to new settlements on the western frontier."[8]

Fort Benton's only white lynching was also its most famous. In 1868 William Hinson drifted into Benton from Helena where he had been charged with a murder but released for lack of evidence. Soon Hinson launched a campaign for a night marshal to patrol Benton's streets. Possessed of a congenial spirit and a persuasive tongue, he soon promoted himself into that position.

In a short time, inebriated drifters complained of losing their money when arrested by the new peace officer. Hinson diverted attention from these charges by loudly urging the formation of a vigilante society to clean out the town. Benton needed a "half dozen hangings," he announced.

Retribution came quickly to the corrupt peace officer. Fort Benton's substantial citizens trapped the marshal with a pretended drunk who caught the officer redhanded lifting his roll. The following day a delegation visited Hinson.

"We've caught the fellow who has been doing these robberies," said the spokesman, "and in half an hour we're going to hang him. Have you got a rope?"

"No," replied the unsuspecting marshal, "but I can get one mighty quick." Good as his word, Hinson immediately purchased a new rope and returned eager to dispatch the victim.[9]

Before the surprised marshal could escape, the crowd hanged

him with his own hemp. Fort Benton had no further trouble with its public servants. But the record does not sustain C. M. MacInnes's charge that vigilantes cleaned out Benton regularly.[10]

Lynchings also occurred across the boundary. On one occasion an angry group of passengers on the Fort Macleod stage shot their driver for compelling them, under the lashings of his long whip, to push the stage up a steep hill.

Equally informal was the lynching of a man who refused to assist some cowboys put out a prairie fire. After they had extinguished the fire, the cowboys "took him out and hung him." [11] In both cases, the penalty seems unduly severe.

Many Montanans blamed influences imported from the southern plains for much of this trouble. The northward drift of Texas cowboys introduced, they felt, a lawless element into the population. Texas law enforcement had a poor reputation in the Whoop-Up country. When Thomas Pool, a Texas cowboy, pulled his revolver and wantonly killed an innocent man in a trivial barroom quarrel, the *River Press* expressed the universal opinion that the Texas frontier "was a good place to become schooled in ruffianism and in the use of the ready revolver." [12]

Western legal values puzzled many observers. Horse stealing and cattle rustling aroused universal condemnation and provoked quick reprisals. Murders of Indians, Chinese, or Negroes, on the other hand, often passed unnoticed or were even praised as ridding the country of undesirables.

In the West, property was safe, believed the famous British correspondent W. H. Russell, "for citizens hunt down with extraordinary energy marauders whose object is simply plunder. It is otherwise with those who assail life and limb." Others were sufficiently perceptive to see that this was an American trait, not a peculiarly western weakness.

Law enforcement, in East or West, rested upon the quality of the county sheriff and the prosecuting attorney. Unfortunately, few sheriffs possessed experience, training, or any particular qualification except the capacity to win political office. Similarly, county attorneys were generally inexperienced young lawyers or incompetent oldsters. Numerous duties reduced the efficiency of both officials. Sheriffs, for example, usually served as tax assessors and collectors, officers of the court serving processes, and jail keepers.

On the whole, the system drew little praise, except from criminals.

III

On the morrow of the Civil War, Chouteau County was larger than the combined areas of Massachusetts, Connecticut, and New Hampshire. The second largest county in Montana Territory, it stretched from the forty-seventh parallel to the unmarked international boundary and from the Judith Mountains to the Rockies. In this vast wilderness, a local sheriff, assisted by a deputy, enforced the laws. Federal marshals and army troops were also present, but they aided local officers only when federal laws had been violated.

During the sixties the Whoop-Up country was virtually without formal law. Winfield Scott Stocking recalled that the Benton he entered in 1866 was a community with "neither village nor city ordinance, neither Territorial nor Federal law, no, not even moral law." [13]

Stocking's recollections somewhat exaggerated the facts. But it was true that the community relied chiefly upon the pressures of social groups to preserve order. Ordinarily, these were powerful forces in shaping individual behavior, but Benton unhappily "was cursed with a floating population of as hard a set of desperadoes as perhaps exist on earth." [14] Lawlessness under these conditions became so common that even Sheriff Hale suffered the loss of his horses to thieves in the early seventies.

In this atmosphere, peace officers were often corrupt. Chouteau's first sheriff, the notorious Henry Plummer, established a tradition that lingered for many years. Plummer began a dual career as sheriff and head of a gang of road agents in the Sun River community in 1863. He ended it hanging from a rope in Bannack when the vigilantes lynched him with his gang.

Succeeding sheriffs were often only a cut above the scheming Plummer. Chouteau's next four sheriffs began their careers in the Whoop-Up country as whisky traders, living on the other side of the law.

Until the seventies, Fort Benton was the rawest of frontier towns with its seamy side showing. By 1875, however, Bentonites became respectable, preferring to forget their past and emphasizing their promising future. The early years seemed unfortunate but the town had outgrown its rough and callow youth.

To John J. Healy belongs much of the credit for this transformation. Indeed, Johnny Healy typified the successful frontier peace officer whose iron-fisted authority was as much a personal regime as it was the rule of law.

Irish-born Healy came west with the Second United States Dragoons in 1858. After two years of a soldier's life, however, young Healy headed for the gold fields to find his fortune. With untiring energy, but without the proverbial luck of his kind, Healy tramped the West. Through Montana's famous gold fields, on into Idaho, and as far north as Edmonton he sought the precious metal.

Next, the ambitious Irishman turned to townsite promotion. This promised a certain avenue to wealth, for shrewd speculators made great fortunes booming insignificant towns into cities. But Healy's choice proved wrong; his little town of Boulder, Montana, remained a little town. Then followed a brief period on the Indian reservation farm at Sun River. When this produced little in the way of financial reward or excitement, he turned to Indian trading.

Healy earned his reputation as a plainsman during these years. Always calm whatever the emergency, completely fearless, a natural leader of men, and unhampered by moral scruples, Healy pushed the whisky traffic north into Canada to establish Fort Whoop-Up. There he presided like a feudal baron over the flourishing trade, but the profits slipped through his fingers to silent partners in Benton. When the Mounted Police ended the whisky trade in 1874, Healy returned to Benton, still lacking the fortune he sought. But he had found adventure and excitement and these were his meat and drink.

For the next three years Healy drifted from one unprofitable enterprise to another. Essentially a man of action, business routine wearied him and financial details escaped his attention. Farmer, trader, hunter, Indian fighter, he was a jack-of-all-trades, but his livelihood became increasingly uncertain. By August 1876 he was desperate. "I am a total wreck financially," he wrote his friend Martin Maginnis, Montana's territorial delegate in Washington. "The grasshoppers got away with *everything* this year and [there is] nothing left for me now but to join Gibbon or some of these Indian fighting fellows." [15]

This seemed a reasonable proposal since Indian fighting always offered a convenient way to tide things over until prosperous times returned. Healy outlined a plan to the territorial delegate in which he promised to defeat the hostile Sioux with only a hundred white volunteers and two hundred Blood Indians. His financial prospects were so poor that any wild scheme seemed feasible and he declared himself "open for any enterprise now that don't necessitate Road agency."

Not road agency but law enforcement rescued the restless Irishman from galling inactivity. For several years Healy had played a leading role in Democratic politics in Chouteau County. As county chairman he earned the gratitude and friendship of Democratic leaders in Montana. The appointment as sheriff of Chouteau County to fill a vacancy in June 1877, therefore, came as a matter of course to this faithful but needy member of the party.

The county commissioners could hardly have made a better choice. Healy's fearless, energetic, and devoted efforts captured the public imagination to establish a legend of law enforcement in the high border country. The visiting British financier A. Staveley Hill joined the chorus of praise, describing Healy a "cool minister of the law" without peer in the Northwest.

Healy earned his reputation. "If any of you is going to steal horses during the next two years," promised the new sheriff, "he had better vote against me, for by God! if I catch him, whether he's voted for me or against me, I'll hang him." [16]

While this political impartiality was commendable, Healy's regime had a personal quality to it that irritated many citizens. Johnny Healy was the law, and the law was what Johnny Healy chose to enforce. Indeed, the sheriff enforced the law against the drifters and the humble as energetically as he had earlier violated it during the whisky trading days. But he only laughed off the frequent suggestions that he seemed blind to the illegal activities of his powerful friends.

Healy took particular delight in bringing horse thieves to justice. His pursuits across wilderness trails filled him with a savage joy and his promise to hang them when captured proved no idle threat. He enforced the law with a brutality that sometimes left the line between crime control and lawlessness vague, though always with a dash and verve that excited attention.

Only once during Healy's tenure of office did Benton's citizens agitate for vigilante action to supplement his actions. In 1879 a gang of horse thieves preyed upon the community with such success that the sheriff faced mounting criticism. The great freighting companies lost so heavily to the horse thieves, however, that they finally imported twenty-five Pinkerton agents, who quickly exposed the gang.

Under Johnny Healy, peace settled over Chouteau County. In contrast to the earlier years, the Whoop-Up country became safe for solitary travelers. Joe Kipp regularly carried sums of money in excess of $100,000 across the plains to Fort Macleod without trouble. Law and order now transformed the county seat from a lusty brawling river town to a respectable commercial mart, intolerant of rowdy transients. By 1881, respectability had so conquered the community that the *Record* thought it newsworthy that one of the town's "fair but frail citizens" fired a pistol shot "just for fun on Main street." Benton's law officers seemed to have forgotten completely the free and easy atmosphere of earlier years. Callous to the whims of frontier conviviality, they arrested the lady of pleasure, and Judge Tattan fined her twenty dollars and costs the following day. Where had the Wild West gone?

IV

Johnny Healy, like most sheriffs, had many official duties. To his responsibilities as a peace officer were added those of tax assessor and collector. These duties bore heavily upon the sheriff, who found them extremely irksome. They undermined his popularity as a dashing peace officer, particularly the onerous task of assessing the property of his fellow taxpayers. When a campaign was launched in 1880 to separate these offices, Healy gladly joined the agitation.

Though his official duties appeared heavy, Healy found time and energy to pursue personal projects. In 1877, shortly after his appointment as sheriff, he joined Judge Tattan in plans to organize a stage and express company. These fell through when T. C. Power blocked the sale of the Gilmer and Salisbury Company to the two Irishmen. But later that same year, the two officeholders purchased the Overland Hotel.

During the following year, Healy became co-owner of the Fort Benton *Record*. This investment was as much political as it was financial, for as local editor Healy vigorously defended the Democratic rule of Chouteau County, especially in the sheriff's office. He also owned a flour mill at Sun River, an enterprise that should have prospered in view of the shortage of milling equipment in the Whoop-Up country. Like the others, however, this investment languished under the indifferent business management of the restless prairie man.

Healy's dream of golden wealth never faded during these busy years. In 1878 he packed up his traps and joined the stampede to the Bear Paw Mountains. His luck failed again but he returned convinced that in the next gold rush he would strike it rich.

The sheriff never found wealth, but he found adventure. One thrilling episode after another filled the columns of Montana's newspapers until the name of Johnny Healy symbolized frontier

117

law enforcement. Many of his exploits were filled with derring-do. In May 1881, for example, while Healy was arresting a Piegan for horse stealing, a friend of the intended prisoner suddenly overpowered the sheriff. Only the timely intervention of one of his deputies saved him from "a horrible and untimely end." Again, in 1882 the dramatic arrival of a troop of cavalry, in approved Hollywood fashion, rescued the peace officer from a large band of intoxicated half-breeds.[17]

Gradually, however, the public tired of Johnny Healy. His irresponsible actions perpetuated an anachronistic order of things in a region rapidly filling up with farmers and ranchers, while his crude sense of humor alienated even his friends. Montanans universally condemned the Chouteau sheriff for a prank played upon Bad Bull, a Blood Indian held in the Benton jail as a hostage to discourage further horse-stealing expeditions. Before releasing the Indian, Sheriff Healy clipped his long hair, thus disgracing Bad Bull and exposing him to the ridicule of his fellows.

"Notwithstanding his protest and piteous appeals," wrote the editor of the *River Press*, "his long black hair was soon clipped and Bad Bull, like Sampson of old, was shorn of his pride and strength. The sheriff laughed. Everybody laughed. It was brave indeed!"

Plainsmen knew, however, that some innocent settler would pay with his life as the Indians revenged the disgrace. "A funny man for sheriff may be a very nice thing on the outside," protested the newspaper, "but he should not endeavor to work up his humor when in the performance of his official duties."[18] And the Bozeman *Avant Courier* joined in denouncing the prank as "very thoughtless and indiscreet and deserves the severest condemnation of all peaceable and law abiding citizens."

The sands of popularity were running out for the sheriff. Mounting criticism so damaged his political prestige that by 1881 he was in trouble. The growing power of the Republican party in the region also cut deeply into his strength.

Ironically, Healy's political enemies seized upon his successes as weapons to unseat him. Charges of corruption were common-place against the sheriff but he weathered them without difficulty. These, after all, were only part of the game. Voters knew very well that he was neither less honest nor more corrupt than William Rowe, former sheriff of the county in the seventies and ex-whisky trader whom the Republicans ran against him in the elections of 1880 and 1882.

But his opponents increasingly emphasized the high cost of successful crime control under Healy's administration. The sheriff's relentless pursuit of evildoers often took him outside Chouteau county. Economy-minded citizens urged Healy to let other units of government capture and prosecute the criminals. All they required of him was that he keep the lawless on the move to prey on other communities.

Even the sympathetic *Record* voiced concern. The expense of punishing for crime exceeded the frontier county's resources; preventing it seemed much too costly. The critical *River Press* worked assiduously to discredit the "energetic, but overzealous sheriff." It seized upon every incident of pursuit, whether successful or not, as an example of Healy's overconscientious and costly law enforcement.

When Healy traveled into an adjoining county to capture an escaped prisoner, editor J. E. Stevens protested vigorously. "It is a pity that Chouteau county is made to pay such heavy bills of costs as the capture of this class of criminals involves. It is a pity, too, that when one of the parties takes the trouble to put himself out of the county, and a good ways out, that he is not allowed to remain. We are sorry that Talbert's rifle failed to kill the party, which would thus have done the county the greatest possible service, by saving it all the costs, that must accrue from his capture and prosecution." [19] Human life was as dust in the balance when weighed against higher taxes.

The construction of a new prison in 1882 was another achievement of Healy's regime that many regarded wasteful. So many prisoners escaped from the ramshackle old jail that in 1881–82 the county commissioners erected a model prison. At first view, the new prison disappointed its many visitors, for it seemed no better than other frontier prisons they had seen. On the inside, however, a huge cage of steel floors, roof, and walls filled the building. Guards patrolled the cage, keeping every movement of the inmates under constant surveillance. Fort Benton's model prison was the pride of the community, for it seemed as escape-proof as "modern science could make it."

But Sheriff Healy did not remain in office to test the new jail's efficiency. Though he vigorously denied the charges of his ene-mies, the colorful sheriff lost his political following. When a Re-publican opponent compared him with Boss Tweed, the angry Irishman denounced his critic as a "skulking, dirty, cowardly, miserable cur." This was exciting, but it won few votes.

In 1882 Chouteau County elected a new sheriff. Johnny Healy, Indian fighter, gold miner, hunter, trader, speculator, prairie man, and adventurer, surrendered his badge to his old friend of the Whoop-Up whisky-trading days, William Rowe. The new Re-publican sheriff promised economy through inactivity, a pledge he faithfully carried out.

Fort Benton and the Whoop-Up country soon seemed too quiet for restless Johnny Healy. His zest for adventure undiminished through the passing years, he headed for Alaska where there re-mained Indians to fight, furs to trap, gold to discover, and em-pires to build.

V

The administration of justice in Chouteau County was as capricious as law enforcement during the early days. Judge Tat-tan, who presided over the local court for many years, later claimed that he was elected "when there was no law or order to speak of in Benton." Since the judge kept no records until the eighties, no detailed evidence exists to reconstruct the character and conduct of his court. It is apparent from other sources, how-ever, that the judge's rulings were as informal as his records. A favorite punishment during the early years offered defendants the choice of a stiff fine and long imprisonment or a speedy departure from Fort Benton. Since most chose to take the stage to Helena or the next boat down the river, Judge Tattan's strategy won approval for "saving the county the money of boarding prisoners."

During the late seventies, Judge Tattan's court could no longer cope with the increasing number of legal cases. Benton's large, though transient, population and the great distance to the district court in Helena provided forceful arguments to create a district court in Benton. When this court was established in 1880, its usefulness immediately became apparent. District Judge D. S. Wade presided over forty trials during the 1881 term, and these were only a fraction of the cases presented to the court but quashed for want of evidence, or other technicalities.

Grand juries showed considerable reluctance to indict, except in cases where the crime was a major one. "In the abstract," observed the *River Press*, "many may conclude that the cause of justice will suffer by this apparent neglect." [20] But Chouteau's poverty dictated that jury trials were too expensive for such trivial offenses as assault and battery. Thus, demands for economical administration, perhaps more than the widely publicized frontier impatience with court procedures, prompted much of the argument for speedy and direct justice.

Minor offenders simply paid a sheriff's fee and were released without a trial. In the name of economy, frontier taxpayers tolerated a dangerous combination of judicial and executive functions in the sheriff's office.

Where local court records exist for the years before 1885, the character of judicial actions and the nature of criminal cases do not differ materially from those of later years. The justice of the peace court dockets for the years from 1870 until 1886 at Sunriver Crossing, a small settlement in a rural setting, reveal the usual offenses characteristic of such a court. There is no way of knowing, of course, what percentage of offenders failed to appear before the court. [21]

As early as 1870, citizens were fined in the Sunriver court for cruelty to animals, an offense not generally regarded as one drawing censure on the frontier. Threats against persons drew good behavior bonds as high as $1250, while cases of disturbing the peace with the use of "insulting and abusive language" also appear in the earliest records. Particularly severe penalties were assessed against those guilty of "indecent and foul statements" in the presence of women.

These records also indicate a passion for legal terms and impressive court phrases not matched by accurate syntax or spelling. "G. W. Wyegand pursonally apeard before me, W. P. Burcher, Justice of the Peace, who being furst sworn deposes and says that on the 29 day of October A.D. 1877 in the county and Territory aforesaid that i have reason to belive and do belive that Ralf Long did with out my knowledge er concent did take Bufelow Robes to the amount of 30 dollers with intent to Robe me of the same and there value and Has left the aforesaid county and naberhood with the above named Robes . . ."

The actions of this particular court, though it existed on the remote edge of settlement, vary markedly from the generally accepted versions of frontier justice. They indicate a concern for due processes of law and for a community orderliness that was effectively implemented, despite the primitive surroundings.

VI

Federal law was also present in the Whoop-Up country. United States marshals and their deputies joined local authorities in suppressing crime. In the early years following the Civil War, their major task was the destruction of the illegal whisky traffic to the Indians, a mission they accomplished with only partial success. The great distances, too few deputies, and public hostility hampered their work. Despite conscientious efforts, the illegal trade with the Indians continued.

Deputy United States Marshal Charles D. Hard was the first to challenge the power of the Whoop-Up traders successfully. Virtually singlehanded, this energetic and able officer put an end to much of the whisky trade. His successes forced the traders to adopt numerous ruses and led many of them to cross the boundary into Canada where his authority could not disturb them. During his four years as deputy marshal from 1869 to 1873, Hard created a tradition of law enforcement that assisted his successors substantially.

Most famous of the Whoop-Up deputy marshals during the following years was John X. Beidler, or X. Beidler, as he preferred to be called. Deputy Marshal Beidler began his career in Montana as one of the leaders of the Virginia City vigilantes. When his work was finished, he had become as much a symbol of law enforcement as Johnny Healy.

Beidler's early youth gave little promise of his exciting life in the West. Born of Dutch parents in Chambersburg, Pennsylvania, young Beidler won a reputation as "the most peaceable and beloved of any young man in the town." But, disappointed in a love affair and restless to see the West, he went out to Kansas.[22]

Frontier Kansas offered ample excitement during the pre-Civil War years. Beidler was soon in the very heart of it, for he joined John Brown's border ruffians. This experience apparently transformed the "peaceable" young Pennsylvanian into a rough and ready frontiersman. But when Brown went east to his disaster at Harper's Ferry, Beidler stayed on the frontier. Through Indian territory, into Texas, and on to Colorado he drifted, eventually finding his way to the gold fields of Virginia City, Montana.

At Virginia City the future marshal attracted attention. Established as a butcher and a cattle drover, he was soon harassed by the region's famous road agents. His outspoken opposition to the gangsters and his relentless efforts to bring them to justice marked him as one of their chief targets.

Soon Beidler played a leading role in hanging these thugs who preyed upon Montana's gold miners. Countless stories, adroitly mixing fact with fiction, surround Beidler's encounters with the road agents. One of his narrow escapes occurred when he was captured by a gang whose members he had tried to hang shortly after he had gone so far as to dig the grave for one of its members.

"You are the man that helped dig my grave," said one of his captors.

"Yes," replied Beidler, "and, by the way, you have never paid me for that yet."

Beidler's experience in the gold fields established his reputation as an adventurer. His unfailing sense of humor and marked storytelling abilities endeared him to fellow frontiersmen, though they sometimes wearied of repetitious stories that made Beidler the hero in every encounter. His selfless generosity, moreover, won many friends for the jovial Pennsylvanian.

Soon Wells, Fargo employed the young Dutchman to ride shotgun on its stages. This, as much as anything, turned Beidler's immense energies to the defense of lives and property. Other men, possessing a similar love of excitement, matched his experiences on the other side of the law.

Beidler's reputation grew rapidly as one story after another went the rounds. Montanans chuckled over Beidler's spirited defense of his failure to protect a stage against a gang of road agents who halted the coach and robbed its passengers. Having somehow learned of the gangsters' plans, Beidler had removed the gold box for a later shipment. But Theodore Tracy, Wells, Fargo agent in Salt Lake City, angrily telegraphed Beidler, "Why in hell ain't you there when our coaches are robbed?"

"Why in hell don't they rob them when I'm there?" replied the indignant Beidler and he immediately resigned. Wells, Fargo rehired its impetuous stage guard, who remained with the company until appointed deputy United States marshal.

As deputy marshal, X. Beidler enforced the law with the same vigor displayed by Johnny Healy. They were a remarkable team, the Dutchman and the Irishman, and they left similar legends of derring-do in the high-line country of Montana.

A multiplicity of duties sent Beidler from one end of the territory to the other. Pursuing and capturing criminals, serving subpoenas, checking federal licenses and permits, searching for army deserters, and protecting federal properties — these and a score of other duties kept the deputy marshal busy. With reckless disregard for danger and complete unconcern for personal comfort, X. Beidler fulfilled his duties.

Sometimes the enthusiastic marshal exceeded his authority. His vigorous harassing of Indian traders and sutlers led to frequent rebukes from his superiors. Many of these traders lived on the margin of the law, operating behind an official façade of military permits and Interior Department licenses. "The law (and you must have read it)," complained United States Marshal W. F. Wheeler to his deputy, "exempts such goods from seizure in the Indian country."

Beidler also fell afoul the confusing lines of legal authority that so often crippled federal marshals. Again Wheeler reprimanded his deputy, this time for arresting traders whose illegal sales had not occurred on federal property. "The sheriff of the county, not the marshal is the one to arrest them under the territorial laws and they should be tried in the territorial courts," wrote Wheeler.[23] Frustrated by this confusion of authority and irritated by the refusal of some sheriffs to enforce the laws, the conscientious deputy frequently overstepped his powers.

By 1879 the years of deprivation and hardship began to take their toll. "J. X. Beidler is here with a batch of U.S. prisoners from Fort Keogh," wrote F. C. Deimling in Virginia City to W. F. Sanders. "Beidler is getting prematurely old from hard riding, exposure, etc. and his services have almost always been but very poorly paid." [24]

By the eighties, his health seriously impaired and his energies depleted, the deputy marshal retired to a well-earned rest. During his arduous years of public service, however, Beidler had saved nothing from his meager pay. Others had enriched themselves while X. Beidler defended their properties and their lives against Montana's numerous gangsters. Now the prematurely aging man lived in poverty, begging drinks from those who would listen to his endless yarns, and existing on the handouts of old friends.

"I can not live in civilization," lamented the broken frontiersman; "if I live I must move onward and God only knows where." [25]

Prompted by the same restlessness, Johnny Healy escaped to Alaska, but X. Beidler remained in Helena, where he lived out his last years in bitterness and neglect.

Fellow pioneers who remembered his contributions to their safety worked to relieve his distress. At public benefits they auctioned off his few souvenirs, buying them at high prices despite their lack of value. Others, like Colonel W. F. Sanders, loaned him money to finance an autobiography they knew he would never write.

In 1889 they introduced a relief bill in the Montana legislature for the old marshal. Economy-minded legislators, as Beidler recorded in his diary, "killed my bill dead." Other efforts to appoint him night watchman of the capitol building or guard at the state penitentiary also failed.

Beidler met these failures with growing cynicism. Bitterly he proposed a toast in the privacy of his diary: "To the oldtimer who never went back on the Legislature. Dam the Legislature that goes back on the Old Timer." [26]

They gave Beidler an impressive funeral when he died the following year. Hundreds of citizens listened in respectful silence to splendid orations that praised his selfless devotion to duty, his manly courage in the public service, and his peerless example to future generations. On his death certificate they sentimentally inscribed: "Occupation, Public Benefactor."

X. Beidler's judgment of his career was somewhat different. "Fifty years from now no one will know anything about it." And his advice to future generations in one of the last entries in his diary differed substantially from the funeral oratory. "Never fear your enemys, but look out for your friends. I had experience." [27]

VII

The United States Army also helped to bring order to the Whoop-Up frontier. Blue-coated troops from Forts Benton, Shaw, and Assiniboine assisted local officials and federal marshals in enforcing the laws.

126

But the army posted to the West was only a shadow of the formidable establishment created by four years of Civil War. Low morale among officers and men accompanied the collapse of American military strength following Appomattox. Recruiting lagged badly, and those who enlisted were often the dregs of society. A high rate of desertion weakened garrisons already reduced by economy-minded congressmen. "Regiments should be one thousand men," General of the Army W. T. Sherman warned the secretary of war, "but the policy of reduction has gradually reduced the Infantry regiment to about three hundred." [28]

Shortsighted policy assigned infantry rather than cavalry units to these posts. Patrols marched out from Forts Shaw and Assiniboine to capture mounted Indians whose fleet ponies carried them many miles from the scenes of their depredations.

Divided authority between the Army and Interior departments further impaired the army's effectiveness. An indifferent public scorned the army that protected it. "There is nothing so little thought of in this part of the country as a soldier," wrote a Montanan to the New York *Herald*. "There are only two creatures who look upon a soldier here without scorn and contempt, and they are little children and dogs." [29]

Despite these handicaps, the army provided many useful and important services. Troops guarded strategic sites from Indian raids, protected vital transportation and communications lines, provided escorts for missions of many kinds, and restrained the Indians along the edge of settlement.[30]

Fort Shaw, established in 1867, was the key base from which the army controlled the high-border country. Strategically situated on the Old North Trail where Piegans, Bloods, and Blackfeet traditionally crossed the Sun and Missouri rivers on raids into the Gallatin valley, it became the western bastion on the plains. General Sherman regarded it the most important post in Montana, for from it the army watched the Crees, Assiniboins, and River Crows as well as the Blackfoot confederacy.

The pressure of settlement complicated army tasks. Troops from Fort Shaw joined civilian authorities in suppressing the extensive whisky traffic to the northern Indians. General John Gibbon stationed detachments along the Whoop-Up trail to capture the traders. But his infantrymen were easily eluded by the well-mounted renegades from Fort Benton.[31]

Other detachments guarded roads between Fort Benton and key towns in Montana. Frequently, patrols went out to repair telegraph lines destroyed by teamsters who solved the problem of the scarcity of fuel in an easy but illegal manner. Buffalo also interrupted telegraphic communication. They found the poles convenient scratching posts and sometimes dragged off miles of wire as they stampeded across the plains.

The construction of these northern posts speeded the economic development of the region. Government spending to construct and maintain the forts introduced considerable currency into this frontier region. Army quartermaster purchases of fresh vegetables, butter, eggs, hay, and grain stimulated the initial agricultural enterprise in the Sun River valley and in the rich, alluvial bottom lands along the Missouri River. Heavy purchases of beef to feed thousands of soldiers prompted the rapid expansion of the range cattle industry on the benchlands and surrounding plains.

Army troops, recruited in the East and transferred to the West at government expense, provided a labor force for the region on a scale comparable only to the Mormon enterprises in Utah. This manpower built roads, telegraph lines, bridges, and other public works and established extensive farms around the posts. Moreover, when released from active service, most of the men remained in the West to continue these activities for private gain.

Army expenditures played such an important role in the region's economy that citizens constantly implored the government to expand its military commitments. They often pictured friendly Indians as hostile and exaggerated isolated depredations into a state of warfare.

Government spending also provided opportunities for fraudulent bidding. General A. H. Terry reported in 1875 that honest and reliable merchants had been forced out by the illegal "straw bidding" and "fly bidding" of dishonest businessmen. "Government contracts," the general lamented, "are not regarded as respectable business transactions." [32]

Post sutlers or traders were also familiar figures at these western posts. J. H. McNight, backed by T. C. Power capital, held the license to operate a store at Fort Shaw for many years, while Colonel C. A. Broadwater included among his extensive investments the post store at Fort Assiniboine.

McNight's operations at Fort Shaw provide a case study of a typical sutler during these years. He carried varied stocks of goods for both soldiers and civilians, served as banker for a community lacking formal banking institutions, and worked closely with the merchant princes of Fort Benton.

From his store at Fort Shaw, McNight supplied the region north of the Sun River. Orders for unusual combinations of goods, both solid and liquid, crossed his desk. But the one from T. F. Morgan must have seemed somewhat strange: "I wish you would send me 500 pounds oats and one rubber nipple for a Bottle."

Officers and enlisted men spent heavily in the sutler's store. Luxury items, clothing, sundries, hunting equipment — the list of purchases by post personnel was endless. But the major offering to the army was whisky, for blue-coated patrons drank heavily at these frontier stores. During General Gibbon's command, McNight was compelled to charge a fixed price for whisky. Enlisted men could buy two shots of whisky for two bits, a modest price but one that provided an ample margin of profit for the sutler. [33]

McNight also conducted a lucrative whisky trade with customers across the boundary in Canada. His records indicate that he counted among his best customers the officers of the Northwest Mounted Police, whose fastidious tastes required the finest of his stock, and usually in impressive quantities. "Captain Crozier wants three gals your best whisky," wrote an agent to McNight from Fort Macleod. "Send it to him with bill, packed securely and marked ©. He is all right on the pay." [34]

That the post traders in the Whoop-Up country were involved

in dubious trading practices characteristic of their kind is also clear. "Come over yourself," wrote Major Upham from the Blackfoot Agency, "and see my new place. Plenty of room for sinching now without being observed." [35]

VIII

While carrying out its primary mission of military protection for the Whoop-Up frontier, the army contributed materially to the social and cultural development of the region. Occasional campaigns took troops into the field for expeditions against hostile Indians, but most of the soldier's time was spent on the post. Western commanders faced serious problems of morale created by the long months of dull and dreary tasks that filled recruits with a disgust for army life.

Officers and their wives escaped from this boredom by creating a society in the tiny forts that seemed as rigid and as formal as the eastern community after which it was patterned. An endless round of parties, teas, literary and musical organizations kept them active and passed the time.

Frequent visits to Fort Shaw by Northwest Mounted Police officers or British officials from across the nearby boundary were warmly welcomed as breaks in the routine. When Lord Lorne, governor general of Canada, visited Fort Shaw, Mrs. Francis M. A. Roe recorded in her diary that a "flutter of excitement passed through the whole garrison." She greatly admired the "gorgeously dressed police with their jaunty, side-tilted caps." But she wondered why the Canadian government forced these splendid troopers to mount "such wretched little beasts."

Behind "filmy curtains" the officers' wives watched the reception on the parade ground for the visiting British officers. The smart appearance of the British impressed them greatly, wrote Mrs. Roe. "Presently without a stop, and as though it was the continuation of a melody, the first notes of 'God Save the Queen' were heard. Instantly, the head of every Englishman and Canadian was uncovered — quietly, and without ostentation or the slightest break in the handshaking and talking. It was like a militia movement by bugle call. They were at a military post of another nation, in the midst of being introduced to its officers, yet not one failed to remember and to remind, that he was an Englishman ever!" [36]

High desertion rates and excessive drinking among enlisted men prompted army officials to take steps designed to relieve the tedium of military life. While some commanders only added further hours of drill and enlarged their guardhouses, others conscientiously sought solutions to these serious problems.

Numerous factors explained the desertions from Forts Shaw and Assiniboine. Disillusionment with military life, the monotony of army routine, the drabness of the surrounding plains, the ease of escape, and the promise of wealth in the gold fields or lucrative employment in frontier enterprises led many soldiers to give the army the "grand bounce." Whatever the motives, most officers believed that the army could lower substantially its desertion rate.

One solution was the recruiting of young farmers and the rejection of workers or immigrants from the urban East. General John Gibbon advised the War Department to abandon its recruiting in the cities and to concentrate "in the small towns, especially in the West, for the reason that a large percentage of deserters were enlisted in and about New York and the other great cities of the East." [37] Others rejected this suggestion claiming that city men stayed in the army while country boys who knew something about farming deserted to work on nearby farms or ranches. For years the argument continued, but few constructive measures resulted.

Many commanders urged reforms to relieve the monotony of daily routines. Some encouraged both officers and men to hunt wild game on the surrounding plains. Others built gymnasiums, bowling alleys, and baseball fields for their troops and encouraged literary, musical, theatrical, and temperance organizations.

A surprising range of social and cultural activities was offered soldiers on the larger posts. At Fort Shaw, in the early seventies, each company of the Seventh Infantry regiment had its own library of "books bearing marks of good usage." The Fort Shaw Dramatic Association presented frequent plays to enthusiastic soldier audiences as well as to citizens in surrounding communities. An excellent band, several active literary societies, and a temperance newspaper edited by W. H. Buck, later editor of the Fort Benton *Record*, were other activities conducted by soldiers.

Perhaps the most interesting contribution to the district was the formation of post schools. Under the direction of officers or enlisted men whose training suggested pedagogical qualifications, day classes were held for the community's children and night classes for soldiers.

Standards were not high in these army schools but they more than equaled those in other frontier communities. A reporter for the Helena *Weekly Independent* believed the school at Fort Assiniboine a valuable experiment and found instructors with eastern college degrees conducting classes.

Official army reports were less optimistic. Inspectors for the Department of Dakota emphasized the shortage of skilled teachers as the most serious weakness of the schools. Equipment at both posts was rated "good," but books at Fort Shaw were regarded as only "fair." [38] By 1884 the inspector could conclude his report with the heartening observation that "good public schools on the posts are now considered almost as necessary as food for the general welfare."

7

One People, Divided

THE INDIANS north and south of the International boundary are one people, severed politically by an invisible line." [1] This observation by Police Commissioner Gilbert M. Sproat in 1878 stated simply the dilemma of the Blackfoot people. North American political development divided them, destroying a regional pattern of living confirmed by generations of experience. And it complicated local problems by making them international.

Blackfeet on both sides of the boundary suffered much the same fate. Smallpox, tuberculosis, measles, trachoma, syphilis, and other diseases from the white man's world took a heavy toll. Whisky, firearms, and the destruction of native resources undermined their self-sufficiency, reducing them to dependence upon the white man's technology. Disruption of native religions and cultures with the accompanying disintegration of tribal life and loss of individual ambition destroyed morale, leaving the Indians spiritually as well as materially poor.

The white man, goaded by imperialistic ambitions, pushed the Blackfeet and their neighbors rudely aside, seizing their lands and wealth. This was accomplished on both sides of the boundary behind the façade of laws written and executed by white men.

In both Wests, the story is one of conflict between primitive and civilized peoples. On the American side, this conflict was continuous, with unceasing guerrilla warfare punctuated by occasional formal military campaigns. To the north, lack of population pressure permitted a more orderly development. But the Manitoba insurrection in 1869 and the Saskatchewan rebellion of 1885 were armed conflicts arising from the same basic friction between whites and natives.[2]

Attitudes toward the Indians in the two countries were not as different as the contrasting experience in the West might suggest. General of the Army W. T. Sherman in his blunt manner reduced all viewpoints to two simple classifications: "one demanding the utter extinction of the Indians, and the other full of love for their conversion to civilization and Christianity." [3] These extremes existed but public opinion was far more diverse than he imagined.

Humanitarian sentiments in eastern North America were aroused by the fate of the plains Indian. Safely remote from the frontier in time and distance, easterners could afford a more objective viewpoint than pioneers who daily faced the problems of living with armed savages. In the United States, the reforming zeal of the pre-Civil War years still burned in many hearts. Just as the abolition crusade brought forth its polemic literature, so this one lead to an outpouring of books and pamphlets. Helen Hunt Jackson's *A Century of Dishonor*, like Harriet Beecher Stowe's *Uncle Tom's Cabin*, struck a responsive note in American hearts.

But men of good will could not agree on the nature of Indian character or on the correct policies to ensure justice to the red men. Most regarded them as children, thus oversimplifying the problems of culture conflict and adjustment. Professor Macoun expressed the popular view that Indians could be educated to the white man's way of life easily and quickly. "There is no reason why an Indian child should not read the same stories, see the same pictures, have the same teaching, and therefore, think the same thoughts as our children." [4] If treated with justice and humanity, Indians would respond with honesty and gratitude. In the end, they could be refashioned in the white man's image, an objective shared by most humanitarians.

Above all, the Indians must be treated with "boundless patience." American experience, wrote Nicholas Davin to Prime Minister Macdonald after his study of Indian educational programs in the United States, proved that "no race of men can suddenly be turned from one set of pursuits to another set of a wholly different nature without great attendant distress." [5]

But whatever their estimate of Indian nature or its future under white domination, humanitarians were agreed that the "Indian problem" could be solved within the bounds of Christian morality.

Sentimentalists confused the picture by creating false images of the Indian and by ignoring the realities facing government officials. To many romanticists the Indian remained the noble savage of James Fenimore Cooper or Jean-Jacques Rousseau, possessing a natural dignity, simplicity, and virtue. "Poor, poor fellow!" wrote the explorer Captain Butler; "crimes he may have and plenty, but his noble traits spring from no book-learning, from no schoolcraft, from the preaching of no pulpit; they come from the instinct of good which the Great Spirit has taught him . . ." [6] From such a comment it was an easy step for remote eastern readers to invest the red man with a nobility that ruled out such traits as cruelty, dishonesty, or guile.

Romanticists publicized naïve views of Indian character and life during the seventies. The British novelist William Black, whose books were widely read on both sides of the Atlantic, typified this tendency. "The Indian by tradition and instinct is a gentleman. Of all the races of the world he is the nearest approach one can get to the good old English squire. He loves horses; he gives up his life to hunting and shooting and fishing." [7]

"Lo, the poor Indian" sentimentalists created so great a gulf between the image and the reality that they did the Indians a disservice. Their writings handicapped the humanitarians by distorting the plea for justice into a caricature. Their apparent assumption that a few thousand savages should remain in possession of the northwestern plains ignored the dynamics of westward expansion.

Officials in Washington as well as in Ottawa sought a humanitarian policy. "The Indian policy of the United States is philanthropical," correctly observed William Shepherd, but efforts to implement it were frustrated by the mores of the frontier community.

Westerners, as we have seen in previous chapters, turned to an extermination policy. This drastic solution, costly in blood and treasure and productive of injustice, grew as much from fear and frustration as from callous greed. But if a rationalization were needed, westerners could point to the doctrine of natural selection, the defense of imperialism so popular in European and eastern circles. The Indian would vanish, whatever the official policy; it was his destiny.

II

Missionary enterprise in the Whoop-Up country was a bright spot in an otherwise dark picture. The selfless devotion of Christian missionaries, both Catholic and Protestant, is in striking contrast to the exploitative character of most white relationships with the natives.

Catholic missionaries began their work among the Blackfeet when the famous Jesuit missionary Father Pierre-Jean De Smet visited them on his trips to the Flatheads in the forties. Though this energetic priest traveled through the Whoop-Up country many times, his dream of establishing a mission among the Blackfeet never materialized.

Father De Smet was the first to learn the difficulties facing Christian missions in this region. The Blackfeet came to trust the black-robed priest. His friendly spirit and genuine compassion won a ready welcome in their camps and he traveled through the Whoop-Up country when other men feared to pass. But the Blackfeet, unlike the eager Flatheads or the receptive Crows and Sioux, received the Christian gospel with little enthusiasm.

Father De Smet knew the plains and mountains of the Northwest and felt the challenge of Blackfoot paganism as few others. During the early forties, he converted several friendly Blackfeet, visitors among the Flatheads. Later, in 1845, during the coldest winter months, he traveled south from Rocky Mountain House into Whoop-Up country hoping to reach the Piegans with his message. He failed to find them and suffered so much from the hardships of winter travel that he was forced to abandon his search.

The following year, however, he resumed his mission. After negotiating a peace between the Blackfeet and Flatheads, he left Father Nicholas Point with the Piegans during the winter of 1846–47. Nearly five hundred children were baptized and a number of marriages solemnized.

Despite these promising beginnings, Catholic missions among the Blackfeet did not prosper. Father De Smet felt that their immoderate use of liquor, their polygamous customs, their many superstitions, and their nomadic character were formidable barriers to the propagation of the gospel.[8]

Later explorers confirmed his judgment and found few lasting effects from early missionary efforts. The Blackfeet looked upon Christian symbols, especially the crucifix, as part of the white man's superior magic, conferring peculiar powers upon the bearer. They were disillusioned to discover that wearing the crucifix did not protect them from harm in battle or give them superiority over their enemies.

The Indians quickly lapsed into their old customs once the missionary departed.[9] Permanent missions were the answer to this problem and two Catholic outposts were established along the edge of the Whoop-Up country. In the fifties, Father Albert Lacombe founded his famous mission on Lac Ste Anne, from which he ministered to the Blackfeet tribes. During the following decade, American Catholics founded St. Peter's mission on the Teton River. While it was also outside the region normally inhabited by the Blackfeet, itinerant priests from the mission went deep into the Whoop-Up country to reach the Piegans, Bloods, and Blackfeet.

Many of the explorers believed that the Catholic ritual and formality created a deep impression upon the Blackfeet. Priestly garb, moreover, set the Catholic missionary apart from other white men, most of whom had come to prey upon the Indians. "What an advantage Rome has," wrote the Earl of Southesk. "Protestants constantly send vulgar, underbred folk to supply their missions, Rome sends polished, highly-educated gentlemen." [10]

One reason for Southesk's judgment was the high caliber of the first Catholic missionaries in the Whoop-Up country. Both Father De Smet and Father Lacombe were illustrious examples. Another factor impressing the Earl was the European background and training of the Catholic missionaries. But the Blackfeet, despite the exertions of dedicated men, were very slow to abandon the faith of their fathers, preferring to cling to a "medicine" that had served them through many centuries.

Protestant missions among the Blackfeet were equally unrewarding until the eighties. As early as the forties, the Reverend Robert T. Rundle began the important Wesleyan missionary work among the North Assiniboins or Stonies. The Reverend Thomas Woolsey continued this work in the fifties and George McDougall and his son John carried it forward through the seventies.

In apparent defiance of scriptural prophecy, the gospel seed scattered among the Stonies prospered, particularly after the McDougalls established their mission at Morleyville on the Bow River at the foot of the mountains. Here from 1873 onward, the Reverend John McDougall preached and practiced a muscular Christianity that greatly influenced the development of the Whoop-Up country, though his work among the Blackfeet was limited.

John McDougall was an unusual combination of vigorous plainsman and man of God. His biting criticisms of the Lord's enemies made him the most controversial man in the region. Despite adverse comment from eastern Methodists, he continued trading with the Indians at Morleyville in partnership with his brother David to combine profits with preaching. To advice that a man of God should remain above the corrupting influences of commerce, McDougall had a ready and spirited defense. Fur trading kept his mission solvent and McDougall was a practical man who believed there "must always be adaptation to conditions, as they are found." [11]

These trading activities brought him into conflict with the free traders in the region. The Fort Benton men, smarting under the parson's bitter invective, denounced the trader-preacher as guilty of the sins he condemned. One critic publicly accused McDougall of ending each sermon with an invitation to the Indians to pass into the trading room where his brother would care for their needs.[12]

These were exaggerated charges but they reflected the distrust raised by McDougall's worldly activities. "Reverend John" further alienated Whoop-Up traders and fellow missionaries by his outspoken defense of the Hudson's Bay Company. This loyalty to the company, cemented by his sister's marriage to Richard Hardisty, the chief factor at Fort Edmonton, expressed itself in many ways.

Frequent reports from Morleyville kept Hudson's Bay officials apprised of Whoop-Up developments. McDougall pleaded with the company to defend more vigorously its interests in the region, and he was greatly disappointed by the company's lack of enthusiasm for his projects. The missionary keenly resented the intrusion of the free traders into Canada. He used his influence among the Indians to divert their trade to the Hudson's Bay Company and urged the Dominion government to intervene. To McDougall, the conflict was one of morality against unrighteousness since the Hudson's Bay Company had abandoned the rum trade.

Religious sentiments were reinforced by national feelings, for McDougall could not forgive the traders for their American nationality. His exaggerated accounts of frontier life in Benton were strongly tinged by this bias, for he could see little good in American society, especially in the West. He even resented the Yankee accents of the Blackfeet when they spoke English! [13]

McDougall's partisanship for the Hudson's Bay Company

aroused the ire of other missionaries. The Reverend William Newton, Anglican missionary at Fort Edmonton, deplored the influence of the Wesleyans with officials at the post and called the company "a trading corporation which existed for gain, and made it at any cost." McDougall's defense of the company he believed was "simply pretentious nonsense. I have myself seen, in the Mountain Fort, a curious arrangement for serving out rum in trade with the Blackfeet, and near Edmonton Fort is 'Drunken Lake' keeping up the tradition of Hudson Bay's most unholy rites — a tradition not likely to be soon extinguished." [14]

"Reverend John's" fearless denunciations of the whisky trade brought results. His books and articles helped to arouse Canadian public opinion, but his harsh indictments of the traders led to numerous unpleasant incidents with his neighbors. McDougall's stout spirit only found these clashes exhilarating, and he ridiculed fellow missionaries who lacked the "manhood" to live an equally dangerous life. Few plainsmen could outride, outhunt, or outshoot the prairie parson who believed that life was forever a struggle. Individuals as well as nations "must war and fight and campaign and struggle and meet disease and calamity in order to be saved from inertia and destruction." [15] None of his critics ever accused "Reverend John" of suffering from inertia.

McDougall pictured the crudity of frontier settlement in exaggerated language. He saw little but the wickedness that accompanied it. "If these were the only products of our modern progress," he wrote of Fort Benton's population, "then, for God's sake and humanity's also, give us barbarism." With thanksgiving he returned to the simplicity of mission life where his will prevailed.

To the south, another Methodist missionary exerted considerable influence in removing the evil that McDougall deplored. W. W. Van Orsdel came west from Pennsylvania in June 1872 to preach to the Blackfeet. Earlier Protestant attempts had failed, notably those under the two Presbyterians, E. D. Mackey in 1856 and George G. Smith ten years later. Despite the unpromising appearance of missionary enterprise among these Indians,

Van Orsdel determined to establish a Protestant mission at the Blackfoot Agency.

The young Pennsylvanian quickly won the respect and affection of the Indians. To them he became "Great Heart," a tribute to his warm understanding and ready sympathy. To white settlers, who recognized the same qualities, he became "Brother Van."

"Brother Van" stayed with the Blackfeet only one year. Then he concluded that he could not conscientiously continue his ministry with the Indians until white society around them improved. Unlike "Reverend John," who fled the evil of his fellow whites, "Brother Van" returned to preach a message of justice for the Indians.

With this decision, Van Orsdel became Montana's famous frontier circuit rider, preaching and singing his way through the territory. With great enthusiasm, though without rancor or bitterness, he devoted his life to making Montana a stable community. He founded nearly one hundred churches, many of them in the Whoop-Up country.[16] But not until 1893 was a permanent Protestant mission established among the Blackfoot people south of the boundary.

Blackfoot slowness to accept Christianity was not due to their lack of interest in religion. Early explorers universally credited them with a deeper and more sincere religious spirit than their neighbors.

Travelers through the region found many reasons for this reluctance. Many deplored the spirit of factionalism and partisanship that confused the Indians. "It is unfortunately true," wrote Captain Butler, "that the jarring interests of different denominations have sometimes induced them to introduce into the field of Indian theology that polemical rancour which so unhappily distinguishes more civilized communities." [17]

Other problems handicapped the missionaries. They experienced great difficulty in expressing the "true character of religious enterprise" to the natives. Southesk discovered an Indian who denied any desire to go to the white man's heaven where he must sit still and sing psalms all day. He preferred to go to hell where "though in great pain, he could walk about." Christian theology baffled many Indians, leading one chief to remark that he could not accept the white man's religion since it was no good. "God came on earth; white man kill him. Indian wouldn't do that." [18]

Lack of concentrated effort further weakened missionary efforts. Both Protestants and Catholics traveled too much in this region; their work was extensive rather than intensive, and suffered as a consequence. Captain Palliser also thought that to be truly successful, missionary enterprise should "commence far away from white settlers." Frequent contacts with the traders demoralized the Blackfeet and kept them in "an unequal competition that must and has always proved fatal to them." [19]

Whatever the causes, Christian missions were singularly ineffective among the Blackfeet in the early years. Few adults embraced the white man's religion.

III

Fifty years after Captain Meriwether Lewis' encounter with the Piegans on the Marias River, the Blackfeet signed their first treaty with the United States. This treaty, one of many negotiated with plains tribes before the Civil War, provided for "perpetual peace" between the American government and the Blackfoot confederacy. It also called for peace between the Blackfeet and their neighbors. Tribal hunting grounds were carefully defined to prevent clashes between the nomadic Indians.

The Treaty of 1855 also exacted numerous concessions from the Indians. Peaceful passage by American citizens was assured and the government was given the right to construct roads, railways, military posts, and other public installations. In return for these rights, the government agreed to pay the Indians goods valued at $20,000 annually and to appropriate $15,000 each year for education in the "agricultural and mechanical pursuits."

Within a short time the peace provisions were violated, for the treaty was not yet ratified in Washington when the Blackfeet were again at war. They remained free of troubles with whites, however, for the filament of settlement reached only a few miles west of the Missouri River. Whoop-Up country was still a red man's land.

During this period of isolation, the Indian Bureau set up machinery to regulate and assist the Indians in their transition to sedentary life. Despite the distractions of the Civil War, the government launched a fourfold program to provide the Indians with the "necessaries of life," to teach them to earn "their subsistence by labor on the soil," to designate reserves where they could reside free from white intrusion, and to protect their lands from greedy whites.[20]

Laudable as these objectives seemed in Washington, they were only partially achieved. Uncertain communications often prevented the Blackfoot Agency from receiving the annual Indian payments and also isolated agents from government decisions.

Indian Bureau officials turned at once to fulfilling their treaty obligations. Within two years after ratification, they established the Sun River farm and sent out an instructor and several farm workers to teach the Indians the rudiments of agriculture. They also began experiments to find fruits, vegetables, and small grains suitable for the region.

During its initial years, the Sun River farm seemed promising. Land was put under cultivation; Indians came to learn the arts of the white man's husbandry; and experiments with vegetables and grains proved modestly successful. Located on the river bottoms where good soil and ample water were available, the farm was considered a major contribution in civilizing the Blackfeet.

In 1864, three separate floods inundated the farm, sweeping away buildings and equipment and ruining the crops. During succeeding seasons, drought, grasshoppers, and untimely frosts killed enthusiasm for the project. In the same year, the gold rushes raised the price of labor more than 200 per cent, making it impossible to retain farm hands on government wages.

A growing disillusionment with the farm as an educational

scheme further blighted the experiment. As early as 1862, the Blackfoot agent Henry W. Reid feared that the hopes held out for Indian agriculture would prove illusory, for the Sun River farm had been of no "practical value to the Indian whatever." [21] Only one Indian, Chief Little Dog, appeared seriously interested in the opportunity to learn "practical farming" from government agents.

By 1864 the farm was virtually unused. When the new agent, Gad E. Upson, arrived to inspect it, he found the buildings in a "dilapidated condition," only a few acres under cultivation, and everything on the reservation displaying "gross neglect, and the utter absence of all effort or interest in the protection of the property belonging to the farm." [22] Soon Blackfoot depredations forced complete abandonment and the Sun River farm joined the long list of noble experiments that failed.

Officials, both in Fort Benton and in Washington, urged reforms during the decade from 1855 to 1865. The reservation system came under considerable criticism. A study in 1863 led the commissioner of Indian affairs to conclude that it was correct in theory but open to grave errors in practice. The "worst classes of our own people" gathered around the reservations and "by means of gambling, the whiskey traffic and every species of vice and immorality," plundered the government and debauched the Indians.[23]

To protect the Blackfeet from this fate, Indian officials discussed the idea of creating an "Indian Territory" in the Whoop-Up country. This reserve, forever closed to white men, would stretch from the Missouri River to the international boundary. Gold rushes made this plan impracticable almost at the moment of its birth. The Sun River stampede in the winter of 1866 brought more than five hundred miners into the Blackfoot country in a few weeks.

During these critical years the Indians were poorly served by their agents. Ten different men held the post between 1865 and 1874, yet at several crucial times the Indians had no agent to protect their interests. After one stretch of eighteen months without an agent, the Indians concluded that the "Great Father" in Washington had forgotten them.[24]

Fort Benton proved a poor choice for the agency. Numerous incidents between transient miners and visiting Indians poisoned relations between the two races. By 1865, a guerrilla warfare settled over the Whoop-Up country. Most of the Indians remained peaceful, but war parties of young braves raided outlying settlements and plundered small parties of travelers.

In this unpromising atmosphere, the government negotiated a new treaty with the chiefs to secure cession of all lands south of the Missouri River. Blackfoot depredations, however, led the secretary of interior to pigeonhole the treaty since the Indians had violated its provisions. Lacking Senate consent, it was not a treaty, a legal distinction the Indians found difficult to understand. White men appropriated the lands but the government made no payments. To the victims, the difference between government policy and unauthorized action by individuals was a phase of American democracy too subtle for unsophisticated minds.

A growing whisky trade in the Whoop-Up country added to the Indian Bureau's problems. Special agent Henry W. Reid reported that nearly every boat ascending the river carried a cargo of whisky. By the Indian Act of 1834, this was illegal, and Indian agents urged the government to send troops, but frontier police duties seemed unimportant to a government engaged in a great Civil War.

The "Blackfoot War" from 1863 to 1870 was part of a general restlessness among plains Indians. It was suppressed with the same ineptitude and disregard for justice that marked Indian administration in other western territories.

Territorial officials were singularly unfitted for these trying times. Many of them prostituted public welfare to individual glory as Indian fighters. Acting Governor Thomas F. Meagher aggravated Indian problems during his brief administration by playing upon public fears to rehabilitate his waning political fortunes. Others, ambitious for economic gain, supported his drastic measures to line their pockets at federal expense.[25] "The public danger is apt to be magnified by parties whose interests lie in the promotion of military schemes that will cause the disbursement of money or will furnish employment for the otherwise idle," General P. R. De Trobriand warned his superiors from Fort Shaw.

This brilliant officer scorned the public hysteria as synthetically created by the self-seeking schemes of dishonest men. "The only Indians within reach," he wrote General Greene in November 1869, "are decidedly friendly, and nothing could be worse, I think, than to chastise them for offenses of which they are not guilty."[26]

General Alfred Sully disagreed with the Fort Shaw commander. From his office as superintendent of Indian affairs in Helena, he urged a firm military policy against the tribes. Perhaps the constant public clamor in the capital city and the promptings of scheming friends influenced his judgment.

The depredations of a raiding party of Piegans in August 1869 finally led to a military intervention. This party, seeking revenge for the murder of two Piegans in Fort Benton, moved deep into the Prickly Pear valley, looting and pillaging. Among its victims was Malcolm Clarke, a widely known and respected pioneer. His murder inflamed public opinion against the Blackfeet just as the earlier killing of John Bozeman had aroused passions against the Indians in the Gallatin valley. Angry and frightened settlers demanded military action.

Disturbed by the mounting agitation in Montana and confused by conflicting reports from commanders in the region, Lieutenant General Philip H. Sheridan sent General James A. Hardie to investigate. His reports emphasized that the depredations were isolated reprisals by hot-blooded youths who could not be restrained by the chiefs. There was no general Indian uprising.

A proper policy under these circumstances was to arrest the guilty individuals. Army officers were unable to execute this program, for no civil court in Montana would convict a white man guilty of an offense against an Indian. General Sully admitted he could lay his hands on the men guilty of the Piegan murders in Fort Benton, but their arrest would be useless since the courts would free them as a matter of course. In the face of these injustices, army officers reported that the Indians were driven to use force to avenge their dead.

General Hardie also learned that the international character of the Blackfeet complicated local problems. When sought by American officials, the Indians simply fled across the boundary into British territory. This easy escape into an unpoliced region irritated American officers. General Sully finally concluded that his basic problem was not in dealing with the Indians but was "more a matter between the United States and English governments . . ." His frustrations led him to propose that military personnel should cross the forty-ninth parallel to capture the red-skinned criminals.

Another source of irritation was the frequency with which Indians from north of the boundary visited Benton demanding annuity payments. Since these nomads recognized no international boundary in their wanderings, to determine their nationality was a fine point. Acting Governor Meagher, however, believed that Indians who fled across the boundary to seek shelter in a foreign country should no longer be regarded as parties to American treaties.[27] His argument later became a familiar one when American officials faced the question of what to do with the refugee Sioux who crossed into the Northwest Territories after the battle of the Little Big Horn.

Frequent charges linked the Hudson's Bay Company to Indian thefts south of the boundary. Sworn affidavits from numerous witnesses convinced American officers that stolen horses and mules found a ready market across the forty-ninth parallel. Whether true or not, army officers suspected company policy of provoking much of their trouble.

To restore peace to the troubled region, Superintendent Sully and United States Marshal W. F. Wheeler called a conference of Blackfoot chiefs at the new agency on the Teton River. Here on New Year's Day 1870, the two officers delivered an ultimatum to the assembled chiefs. They must keep their young men under control and raids against white settlers must cease. Stolen horses and livestock must be returned to their owners and the murderers of Malcolm Clarke surrendered within two weeks. Unless these demands were met, the government would consider that a state of war existed with the Blackfeet.

General Sully exceeded his orders in his effort to intimidate the Indians. Without authorization from Washington, he blandly informed the chiefs that the British government had granted him permission "to cross the line with our troops." Later he reported that this threat affected the Indians more than anything else he said.[28]

General Sully hoped to coerce the Indians without resort to force. But his action embarrassed army officers, who quickly came to the conclusion that an unenforced ultimatum would encourage further depredations. Even General De Trobriand reversed his earlier position to urge "a sharp and severe blow upon some guilty band as an example to the rest."[29]

Blunt warnings to the Indians had failed and more raiding parties than ever roamed the Whoop-Up country. To harassed army officers the argument for a punitive expedition became increasingly attractive. A surprise attack upon an unsuspecting band, thought General De Trobriand, would not only be a punishment for past crimes but a move to prevent further aggressions.[30]

In Chicago, General Sheridan welcomed De Trobriand's advice for a preventive war. In October, the fiery cavalryman had planned that kind of a campaign. "About the time of a good heavy snow," he wrote General E. D. Townshend, "I will send out a party and try and strike them. About the 15th of January they will be very helpless, and if where they live is not too far from Shaw or Ellis, we might be able to give them a good hard blow, which will make peace a desirable object."[31]

Meantime, General Sully also reversed his position. Concerned

148

over the possible consequences of a military campaign, he now urged moderation toward the Indians. "For the present," he wrote General Hardie on January 13, "no blood should be shed, if it is possible to avoid it."

Two days later, General Sheridan dispatched his orders to De Trobriand. "If the lives and property of the citizens of Montana can best be protected by striking Mountain Chief's band, I want them struck. Tell Baker to strike them *hard*." [32]

On January 19, in subzero weather, Major Eugene Baker led his column out of Fort Shaw "to strike them hard." His orders commanded him to attack the Piegan band of Mountain Chief, but to avoid the friendly Piegan and Blood bands camped near by. Scout Joe Kipp, half-breed son of the famous American Fur Company trader, guided the expedition. Complete secrecy prevented the whisky traders at Fort Benton from warning their Indian friends of the impending attack.

At eight o'clock on the morning of January 23, Major Baker attacked an Indian camp on the Marias River. When the smoke of battle cleared away, 173 Indians, men, women, and children lay dead. But they were not Mountain Chief's Piegans. This was Heavy Runner's camp of friendly Indians, then suffering from a severe epidemic of smallpox.

News of the brutal attack prompted immediate protests as a wave of resentment swept the country. Humanitarians quickly labeled it a "massacre," which indeed it was.

Army officers, always reluctant to admit combat errors, denied that a mistake had been made! Mountain Chief, they claimed, had escaped in the confusion. Since this was transparently false it cast a shadow of doubt on all army claims and encouraged wild rumors. Major Baker was accused of being drunk during the attack and of deliberately destroying a friendly camp despite Joe Kipp's warnings. Story after story went the rounds but army officers dismissed them all as fabrications of the corrupt "Indian ring."

Captain W. F. Butler, innocent of the facts and anxious to

discredit American Indian administration, recorded one of these fictitious yarns as a factual account in his *Great Lone Land.*

"Here is the story of the raid as told me by a miner whose 'pal' was present in the scene," wrote the British explorer.

"It was a little afore day when the boys came upon two redskins in a gulf near-away to the Sun river. They caught the darned red devils and strapped them on a horse, and swore that if they didn't just lead the way to their camp that they'd blow their b.... brains out; and Jim Baker wasn't the coon to go under if he said he'd do it — no, you bet he wasn't. So the red devils showed the trail, and soon the boys came out on a wide gulf, and saw down below the lodges of the 'Pagans.'

"Baker says, 'Now, boys,' says he, 'thar's the devils and just you go in and clear them out. No darned prisoners, you know; Uncle Sam ain't agoin' to keep prisoners, I guess. No darned squaws or young uns, but just kill 'em all, squaws and all . . .' I say, mister, that Baker's a bell-ox among sodgers, you bet." [33]

Later Captain Butler was surprised to discover that the surviving Piegans spoke of the attack as "the fortune of war." This attitude the explorer could forgive, but for the American "outscourings of Europe" he had only contempt. Had he truly sought an understanding of the tragedy, he would have questioned the Indians carefully about their hatred for Joe Kipp. To the Piegans, the half-breed Kipp was responsible, and they never forgave him.

Eastern critics denounced the incident as another "Chivington massacre," a disgrace to American arms. Many eastern newspapers cited it as further proof that civil affairs must never be placed under army administration, for the army's training was to fight. If problems were not easily resolved by other means, impatient army officers were quick to cut Gordian knots with the sword.

Westerners, however, applauded the army's direct methods. General De Trobriand's argument that the expedition was a salutary lesson to the Blackfeet struck a responsive note. During later years, pioneers pointed to the lack of serious Indian troubles in the Whoop-Up country as proof that Major Baker solved the problem once and for all.

IV

"It is fair to assume that no Indian policy could be worse than that maintained by the United States . . . It is the great evil of the day." [34] This judgment by a Montana editor in 1877 summarized accurately public sentiment throughout the nation.

Ironically, public opinion indicted a policy that had grown out of a genuine concern for the Indians' welfare. Condemned from that day to this, the program was launched as a "Peace Policy" to quiet the strife between white man and red, and to bring justice to a forgotten people.[35]

The inauguration of Ulysses S. Grant in 1869 brought a new approach to the "Indian problem." Distressed by the sordid story of America's mistreatment of her aborigines, the soldier President turned to humanitarians for advice. A commission composed of ten distinguished citizens was appointed and a full-blooded Indian, Genral Ely S. Parker, guided the new policy as commissioner of Indian affairs. A cooperative Congress appropriated $2,000,000 to finance the program.

Grant's "Peace Policy" introduced four important changes. The plains Indians were to be dismounted, disarmed, and placed on suitable reservations where they could take up the white man's agriculture. Educational programs were devised to dissipate the "clouds of ignorance and superstition" and to teach them agricultural and mechanical skills. Further, the unrealistic treaty system based on the fiction of tribal sovereignty was abandoned in 1871. Finally, the government sought to assist the individual Indian directly rather than through the tribe.[36]

To execute this high-minded program, the President called in religious leaders. Church groups, especially the Quakers, recommended agents for appointment. President Grant also looked to the army to provide agents, particularly in the Dakota superintendency and in the Pacific Northwest.

The "Peace Policy" promised much; yet within a few years

Indian affairs were in a worse state than ever. Secretary Parker resigned, falsely charged with corruption; the Commission's personnel was radically changed to make it a pliant tool; and open scandals discredited the Indian Bureau. When President Grant retired from office in 1877, only the wreckage of his policy remained as evidence of his good intentions. On the plains, the Indians were in open revolt, ready to launch the last of their great wars against white imperialism.

The fate of the Blackfeet was typical of the failure of the entire policy. A fundamental administrative weakness paralyzed Grant's program by dividing authority between the Interior and War departments. Conflicting lines of responsibility frustrated conscientious army officers in their efforts to assist the Indians, while politically appointed agents remained virtually free of effective supervision. The Indians were the chief victims in the resulting confusion.

Widespread corruption among Indian agents further undermined the "Peace Policy." The low morale of government service during Grant's administration was particularly evident in the Indian Bureau, where numerous opportunities for pelf attracted dishonest men. The Reverend John McDougall concluded after his several visits to the Blackfoot Agency in the seventies that "the government and the Indians were, both of them, looked upon by the ordinary Government employee as legitimate prey." [37]

This corruption was universally known throughout the West. "The utter mismanagement of Indian affairs in general has become a by-word in the community," commented the editor of the Fort Benton *Record* in 1875. Later, the newspaper listed some of the favorite methods of cheating the Indians — steel spades made of sheet iron, cast-iron axes, pasteboard shoes, rotten clothing, forty dozen elastic garters to a tribe "which did not boast a single pair of stockings," diseased cattle and spoiled flour for rations. "It is no great wonder that the Indian sometimes grows restive under such treatment and occasionally sharpens up his little tomahawk and goes for the scalp of some struggling settler." [38]

Army officers resented Indian Bureau mismanagement, for subsequent Indian uprisings forced their troops into hard campaigns. While commander at Fort Shaw, General John Gibbon filled his reports with sarcastic comments about Indian Bureau inefficiency. "The wonder is not that peculation should sometimes occur," he wrote, "but that it does not happen in *all cases*." [39]

Frequent scandals involving Indian agents appointed through religious organizations led the churches to deny responsibility for the "Peace Policy." The Rocky Mountain Conference of the Methodist Episcopal Church announced in 1876 that it had "no control over Indian agents supposed to be under her care, and is in no way responsible for the manner in which the agencies are conducted." [40] In the public mind, however, the churches suffered great loss of prestige. J. H. D. Street's complaint to Territorial Delegate Maginnis of "the high handed robbery of these Preacher Agents & their Fellow-partners" [41] was widely shared throughout the West.

In general, westerners took a dim view of the "Peace Policy." Newspapers ridiculed it as "expounding gospel truths to squaws and papooses, while thousands of blood-thirsty cut-throats are permitted to roam the country at will . . ." [42] Protests against eastern ignorance, indifference, and sentimentalism filled their columns. When it was all over, the Fort Benton *Record* composed its epitaph: "The paternal Government has tried very many means of pacification — whiskey, agencies, missionaries, Quakers, the clergy, the Bureau of the Interior, excursion trips to Washington to see the Great Father, liberal appropriations for gunpowder, mowing machines, patent churns, Spencer rifles and shoddy clothes . . ." [43]

A major Blackfoot grievance against the government was the steady reduction of their reservation. The failure of the treaties of 1865 and 1867 to win senatorial consent left the reservation a vaguely drawn territory north of the Missouri River, lacking precise legal definition. In 1873, and again in 1874, presidential orders reduced it to the region lying north of the Sun River; then to the area north of the Marias.

These changes were effected without compensation to the Indians, thus laying the basis for later claims against the government. Moreover, the second executive order in 1874 was vigorously opposed by the Indians. "The Indians residing upon this reservation are unanimous in their opposition to the change of the line," wrote agent R. F. May to Major Maginnis in Washington.[44]

Nor did the alterations satisfy the cattlemen, businessmen, or land speculators who coveted the rich grasslands of the reservation. A steady stream of letters, petitions, and memorials flowed to Washington urging further cessions. Typical of the pressures exerted upon officials was C. A. Broadwater's plea to Martin Maginnis to have the boundaries redrawn to promote his speculative interests in "choice spots on the Reservations." Broadwater also demanded support for larger appropriations to Fort Assiniboine, since he was the post trader for the northern garrison. "Both I must have," he warned the delegate, "or damned if I don't go back on you next election." [45]

By 1876 the entire plains frontier was aflame with a general Indian war. The Blackfeet remained peaceful during the Sioux and Nez Perce wars, despite their many grievances against the white society around them. Frequent rumors of alliances with the hostiles frightened nervous settlers, but nothing came of them.

Fort Benton lived through one alarm after another during these years. Unfounded rumors that Sitting Bull and his Sioux were moving into the Whoop-Up country often agitated the community.

Excitement reached its zenith when Chief Joseph's Indians crossed the Missouri River at Cow Island on their journey north to the Bear Paw Mountains. Frightened citizens hurriedly organized a volunteer unit under the command of John J. Donnelly which rode off to relieve a beleaguered wagon train. Chief Joseph was gone when the Benton men reached the island, but they returned to a hero's welcome. Later they formed the "Benton Home Guards" to protect the river town. "Colonel" Donnelly, "Lieutenant" Johnny Healy, and "Second Lieutenant" John H. Evans commanded this troop of former Whoop-Up traders, who revived for a brief moment the Indian fighting thrills of earlier years.[46]

These were only temporary flurries of excitement. More serious were the raids and depredations by Indians along the international boundary. Cattlemen, Indian agents, army officers, and the American tribes resented these intrusions by Canadian Indians who raided their herds or killed their scarce game. "The advantages of the 'Iron Line' so called by the Indians, are now well understood . . . It enables them to leave their families in safety with their Grandmother while they are roaming America in search for horses and scalps," complained the *Record*.[47]

Mounted Police officers tried to stop these "pinto buffalo" hunts and carefully returned stolen property to American owners whenever possible. The incursions from the north were on too great a scale, however, to be regulated by the police. American officials estimated that more than five thousand Canadian Indians still roamed their plains in 1881. Canadian officials placed the number at twelve thousand![48] Diplomatic protests to the British minister expressed American indignation, but the Canadian Indians remained where they could find buffalo.[49]

Americans suspected that the Canadian government deliberately encouraged the Indians to remain south of the boundary. These suspicions were well founded. Lieutenant Governor Edgar B. Dewdney later admitted to his friends in Ottawa that he had encouraged the Indians to enter American territory. When Blackfoot chiefs came for help during the starvation period in 1879, he "advised them strongly to go and gave them some provision to take them off." Again in 1880 he repeated the advice, defending his action with the argument that his shrewdness had saved the Dominion government "at least $100,000."[50] These Indians were annuitants under Treaty Seven signed at Blackfoot Crossing in 1877, but the longer they lived from the yields of the chase, the longer the Canadian government could defer the expense and difficulty of settling them on their reserves.

Conflicting interpretations of the Indians' role during the eighties led to unpleasant incidents along the international boundary. In Ottawa, officials viewed the American West as the same uninhabited wilderness as their own Northwest Territories and argued that the Indians should continue to follow the buffalo freely, ignoring the political boundary in their hunting.

American officials, prompted by the rapid growth of the range cattle industry in Montana, rejected this Canadian doctrine of "free passage." Eventually the Canadian government proposed a system of passes for individual Indians to visit "relations and friends across the boundary." This program was no more acceptable to the American government, however, than unrestricted passage, for it did not promise to halt "the incursions and depredations of bodies of Indians." [51]

In 1882 the American government acted unilaterally to end the free movement of Canadian Indians and half-breeds across the boundary. Army troops forced them to return to their own hunting grounds, destroying their lodges and confiscating their goods if they returned. This drastic policy finally made the forty-ninth parallel a barrier to the northern Indians. From that time onward the Blackfeet were truly one people divided by an invisible line.

8

Chicago of the Plains

WHILE a great Civil War raged far to the east, Fort Benton emerged a hustling commercial center, abandoning forever its modest role as a fur trading post. Few towns have played so important a part in the growth of a region, for through Benton flowed the commerce of a great inland empire. From Wyoming deep into British North America, the plains country paid tribute to the little inland port.

Gold unleashed the forces which transformed Benton. The Montana village was the end of a long trip up the Big Muddy; from Benton the gold-seekers rode or walked. Virginia City, Bannack, Last Chance Gulch — these were the magic names which lured thousands to the Shining Mountains. And most reached these El Dorados by the slow and hazardous, but preferable, journey up the winding river.

"All trails lead out of Benton" was a familiar saying on the northern plains. To a surprising degree it was true. Benton was the anchor end of the famous Mullan road to Walla Walla, as well as the terminus of the Helena road to the gold fields, of the Minnesota-Montana road to St. Paul, of the Whoop-Up Trail reaching into British North America, and of lesser known but important trails to other frontier posts.

Like countless frontier towns before it, Benton was a city of great dreams, for it lay on that restless edge of settlement where reality meets fantasy and the boomer is often indistinguishable from the conservative man of business. "Who can tell of the future," wrote the village's first newspaper editor. "A few years ago and what was Chicago, St. Louis and Omaha? Examine their history. Once trading posts similar to Benton, now great commercial marts, the centre of trade, wealth and manufacture." [1] With thousands of gold-seekers passing through their town, little wonder Bentonites dreamed bold dreams and saw great visions. With the river reaching like a giant umbilical cord tying it to the industrial strength of the East, and with trails stretching into a hinterland of unknown mineral and agricultural wealth, few Benton residents defied the universally accepted gospel of unlimited expansion which illumined their future. "Chicago of the Plains" was their name for a dream which gave every promise of coming true.

To the casual visitor in the 1860s, Benton gave few hints of future greatness. Most travelers saw it as a crude little frontier town with its rude adobe and log huts scattered capriciously along its single street like toy houses in a child's sandbox, or thought it wretchedly uncomfortable in its dusty, treeless setting, with its strongly alkaline drinking water, made the more uncomfortable by the inescapable odors of the twenty thousand oxen and mules which hauled its commerce and by the extremes of heat and cold which plagued it. Official army reports of Fort Benton's physical setting are in striking contrast to the glowing descriptions of its citizens. "The surrounding country is mostly prairie with good grass, but without timber. The land is not adapted to agriculture . . . Climate considered healthy. Extremes of heat and cold generally very great." In contrast, the warm and vivid phrases of the native sound suspiciously fulsome: "Pleasantly located on the banks of the Missouri; encompassed on either side by the beautiful and fertile valleys of the Sun river, Teton and Marias, whose broad acres, untouched by plough share or scythe, yield abundant sustenance to the myriads of animals that roam their grassy wilds; protected by the thickly wooded sides of the Highwood." [2]

Nor was there much to indicate greatness in the character of the town's activities. At first glance, the visitor saw only a mile-long levee piled high with commercial goods, a few unimpressive adobe or log huts housing small business establishments, and a row of disreputable saloons or hurdy-gurdy houses, boisterous and wicked. The quality of many of the town's citizens was unmistakably revealed in their sobriquets: "Kino Bill," "Bedrock Jim," "Whistling Jack," "Buckskin Joe," "Four Jack Bob," "Toe String Joe," "Sweet-Oil Bob," "Summer House Charlie," "Slim Jim," "Spring Heel Jack," "Liver-Eating Johnson," "Slippery Dick," "Smoothy Bill," "Gros Ventres Johnny," and "Whiskey Brown." This informal census was hardly calculated to inspire confidence in the social or economic future of the community.[3] Some years later when it was safe to do so, the Fort Benton *Record* candidly admitted that during its early years "Benton was a squaw town, a scalp market, the home of cutthroats and horse thieves; the military denounced it as an ammunition depot and whiskey trading post for hostile Indians; the Mounted Police had broken up the fur trade, arrested and prosecuted the Benton traders and diverted the robe trade from Benton to the Winnipeg market; there was no safety or protection for settlers . . . the town itself was unpopular . . ."[4]

During the following decade, however, Benton underwent sweeping changes. The rapid decline of the fur trade, the appearance of the Mounted Police who stopped the illegal whisky traffic north of the boundary, and the playing out of the gold rushes brought economic alterations that profoundly changed the character of the river town. Rather than a small fur trading post employing a handful of men, Benton became a commercial center where financiers, freighters, wholesalers, and jobbers created new economic empires under the dynamic leadership of T. C. Power and I. G. Baker.

As Benton changed from a rough border town to a community of merchant's account books and manifest lists, wealthy merchant princes demanded stability and order. As their wealth and power grew, their interests dictated a respect for property characteristic of a more complex economic life. At the same time, social and cultural activities developed as wealth paid its tribute to culture. "Those who at first were careless of their reputations, and desirous only of accumulating fortunes and leaving the country," observed the *Record* in 1878, "are now eager to become reputable citizens and to establish permanent homes."

Benton's metamorphosis attracted national attention. "A person who has not visited the place since its earlier days will be astonished at the change which has been wrought there within so short a time," commented a Chicago writer in 1879. "A wonderful change indeed! A population of uncertain character, with doubtful means of support, has changed into a well-to-do community of solid businessmen, with a legitimate trade." [5] Years later, W. S. Stocking recalled that these changes were so radical they comprised "an absolute transition from rudeness, lawlessness, violence and border warfare to a permanent condition of tranquility and high civilization." [6]

By 1877 the Fort Benton *Record* filled its columns with praise for the town's new career. With unconcealed pride the editor warmly congratulated his fellow citizens for effecting these changes without the intervention of vigilantes or "illegal bands of Regulators." "It is doubtful," argued its editor, "whether in any town of the Territory there are now better order, a healthier morality, a greater immunity from unpleasant sights and sounds . . ." [7]

These roseate judgments undoubtedly exaggerated the rapid rise of virtue and the collapse of vice. Still without a church building or a resident clergyman by 1877, Benton required more years than had yet passed to make the transition to a stable community life, particularly in the face of determined resistance from many of its transient citizens.

Yet it was obvious that the old Benton of wolfers and whisky smugglers was gone. Traders whose whisky and guns had demoralized Whoop-Up Indians retired to more peaceful pursuits. Some joined the growing numbers of businessmen in Benton, others turned to agriculture in the rich valleys surrounding the town. Stock raising, farming, and business enterprise more and more absorbed the energy of men who had written lurid chapters in the Indian trade.

II

Through the years Fort Benton was also a military post. Troops were briefly stationed there in the winter of 1866–67 but were withdrawn in the spring. Later in 1869 the army posted Company B of the 13th Infantry to the river town to guard its lines of communications on the northern plains. Until 1881 small detachments of troops remained in Benton to protect this vital communications center, for Benton was the linchpin of the army's logistic planning in northern Montana. Through Fort Benton passed the supplies and equipment for Forts Ellis, Shaw, and Assiniboine and its telegraph linked the northern posts to Forts Buford and Abraham Lincoln down the river.

But Fort Benton was never a major military post. During the early years of army occupation, troops were quartered at the old fort built by the American Fur Company. After 1874, however, the troops abandoned it as uninhabitable and the government leased buildings in the town for quarters and storehouses. Only two buildings on the military reservation remained in government hands, one as quarters for laundresses, the other as stables for army mounts. The buildings of the old fort, as well as all the land reaching to the river, were claimed by the legal successors of the fur company.

For many years the military reservation was a source of grievance to Benton's ambitious businessmen. With choice land tied up by the government, expansion was costly and difficult. As a consequence, they kept their territorial delegate in Washington under constant pressure to have the reservation thrown open for sale. Led by S. T. Hauser of Helena, a group of merchants sponsored a scheme to open the reservation as a single block of land. "I wanted particularly to talk to you *about* having the *reservation* in *Benton sold*," wrote Hauser to Martin Maginnis in Washington. "As the troops have been ordered away from there, there can be no earthly use for the Government holding

161

the land. Can't you have it sold in lump as Ft. Logan Reservation has? Please let me know as there's money in it. Millions in it. Powers, Conrad and myself are anxious to get a *chance* to purchase it, but whether we do or not, have it sold, as it will help *Benton*, particularly the *north* end." [8]

When the government finally opened the land to settlement in 1882, Benton was the scene of a wild stampede. Visions of quick wealth touched off a miniature land rush as the town's prominent citizens scrambled with the floaters and ne'er-do-wells for choice lots. The invaders launched their assault with wagons of lumber, wire fencing, and stakes to mark out and enclose their lots. Bitter fights broke out as men struggled for possession of the best sites and Benton watched an exciting spectacle which briefly recaptured the hectic spirit of the gold rush days. So determined in their acquisitiveness were the claimants that an amusing situation developed in which Main Street was "bounded on each side by a fence clear to the bluffs and no streets have been left intersecting." [9] In the mad rush for property, who could afford to wait for a proper survey to mark off side streets?

Feverish expansion was the theme of Benton's growth for two decades after the Civil War. These were indeed prosperous days for this "Queen city of the Northern Plains." From an unimpressive frontier village of only twenty-seven log or adobe huts in 1866, Benton mushroomed into a bustling town of great warehouses and business firms, hotels, and public buildings. Front Street facing the river no longer remained the town's single thoroughfare as rows of streets lined with busy shops and service industries fanned out from the water front. The tiny Overland Hotel was soon overshadowed by the more impressive Centennial, and blocks of business buildings were constructed to accommodate such growing business firms as the T. C. Power, I. G. Baker, Murphy-Neel, W. S. Wetzel, and Kleinschmidt companies. Brickyards, carpenter shops, blacksmiths, wheelwrights, harness makers, boot and shoe makers, tailors, barbers, grocers, and butchers quickly appeared to provide goods and services to the boom town's population.

This rapid expansion touched off a runaway inflation of building costs. Real estate values skyrocketed more than 500 per cent in the single year of 1879 and rents realized from 25 to 50 per cent on capital invested in dwellings and business buildings. Prices remained high through 1882, but by 1883, in the face of Benton's waning commercial position and the national economic depression, real estate values declined.[10]

III

Life in Benton matched this hectic expansion with its excitement and suspense. Bentonites, especially in the early years after the war, lived in fear of fires, floods, and Indian alarms or anxiously waited for the spring breakup of the river, for the arrival of steamboats, for news of great gold discoveries, or for the autumnal freeze-up and the ending of the navigation season.

Indian alarms often swept the river community until the infamous Baker massacre in January 1870 destroyed Indian power in the Benton region. Until that cruel incident, Blackfeet and Piegans kept Benton in frequent states of excitement with their horse-stealing expeditions and war parties. Numerous isolated settlers or members of small parties lost their lives during these troubled years. Occasionally, Benton itself suffered from Indian depredations. On one occasion, a large band of Crows drove off all the livestock from the farther side of the river while Benton citizens, lacking long-range rifles or sufficient boats, raged and cursed helplessly at the redskins as they watched their cattle disappear over the horizon.

Not all experiences with Indians were as grim or as costly. One of Benton's most famous folk stories came from efforts of the town's citizens to impress the Indians with the white man's magical powers. The instrument by which they were to be awed was an ancient brass cannon lashed on the back of a mule. In the presence of a crowd of several hundred, both white and red, the cannon was loaded, primed, and prepared to fire at a target in a cutbank across the river.

With great ostentation and proper solemnity, a spot was care-

fully marked on the far bank and the Indians were warned of
the great power of the weapon. Presently, the fuse was lighted
and the mule held firmly with the cannon trained on the target.
The hissing sound of the burning fuse frightened the mule, however, and the alarmed beast tore loose from his handlers to in-
scribe a circle as he pitched and bucked, always with the cannon
pointing its deadly charge at the crowd.

This was too much for the white men who had come to demonstrate their great powers. With a frenzy born of panic, the
representatives of the master race broke and ran, hurling themselves headlong into the river or sprawling on the ground to escape
the impending explosion. Though baffled by the strange antics
of their white friends, the Indians calmly held their ground,
thinking that the whole performance was somehow part of the
white man's magic. When the cannon finally exploded harmless-
ly into the ground, the Bentonites sheepishly returned, but some
of them never outlived the ignominy of their undignified flight.

Fires were always a threat in this little frontier town, as indeed
they were in all of America's cities during the nineteenth century. So great was the danger that steps were taken by an
aroused community to reduce the hazard. In 1877 John Evans,
the popular saloonkeeper and former Whoop-Up trader, was appointed fire warden. At once overdue reforms were launched.
Haystacks were ordered off Main Street and the custom of burning trash in the public thoroughfares was discouraged.

That fires were frequent and costly is eloquently revealed in
the front-page stories of the local newspapers. The tragic death
of an infant in a fire caused by an exploding kerosene lamp
touched off a community project to raise money to relieve the
stricken family and reminded the town of the urgency of its
problem. Nearly all buildings in Benton were slight wooden
frames, many without chimneys. The clumsy bucket brigade and
the out-of-date hand pump were inadequate protection against
a major conflagration, and Benton citizens lived in constant
dread of fire. When a cruel prankster cried "fire" in a crowded
hotel room during the sermon of a visiting Scottish divine, the

congregation stampeded for the exits, injuring and bruising many. "If a fire once obtains headway in or near the centre of town," warned an alarmed *Record*, "Goodbye, Benton!" [11]

To meet this threat, Benton's leading merchants finally forced the town to act. In 1880 the city fathers proudly ordered a new steam-powered hook and ladder truck to replace the overaged and nearly useless hand pump. With great enthusiasm the town's young men organized the "Pioneer Hook and Ladder Company" to use the equipment when it arrived. Eagerly the entire community awaited its new engine, but endless delays gradually blunted their enthusiasm. When the steamboat carrying the new machine reached the upper river, low water stopped it at Cow Island. There the engine lay exposed to the elements for many months. When it finally reached Benton, instead of welcoming a brightly painted and shiny fire engine, discouraged citizens found an engine on which the paint was badly peeled, the ladders cut in half, and one wheel missing. In the face of this disaster, the "Pioneer Hook and Ladder Company" never drilled, but its social activities continued undiscouraged.

Pioneer Benton was bleak and unattractive. For many years no tree grew in Benton and careless citizens added little to the town's beauty by throwing their garbage, slop, and trash into the streets or over the river bank along the levee. Outraged protests from civic-minded citizens did little to discourage these practices until the late 1880s. During lengthy dry seasons the plains dust covered Benton like a blanket, while rainy spells converted its dirt streets into seas of mud. Unkind critics visiting Benton during a wet season complained bitterly of the town's "succession of hog wallows," though the construction of wooden sidewalks in 1883 moderated these charges somewhat. On top of all this, the spring breakup of the river often created ice-jams near the city, threatening the town with floods and adding to the cost and discomfort of life on the Great Plains.

Untimely chinook winds sometimes created flood hazards. In February 1884, a particularly serious flood backed up from an ice-jam following three days of warm winds. Flood waters inundated much of Benton's business district, filling many of the shops and stores until the ice, which had choked the river at Shonkin Bar, was blasted free with dynamite.

This flood interrupted a large Methodist service being conducted by a visiting clergyman. His account of the event to the *Montana Christian Advocate* was an exciting piece of news reporting: "Our services were about half through when the alarm was given and about one minute sufficed to empty the church of its congregation. The night was dark and to see the lanterns swinging, to hear the rumbling of wagons, the crying of children, the screaming of some men who were more likely to overflow with 'Jersey Lightning' than were the river banks with water, made the scene rather exciting."

Nor could the saintly reporter fail to point out the moral lesson of his Benton experience. "It does seem strange," he speculated, "that people who profess to be endowed with a fair share of human reason should make such earnest efforts to save their lives and property as were exhibited and suffer month after month to pass away without making any effort whatever to seek their soul's salvation." [12]

Supplying fuel for Fort Benton was yet another serious problem. Long winters with periods of intense cold compelled northern plainsmen to provide adequate heating for their homes and public buildings. Fuel was always dear in Fort Benton. Scarcity of timber on the surrounding plains made wood costs prohibitive and local coal deposits never supplied the little city's needs. This scarcity created high prices and fuel famines which sometimes closed Benton's shops and public buildings. Visitors with legal business during November 1883 were greeted at the city hall with the cold, inhospitable placard: "No fuel — Froze out!" Bentonites willingly paid high prices for the output of Nicholas Sheran's mines at Coal Banks near old Fort Whoop-Up.

IV

Community building was a painfully slow process on every American frontier due to the transient character of our people, but Fort Benton's role as the entrepôt to the northern plains aggravated familiar problems. The constant parade of gold-seekers, freighters, adventurers, speculators, and fugitives from justice argued against stable and orderly growth.

Eloquent testimony of the excessive mobility of northern plainsmen lay in the violent fluctuations in Fort Benton's size from season to season and from year to year. Rumors of gold often filled the town with prospectors hurrying to the scene of the latest stampede. The opening of the navigation season each spring added thousands to the town's permanent population of seven hundred. But with the ending of the shipping season, the town again lapsed into comparative quiet as only its permanent residents remained to carry on the city's business.

Housing facilities were never adequate during the freighting season and men took whatever quarters they could find, adding to the confusion and disorder of the overcrowded town. Young S. C. Ashby was amazed to discover that his companion for the night in a cold, uncomfortable warehouse was Jonathan Levy, wealthy Helena merchant, waiting for a consignment.[13] These primitive conditions forced a rude equalitarianism upon rich and poor which was later falsely hailed as evidence of a conscious leveling movement.

Fort Benton, like other boom towns, suffered from the disinterest of transient residents who felt few ties of loyalty to the local community. Nor did they recognize the restraints of tradition or sentiment which influence behavior in established communities. In such an environment, there were few incentives to create or support schools and churches, or other institutions usually identified with the public welfare in mature societies.

Speculation, not community building, was the cement which held much of Benton society together in the years immediately following the war. Visitors to the river town frequently expressed their concern over this lack of community spirit and were impressed by the consuming spirit of acquisitiveness which motivated many of its citizens, whether at the gambling table, in real estate, or with the goods and services of commerce. Even

the wealthiest preferred to invest their fortunes in further speculations rather than build "a great house." "The people who live
here are only living to make money and not to make things look
pleasant and comfortable," complained a distressed observer in
1879.[14]

Numerous social tensions existed in the cosmopolitan character of the city's population. Transients from every state in the
Union and from every Canadian province passed through Benton. Census statistics also revealed that southerners came in
considerable numbers in the years following Appomattox, and
more than one saloon fight broke out after an indiscreet use of
the words "Johnny Reb" or "Damn Yankee." The polyglot character of Benton's citizenry is further suggested by its high percentage of French-Canadians and half-breeds, as well as its representatives of nearly every nation and language of Europe.

Irish immigrants, in particular, sought out Fort Benton as
peculiarly congenial to sons of the Emerald Isle. Benton's streets
were filled with Irish swagger and its saloons hummed with the
pleasant accents of the "ould country." Alone among the immigrant groups, the Irish seem to have achieved a certain economic
and social status in Benton without great difficulty and num-
bered among their successful countrymen such well-known citizens as the Healy brothers, Matthew Carroll, J. J. Donnelly, and
Judge Tattan.

With characteristic vigor and enthusiasm they quickly dominated the Democratic party as completely as ever they did in
any New England industrial city. Soon the Irish bloc and the
Democratic party appeared to be synonymous, though important leadership also came from the large numbers of southerners
who joined the party of the Democracy in their new home.

This Irish hegemony in the Democratic party aroused keen
resentment, both within and outside the party. Republican critics not only played upon the traditional fear of the immigrant,
but also hurled savage attacks upon the "Whoop-Up Democrats" whose Irish origins and whisky trading north of the
border marked them as fair game for political ridicule. But the

struggle within the party was quite often as bitter and as violent. Non-Irish Democrats frequently voiced deep resentment at what they regarded as the Irish dictatorship in their party. This was especially true of southern Democrats, who found their party a somewhat different organization in frontier Montana from the one they had left in Virginia. This bitterness was fully expressed in a famous letter from John P. Bruce to the colorful Baron O'Keefe in 1874:

"But bear in mind, Baron, that when the day and opportunity comes, I shall make the experiment of being elected without Irish votes, unless your countrymen reform and act better in this regard in the future than in the past. It is the only tarnish on their proud escutcheon, and for their sake and the good of Montana, I do sincerely trust that, having all the rights and privileges of American citizens themselves, they will let myself and others, who happen not to be born in Old Ireland, have an equal show for the honors and advantages of our Government. 'Equal rights to all — exclusive privileges to none.' " [15]

Fort Benton was also a Fenian stronghold. Here this secret Irish brotherhood nursed its wrath against the British empire and planned militant campaigns against its North American dominion. Led by Colonel J. J. Donnelly, whose career already boasted two efforts to invade Canada, the Fenians noisily urged the annexation of Canada to the American republic and dreamed of the day when Irish passion would join American power to humble the proud British empire whose most valuable possession seemed to lie within their grasp just across the forty-ninth parallel.

Racial tensions created numerous unpleasant incidents. Many of the fights and acts of violence occurring during these years were prompted by racial rather than by frontier tensions and Benton's reputation as a "tough town" was similar to that of many towns along the Ohio or Mississippi rivers during the steamboat era.

Indians frequented Benton in large numbers, particularly while the Blackfoot Agency was located in the town. Distrust and hatred for the red men prompted disturbances which widened the gulf of misunderstanding and suspicion separating the two peoples. Finally in 1870, the federal government shifted the agency headquarters, which eliminated the occasion for much disorder within the city.

Negroes were also in the town in large numbers serving as roustabouts on the river front or as crewmen on the steamboats. Many frontier towns in the Far West suffered from anti-Chinese sentiment and riots, but Benton was one of the few which also bore the burden of anti-Negro racism. By 1882 this hostility reached such heights that the town's leading citizens petitioned the local school board to establish a separate school for its colored children.

Social disorders were thus as often the result of diverse national origins and heterogeneous racial composition as of the instability of a new community on the edge of settlement.

Social stability was further delayed by the predominately masculine character of this frontier through its successive stages as a fur trading, gold mining, military, freighting, and ranching economy. Many of these men, moreover, were Civil War veterans who found freedom for their restless spirits in the primitive society of the West. Here they continued the camaraderie of the war years and perpetuated the unrestrained life of a masculine society, joining in a drinking bout, a fight, or a frolic with equal enthusiasm.[16]

Family life exerted slight influence upon this region's social structure for many years. There were several half-breed families, but they occupied an insignificant position in the town's social structure. Until Benton's expansion as a commercial and business center in the 1870s, Mrs. G. A. Baker and Mrs. W. S. Stocking were the only white women residing permanently in the town. Most of the white women in the community were euphemistically referred to in the newspapers as "our fair but frail citizens." Obviously these added little to the town by way of community uplift.

Much of the crudity and vulgarity of frontier life can be

traced directly to this absence of the family as the basic social unit. Frequent protests appeared in the local press condemning the general disrespect for social niceties or denouncing the barracks-like atmosphere pervading the community. The universal disregard for cleanliness, the general want of concern for personal appearance, the inordinate use of chewing tobacco and alcohol, and the shocking use of profanity were the usual targets of criticism in this masculine society. Occasionally, however, other customs aroused editorial ire. In 1876, for example, the *Record*'s editor protested that the practice of bathing in the river at the levee's end was unseemly. With good-natured indignation he urged the town's many bachelors to go farther up the river from Benton to perform their ablutions, since "they don't look well with their clothes off, and might be mistaken for catfish." [17] Yet another type of offense against good taste drew editorial fire as the paper warned that "making love to a squaw across a hotel fence, in broad daylight, is something that even the good-natured proprietors of the Overland must condemn." [18]

A chronic shortage of marriageable women led to the use of advertising in eastern journals for wives. "Lonely hearts" columns in magazines and newspapers illumined masculine hearts from Benton to Calgary with the promise of romance shining through their pages. *Heart and Hand*, a Chicago publication, was a favorite for this purpose and its many letters and messages from the "lovelorn" and "lonely hearts" were eagerly read by northern plainsmen. Numerous marriages were contracted, sight unseen, through the good offices of such a journal.

Occasionally, however, these mail-order romances failed to produce a desirable soul-mate. To prevent this, one cautious Northwest Mounted Police officer, equipped with a powerful glass and ensconced on a nearby hill, coolly surveyed the unsuspecting picture bride arriving by stagecoach before committing himself. After careful scrutiny, he dispatched his orderly with a note of regret and sufficient funds to pay for a return journey to the East.[19] Not all prospective husbands were as farsighted as this.

V

Few centers for social life existed in Benton except in hotels and saloons. These quickly assumed characteristic frontier importance and served as convivial oases for the entire northwest plains, since Benton was the social as well as the economic hub of the region.

Hotels played a uniquely important role in Fort Benton's growth. With thousands of transients passing through the river town annually, they were also of considerable consequence in the development of the entire region. Hotel services ranged widely from the rather primitive accommodations available in the Overland immediately following the war to the impressive Grand Union in the 1880s. From the Overland, through the opening of the Centennial, the Chouteau House, and finally the Grand Union, the quality of service and accommodations steadily improved.

As early as 1867, however, many travelers found Benton's hotels better than those usually available in frontier towns. One feminine traveler discovered to her surprise that her "rooms were on the ground floor [and] open directly into the street. The walls were neatly whitewashed and the whole interior of the rooms wore an air of comfort to which we had long been strangers." [20]

In November 1882 the Grand Union proudly opened its doors, with A. Staveley Hill, British capitalist and member of Parliament, as its first guest. This hotel was regarded by many visitors as superior to most western hotels and the equal of many eastern hostelries. [21]

Most travelers, however, found accommodations inferior. Some, forced to share their rooms with fellow travelers, found the experience intolerable. Much depended, of course, upon the season and the crowded state of the city. In general, Benton hotels offered "first class" accommodations to those who could afford an extra fifty cents charge and "second class" facilities to all others. The indefatigable British traveler Major William Shepherd claimed that these western hotels and restaurants were "wonderfully good, considering." [22] But this apparently was a sufficient qualification to allow for a monotonous diet of poorly prepared food, plainly served under conditions deficient in sanitation and wanting in style.

Saloons were even more important in the social life of the town since they were the community clubs, providing relaxation and social intercourse for the fraternity of plainsmen. Frontier life, like that of the soldier in wartime, had its moments of high excitement, but these were few in contrast to the long periods of drab monotony and hard work. The saloon was a central institution in every town or village and communities vied with each other to claim the largest and most ornate in the West.

By the 1880s, Benton was widely known for its numerous, gaudy, and wicked saloons and "hurdy-gurdy" houses. Few visitors passed through this western Sodom without critical comment on Benton's open wickedness and conspicuous sin. But in the early years Benton's saloons, while numerous, were far from luxurious. As late as 1878, not a saloon in Benton hung shades or curtains to hide its shame and the main street was often littered with soiled and torn playing cards carelessly swept out the front doors.

After this inauspicious beginning, however, Benton publicans built bigger and better saloons to keep pace with the town's growth. By the mid-1880s, the town's primacy in this field of achievement was undisputed on the northern plains. Whether the thirsty traveler stopped at the "Jungle," the "Extradition," the "Break O'Day," the "Medicine Lodge," the "Exchange," or any other of Benton's numerous public houses, he found much the same atmosphere in each, with its neatly papered walls, from which looked down, in apparent unconcern, the stern visages of the Father of His Country and the Great Emancipator.

Behind the muslin curtains which mercifully shielded convivial spirits from public scrutiny, an affable Charlie, Bob, or Bill dispensed his potions. Saloonkeepers were indeed a distinct type and were universally recognized as such by those travelers who recorded their impressions for credulous readers. "The saloonkeeper," wrote one enthusiastic visitor, "is always tidily dressed, appears in a white shirt, his sleeves and wrist bands protected by calico cuffs; his cleanliness, and his not wearing a hat, at once separate him from his customers." [23]

To his nominal functions as bartender, the successful publican added other duties of a thoughtful host. His unlimited stock of stories, his familiarity with local personalities, and his fund of news, both social and political, made him a popular figure in the community. Since most frontiersmen disdained mixed drinks, the professional skills of the publican were often limited, but with ready wit and untiring tongue, most were able to satisfy their uncritical customers. When mixed cocktails, slings, or other exotic drinks were required, artful barkeepers disguised the poor quality of the spirits with a stimulant of a pronounced flavor, usually bitters, and the mixture was then kept in subjugation by the liberal use of ice. This universal use of ice in western saloons amazed visiting Europeans, one of whom gravely informed his English readers that "iced drinks are consumed by classes in America far below the social level of those who never taste them in this country." [24]

Dancing saloons, or "hurdy-gurdy" houses, also provided amusement for Benton's masculine population. Here "bedizened wrecks of women" lightly danced away the hours with partners willing to pay a dollar a dance. Custom also dictated that the patron "balance his partner up to the bar" once the dance was finished. There the willing guest paid generously for his drink as well as for the pink lemonade his companion sipped as she computed her share of the profits in his empty glass.

Gambling saloons were more numerous and more popular. These were usually of two types: one catered to local talent and was known for its "square deal," while the other preyed on inexperienced strangers with its "hogging" tactics. In each, however, games of faro, blackjack, and poker were presided over with appropriate rituals by professional gamblers whose skills and colorful demeanor have made them favorite subjects for pulp magazine writers and Hollywood directors ever since.

With few other amusements to while away their time, plainsmen came to place a high regard upon skill at cards or at tippling. Drinking and gaming, as John Murphy tolerantly recorded, attracted even the "higher social personages of the town, for drinking is a virtue with those who would be considered genial or popular." [25]

There were those, however, who regarded this free flow of liquor as the curse of frontier life. In protest against it, and to redeem its many victims, they formed temperance societies in the Fort Benton vicinity. Of these, the Independent Order of Good Templars and the Order of Jonadab were the most important. The Jonadab pledge, however, was of such strict character and the oath such a solemn one that all but the most determined teetotalers were frightened away and its membership remained small.

Of greater influence as well as larger membership, the Order of Good Templars led in the battle against King Alcohol. Organized in the Sun River district in 1872 and during the following year at Benton, Good Templar chapters grew rapidly in membership and strength. Within a year, the Sun River chapter counted 115 members in good standing, largely recruited from the army forces stationed at Fort Shaw.[26]

These societies were more than organized efforts to moderate the evils of the whisky traffic in the Whoop-Up country. They were serious attempts to fill the social vacuum in this sparsely settled region by sponsoring musicals, dances, dinners, amateur theatricals, debates, and lectures. Good Templar meetings, with their elaborate ritual and colorful regalia, relieved some of the drabness of frontier life, and their journal, *The Good Templar*, provided reading material on diverse topics of universal interest as it preached, with conviction and passion, the doctrines of temperance.

For those who sought entertainment and relaxation without the degrading atmosphere of the saloon or hurdy-gurdy house, the Templars filled an urgent need. While the society's records clearly reveal that only a small minority of "those who had fallen through the vices of intemperance" ever signed the pledge, the Templars achieved considerable success in their efforts to provide nonalcoholic entertainment, thus contributing materially in stimulating cultural interests among enemies of demon rum.

VI

It is unfortunately a fact that too many historians, along with storytellers of indifferent veracity, have overemphasized the cultural crudity of the West. Fort Benton's social history is indeed a case in point. If the focus of historical attention centers only on the human flotsam and jetsam passing through the town, little of cultural activity is observed. These men seldom added much to the town's cultural life, nor had they much to offer despite their antecedents in the older and civilized communities. As one Canadian observer wisely pointed out, "The scum of the westward floating population is on the surface. We do not find the quiet, industrious workers of new frontier towns in poker rooms or at billiard tables." [27]

Beneath this floating population rested the town's permanent residents comprising the business and professional men, the artisans and workers and their families. These were the men and women whose devotion and energy created a stable community in the face of discouraging odds. These were the men and women whose tireless zeal to build a community in the cultural image of their past led to substantial achievements in the realm of the mind and the spirit. These were the men and women whose concern for the arts, for learning, and for what they called "the finer things of life," prompted them to organize musical, literary, or debating societies and social clubs, as well as the more familiar religious and educational institutions.

Newspapers played an important role in this transfer of culture to the frontier. Their catholicity of interests and universality of coverage provided for readers a fund of information supplied in more complex ways to our modern generation. Fort Benton supported two of these newspapers during most of these years, the *Record* and the *River Press*. In the manner of their time, they did far more than publish sensational headlines or local gossip. Columns of solid print, unbroken by boldface type or by single sentence paragraphs and unrelieved by photographs of Miss Universe, brought stories from the far corners of the earth to frontier America. Essays on moral philosophy, aboriginal life in South America, or court life in Europe were not uncommon, though they were sometimes pirated from eastern journals without credit. Political news was paramount; so much of it was printed that readers could hardly escape partisan indoctrination. Benton's newspapers were a vital link with the outside world and were cherished the more for Benton's relative isolation from the national scene.

With characteristic North American concern for education, Benton citizens established a school for their children very early in the town's history. The first school appeared in 1868 under the direction of Miss Fannie Culbertson, daughter of the famous fur trader. But this school suffered so seriously from inattention and from Benton's declining fortunes in the early 1870s that it collapsed.

By 1873, however, Benton's population was sufficiently stable to prompt the organization of a permanent school. In that year the defunct school was reopened in the courthouse under the tutelage of J. A. Kanouse, reportedly a Yale graduate. This arrangement was most unsatisfactory, for proximity to the courtroom necessitated rules which "hampered the children." Moreover, heavy rains seeped through the roof of the adobe building, much to the delight of the scholars, who gained extra holidays from their studies on these occasions.

Community pride soon demanded more adequate quarters for Benton's children. In 1876, a campaign was launched to build a permanent school, and in May a special election approved the project. By 1877, the building was under construction and in January 1878 Benton's school children proudly occupied their new two-room brick building and the housing problem was solved.

More difficult was the problem of securing competent teachers.

Qualified schoolmasters drifted through Benton from time to time, but few stayed very long. Pay was low and other inducements were few; hence the men sought other and more lucrative employment. When the school board turned to employing women teachers, the problem remained, for marriage often claimed them before the term expired. Thus, the school was sometimes forced to close before the completion of the term, and the quality of instruction was often less than inspired.

Physical equipment steadily improved in the Benton school as the little community sought to create a system "which has only one superior in the world, that of Prussia." By 1881, schoolmaster E. R. Clingan proudly reported to the school board that his classrooms were "furnished with the best of seats and teachers, desks, an organ, maps, charts, globes, good black boards and other furniture necessary to constitute a first class school." [28]

But slight advance was made in these years in solving the most serious of all problems of elementary education in frontier communities, the small percentage of eligible children who attended school. Benton made little headway in meeting this problem during its early years. The census of 1880 revealed 512 children of school age in Benton, but the enrollment of the school did not exceed 100 pupils.

Other activities of a cultural nature were also apparent very early in the town's history, though many of these were sponsored by organizations of an essentially social character. Bentonites, like Americans everywhere, were great joiners, associating themselves for many purposes. Familiar organizations such as the Masonic lodge appeared as early as 1874 and were soon followed by societies unique to the local community, such as the Frontier and Chouteau clubs.

These organizations sponsored serious cultural programs along with their many social and recreational events. In the early years, for example, the Masonic lodge presented annual lectures featuring visiting dignitaries. A rather typical series for the enlightenment of Benton's social elite was that delivered in 1875 by General John Gibbon entitled, with satisfactory vagueness,

"Other Worlds Than Ours." It must also have surprised many visitors to find as early as 1879 an oil painting gallery in the local courthouse maintained by the town's leading citizens.

Frequent theatrical performances were a favorite entertainment during the long winter months. Most of these were enacted by touring companies whose extensive repertoire was in striking contrast to their limited ability, meager scenery, and ancient costumes. Favorite troupes, such as the Taylor, Frank Hall, and Billy Arlington companies, were eagerly greeted season after season. Individual performers also appeared on local stages with their acts of magic, music, and drama. Novelty acts comprising mind reading, mesmerism, and ventriloquism frequently advertised their presence in the river town, but these excited considerable suspicion and eventually came to be regarded as "traveling humbugs" whose only skill lay in "fooling the public out of its surplus cash." Occasionally, however, a performance received warm praise from local critics. Great enthusiasm greeted Mr. William Hyde's show, which brought to Benton a stereopticon exhibition featuring "a variety of beautifully colored pictures, representing statuary, scenes from nature, life-like portraits of noted men and women and a large collection of the funniest kind of caricatures." [29]

More interesting, at least in retrospect, was the frequent staging of local productions. Serious drama as well as minstrels, comedies, and novelty shows offered local thespians an opportunity to display their talents and provided a welcome change of fare in the succession of humorists, lecturers, and professional exhibitionists passing through Benton. All in all, the local theater played a far more important role in the life of the frontier community than it has more recently as cultural standards have matured in motion pictures.

Holiday festivities provided a convenient excuse for the community to enjoy mass entertainments. Fourth of July oratory and fireworks were as familiar and exciting in Benton as elsewhere during these years. Athletic contests, spelling bees, shooting matches, and public dances made Christmas, Thanksgiv-

179

ing, and every other holiday brief interludes of excitement and pleasure.

In marked contrast to the raw environment about them, and perhaps in defiance against it, Benton's social leaders planned frequent and highly formal social events. Teas, receptions, and colorful balls highlighted the social seasons, and the graceful and elaborate invitations which remain in historical archives eloquently testify to the studied formality of these occasions.

During the hot summer months many of these events were held aboard visiting steamboats with proud captains contending for social honors. During the winter months the Frontier Club and the Chouteau Club greatly impressed visitors with the style and elegance of their dinners and dances. William Bross, one-time editor of the Chicago *Tribune*, confided to his diary in apparent surprise that he found the members of the Frontier Club "very intelligent, cultivated people," while Sir Cecil Denny of the Northwest Mounted Police remembered his honorary membership in the Chouteau Club as one of the reasons for his "very pleasant visit in Benton." [30] Army officers and Mounted Police officials were lionized by Benton hostesses, and Generals Gibbon and Ruger and Colonels Macleod and Irvine found a cordial welcome on their frequent visits to the river metropolis.

VII

Like other boom towns on the Great Plains frontier, Benton suffered a chronic shortage of professional men and skilled artisans. Few doctors or pharmacists ventured the healing arts so far from established communities. As surprising as it now seems, even lawyers were slow to hang out their shingles in this distant town. The shortage of doctors and druggists remained for many years, but the appearance of a rash of amateur Blackstones in the late 1870s provided legal talent of indifferent training and ability.

Far more critical in the town's rise to prominence was the consistent shortage of skilled artisans. Carpenters, wheelwrights, masons, brickmakers, tailors, shoemakers, and tinsmiths commanded high wages in the Whoop-Up country, but the shortage remained unrelieved. Despite wages ranging 50 per cent higher than eastern pay scales, Benton's entrepreneurs were unable to solve their problem. As late as 1886, the *River Press* lamented the absence of sufficient skilled workers despite "advantages for the poor and industrious classes of the crowded cities of the East which no other country on the face of the earth can possess." [31]

This problem excited considerable discussion among Benton's capitalists. Numerous schemes were proposed to the Benton Board of Trade, but none got beyond the talking stage. Most lived with the hope that time would solve this distressing problem, for any plan which promised action required capital. Obviously, some scheme of assisted passage was necessary but few were willing to support any such program since there was no guarantee that once the artisan reached Benton, he would stay. Too often promising craftsmen appeared, only to drop their tools in favor of a miner's shovel.

An equally serious barrier to the westward migration of skilled artisans lay in the high cost of moving an entire household to remote Benton. Once the craftsman reached the river town, moreover, there was only the promise of seasonal employment with high wages in the summer months and unemployment and idleness during the winter season.

This absence of a sufficient supply of skilled labor on the frontier disturbed many visitors whose concerns turned to economic questions. Of these, the most searching observations were left by Peter O'Leary, a British worker, who viewed western problems through the eyes of a skilled craftsman. O'Leary's conclusion after months of careful study was an indictment of American policy and an interesting footnote to a tragic chapter in the history of American immigration during the Gilded Age.

"It might, indeed, be said," he wrote, "that emigration to those fertile western wilds is an extension of the empire of civilisation; I am astonished that the UNITED STATES GOVERNMENT do not encourage it by giving to the multitudes who arrive daily from European countries at New York, Boston and Philadelphia, facilities to go West instead of leaving them to loaf about the great cities where they can never rise above poverty. I do not know anything about the internal statesmanship of the United States, but I believe it is A VERY SHORTSIGHTED POLICY not to assist the poor, but strong and willing, European emigrant to settle on the land." [32]

If the northern plains acted as a "safety valve" for eastern urban proletarians by providing mass employment, thus draining off discontent and frustration, O'Leary did not discover it. It is perfectly clear, moreover, that such a mechanism did not exist. The frequent pleas for skilled workers and the constant emphasis upon schemes to draw them into the Whoop-Up country argue that the economic opportunities of the West attracted few from eastern cities. Benton freighters, muleskinners, bull-whackers, carpenters, and wheelwrights were drawn chiefly from contiguous western and middle western communities where the tradition of westward migration was yet strong and proximity gave easy access.

9

Life on the Trail

TRANSPORTATION was the key to western empire and the foundation of Fort Benton's prosperity. But no obliging rivers coursed the Whoop-Up country to provide those natural arteries of commerce so familiar in the forest regions of North America. Consequently the region between the Missouri River and the North Saskatchewan was a land of carts, wagons, buckboards, prairie schooners, and stagecoaches. In the Whoop-Up country, the wheel ruled supreme.

On a dozen trails reaching out of Fort Benton, wagon trains carried the commerce of the plains. Toiling men drove oxen and mules to northern destinations carrying the commerce that linked the Canadian with the American West. Around this lowly industry developed a community uniquely western, though international in character. It comprised a West within the West, a social group within a larger society.

Confusion, even serious misunderstanding, marks much that is believed about the plains West. Much of this stems from a failure to recognize the sharp differences between life in the rural West and life in the frontier towns. Generalizations describing the thought and actions of men on the trail are often misleading when applied to men and manners in the towns. Life on the trails, in the prairie camps, on the ranches, or at the remote posts was very different from that in Fort Benton. Despite its many primitive qualities, the little river town was a sub-metropolis, offering an urban environment foreign to the rural community around it.

Great freighting companies were the mainsprings that kept the wagon trains moving along the trails. The Hudson's Bay Company first sent shipments of furs down the Old North Trail to Fort Benton in an effort to find a cheaper route to eastern markets. Bentonites, familiar with the great bulltrains of the plains, stared with astonishment at the squealing, two-wheeled Red River carts that entered their city in 1870. This experiment failed, however, and never again did these carts move down from the far north with their precious cargoes.

With the opening of the trading posts in the Whoop-Up country and the arrival of the Northwest Mounted Police, wagon wheels turned north. To supply the expanding population with goods and equipment, bulky bulltrains and creaking muletrains headed for the border. To furnish transport for men and mails, speedy express wagons followed the same trails.

I. G. Baker, T. C. Power, Murphy, Neel and Co., and Diamond R built great corporations in the prosaic business of freighting. Individual contractors also entered the freighting business, though they often leased their equipment to the larger freighting companies. Murphy, Neel and Co. sent more than one hundred wagons over the trails to Forts Macleod and Walsh, and the Baker and Power firms dwarfed these operations. Each sent hundreds of wagons out every spring and owned several thousand oxen and mules to keep their trains moving.

These operations represented considerable capital investment. The T. C. Power Company estimated that a single wagon train required a $25,000 to $30,000 investment, while annual expenditures for the wages and subsistence of several hundred men involved impressive figures. Care of animals demanded extensive stables, warehouses, hay and feed, while concern for employees led the Power firm to erect "an elegant boarding and lodging house for their small army of teamsters, freighters and other employees." [1]

The cargoes reflected the complex economic interests of the great mercantile companies. Baker and Power wagon trains hauled tons of goods to their stores north of Fort Benton. Supplies for the Northwest Mounted Police and for United States Army troops, and food and clothing for thousands of reservation Indians on both sides of the boundary comprised the bulky cargoes that made great fortunes for their owners. Occasionally, manifest lists showed shipments peculiar to the region. In October 1880, for example, I. G. Baker bullteams hauled 40,000 pounds of pemmican to Fort Macleod and Battleford to feed Indians at those points.

Independent shippers often followed more diverse schedules. In September 1882, Clark Tingley's seven teams, each pulling three wagons, hauled flour to Fort Edmonton for the Baker Company. This substantial load of flour must have reminded many Bentonites of the familiar western story of the bulltrain that arrived in a frontier town with forty barrels of whisky and one barrel of flour. "What do they want of all that flour?" inquired one curious bystander.

At Fort Edmonton, Tingley's wagons took on a cargo of imported English goods for Fort Macleod. Since no bills of lading awaited him there, Tingley moved his teams over to Coal Banks, near Fort Whoop-Up, to take on a load of coal with which he returned to Fort Benton. The freighting enterprises of this modest owner thus demonstrated both the diversity and the international character of commerce in the Whoop-Up country.

II

Stagecoaches, and their individualistic drivers, wrote a colorful chapter in western history. By the 1880s, daily Concord mail coaches wheeled out of Benton for Helena. But trips to Fort Macleod and Calgary were slower in reaching this level of service.

With considerable exaggeration, the "Benton, Macleod and Calgary Stage Co." advertised regularly scheduled departures of "four horse coaches." This company, another I. G. Baker subsidiary, provided the vital link between Benton and the Canadian towns. But travelers who believed the advertising faced a surprise when the call "Coach" rang out from the Overland Hotel on the fifth, fifteenth, and twenty-fifth of each month.

Instead of a Concord coach drawn by a prancing four-in-hand, they climbed aboard an open wagon drawn by four mules. In this informal rig they braved the dust and heat of summer or the sleet and snow of winter. From Benton to Rocky Springs near the boundary line this light wagon carried them over the plains. At Rocky Springs the travelers looked forward to a different vehicle. Unhappily, it proved to be a duplicate of the rig they had just ridden from Benton, and the trip from Rocky Springs to Macleod was no more pleasant or comfortable.

By the mid-eighties, however, Concord coaches came into use on the northern runs. These marvels of nineteenth-century craftsmanship possessed the durability, weight, and sturdiness to withstand the hazards of western travel. Neither sleet nor snow, swollen streams nor seas of mud could prevent their appointed rounds, though delays often mounted to days as coaches waited for impassable barriers to disappear.

The introduction of the Concord stage, built for sturdy travel and not for comfort, marked a genuine improvement on the Whoop-Up Trail. Yet bruised and weary travelers recorded their recollections of the discomfort and tedium of crowded coaches, rough rides, dust or mud, gnats and flies. From some accounts the inference is clear that western travel revived the plagues of ancient Egypt. Few travelers really understood that the stages operated for mail and express revenues. Passengers were only surplus cargo.

Considerable skill was required to handle a Concord stage and veteran drivers were widely known for their techniques. An improperly loaded stage meant trouble for an entire trip. Too heavy a load in the front made it impossible to hold on a downgrade, while too heavy a load on the hurricane deck might throw the stage over when it hit a rock.

Most drivers fully appreciated the important role they played in western life, displaying in their demeanor and manner of dress a pride equal to their station. Veteran drivers boasted they could trail a coach where most men "couldn't trail a whip." Stagemen learned their routes thoroughly, charging through

shifting fords with what impressed many riders as uncanny instinct. Experienced drivers took great pride in their skill with
the ribbons, their complete understanding of their teams, and
their intimate familiarity with each rise and roll of the prairie
road. John D. Higinbotham, Fort Macleod druggist, who traveled the Whoop-Up Trail many times, thought the drivers "were
artists in their line." [2]

Whoop-Up stagemen were part of a larger western fraternity.
Their manner of dress, with buckskin gloves, Stetson hat, and
ever-present vest, fitted the habiliment of their order. Unlike
southern plainsmen, however, Whoop-Up drivers wore heavy
buffalo coats and Scotch caps against the winter's rigors. Newspapers in Fort Benton and Fort Macleod chronicled the arrivals
and departures of every stage, never failing to record that such
a well-known driver as Z. D. Holmes, Jack Lee, "Polly," "Silver"
Johnson, or "Scotch Bill" Atkins was on the box.

Perhaps in only one regard did Whoop-Up stagemen excel.
They earned a universal reputation as hard drinkers while on
the trail. Travelers returning from Whoop-Up country frequently mentioned that the trail was clearly marked, when all other
signs failed, by the "dead soldiers" along the route. These head-
less bottles testified eloquently to the universal habit of scorn-
ing the use of bottle openers and of simply decapitating the
bottle on the sharp steel tires of the coach.

Mail seemed far more important than passengers, both to the
stagecoach companies and to the general citizenry. Relatively
few plainsmen traveled the stages, but everyone depended upon
the United States mails they carried. Companies welcomed the
revenue that made the trips profitable, though there is no evidence that the I. G. Baker Company resorted to the star route
frauds so common throughout the West during the years of the
Grant administration.

Plainsmen eagerly greeted each stage for the news and personal messages it carried. The arrival of the coach touched off
a minor celebration in every community. Similarly, many travelers expressed excitement at meeting a mail wagon on the trail.

The commonplace wagon, with its four mules and canvas top, somehow became a symbol representing personal ties and national sentiments.

Horace Greeley professed to see "Bunker Hill, Saratoga, Yorktown, Plattsburgh, New Orleans, the starry flag and the American Union" in the mail wagon that he met on the plains.[3] Unimaginative plainsmen seldom possessed the warm emotionalism to discern all this in the four mules carrying their mail, but they welcomed the rig warmly just the same.

Whoop-Up mail service suggests an unexplored footnote to the history of the United States postal service. Until the construction of the Canadian Pacific Railway, mail from Macleod and other Canadian points went east via Fort Benton. Thus during these years outgoing letters bore United States postage stamps. Fort Macleod had the unique distinction of possessing an informal United States post office on Canadian soil. What would a United States stamp, canceled at Fort Macleod, Northwest Territory, Canada, be worth to a modern philatelist?

III

Freight made the profits, and long trains of wagons drawn by oxen or mules hauled it. Bulltrains, so common throughout the West, always excited visiting pilgrims as a novel sight. Bulltrains were unique to the West, and the spectacle of twelve or fourteen yoke of oxen plodding across the plains stirred more than one traveler to record his impressions.

"We were approaching Fort Whoop-Up from the east," wrote one visitor, "and it was toward evening as we topped a small rise and looked down upon the plain beneath us. Some distance away, it must have been at least five miles, we could hear the sound of voices, ever and anon raised in hoarse shout. At first we could see nothing. Then, from a large coppice or clump of trees we saw emerge some toiling, plodding oxen. We could see them plainly through our field glasses, swinging along in that peculiar gait of the bovine. As they walked, the dust drifted from their plodding hoofs in little clouds. Team after team came into view, until there was nearly half a mile of them stretched out. A man on horseback rode up and down the line. The sun was nearing the horizon and we stood and watched them until the plodding, swaying oxen, dragging their wagons behind them, were lost in the haze of the autumn sun." [4]

Bulltrains often consisted of eight to ten teams with twenty-four to thirty wagons. Harnesses were simple, seldom more than hickory bow yokes with stout chains. Wheel oxen were first driven into place, then the rest of the team hitched to the wagon. Ahead of the "wheelers" were the first "pointers," while the next pairs were called first, second, and third "swings."

Wagons were hitched in tandem behind the teams. Usually three heavy, five-foot gauge wagons, "lead," "swing," and "trail," comprised a team, with ten to twelve yoke of oxen out in front. Heavy loads, ranging from 7000 to 9000 pounds of freight, filled each wagon, with the trains often carrying more than 200,000 pounds of cargo across the plains. Travel, of course, was tediously slow. Ten to fifteen miles seemed a good day's journey, and the bulltrains required fifteen to twenty days to complete the trip up the trail from Fort Benton to Fort Macleod.

Muletrains traveled faster and made a smarter appearance. But they cost considerably more. A good yoke of oxen cost only $300 in the eighties, but a team of mules usually sold for $500 or $600. At the height of the freighting season, a mule team and wagon sometimes brought as much as $800.

Bullwhackers invariably walked alongside their plodding teams. To keep the slow-moving oxen at a steady gait, drivers swung their long whips at the animals' flanks, snapping them in the air with an explosive report which from a distance sounded like the crack of a pistol shot. Loud cries of "Gee" and "Haw" punctuated the noise and confusion as drivers turned their animals to the left or right.

Muleskinners, on the other hand, generally rode the left wheel animal. Most drove jerkline, a single line running out to the lead mule which the skinner jerked hard for a left turn or gave a steady pull for a right turn. Trained "leader" mules cost considerably more than others and were difficult to replace on the trail. Many drivers mounted chime bells to the harness hames that tinkled musically with the swaying of the animals. Each little settlement along the trail turned out in excitement when the long trains moved through their dusty streets with whips cracking, wagons creaking, and bells tinkling.

Westerners regarded the mule with mingled emotions. Some professed to believe that his stubborn, intractable spirit came from the fact that he was the only animal Noah did not take on the Ark. Others claimed that his innocent appearance concealed a stubborn deafness to command and an implacable hostility to work causing frustration and despair to drivers, unless periodically relieved by sulphuric language and impetuous outbursts.

In command of the outfit rode the train boss whose reputation as a skinner or whacker, as well as a driver of men, recommended him for the job. Baker, Power, Diamond R, and Murphy, Neel each had their favorite wagonmasters in whose hands they entrusted valuable cargoes and equipment. Pink Wilson, Dave Jenks, Milt Emsley, "Dutch" Patrick, Howell Harris, John O'Conner, and Ed Trainer won reputations as able, if hard, train bosses who kept their wagons rolling along the Whoop-Up Trail.

IV

Wagon freighting was a specialized industry which developed its own techniques and its own master artisans. Bullwhackers and muleskinners played their part in developing the West along with pioneer merchants, bankers, ranchers, cowboys, preachers, grangers, and politicians.

Three wagons hitched in tandem behind ten span of mules or twelve yoke of oxen were more than a match for an inexperienced pilgrim just out from the States. Only a seasoned veteran with complete mastery of jerkline or ribbons and an artistic use of the black snake could keep the train moving steadily. On top of this, the driver who lacked the lung power to fire a volley of expletives at the psychological moment to stir the beasts to action was helpless before the stubborn mule or sluggish ox. Motions of whip and line and sound of oaths, it is maintained, had to be as skillfully coordinated as a symphony and as unyielding as steel.

Travelers who left a record of their experiences on this northern trail paid tribute to the bullwhackers as unique western figures. And no skill attracted greater comment than the bullwhacker's profanity, an art so highly developed that even the pious were moved to admiration. One Canadian clergyman, touring the West for the first time, was so impressed that he was impelled to write:

"The fully developed bull-whacker never pauses or stutters when he is once roused by surrounding influences to a full display of his powers, but launches forth in a torrent of the fanciest expletives, dressed in colors wonderfully gorgeous and eloquent, incandescent and irresistible. The principal portion of the existence of the bull-whacker is occupied in composing profanity of startling originality into which neither iteration nor plagiarism ever creeps." [5]

Another visitor to the Whoop-Up country argued that he could determine without difficulty the religious background of the muleskinner by listening to his swearing. Some of the oaths, he believed, derived their rich flavor from camp meeting reminiscences, while others demonstrated a closed communion background. This appeared obvious since the drivers, after damning their mules, superfluously damned the man who would not damn them with him. Still other oaths possessed the grand and reverent phraseology of the Prayer Book, while there were even those "Godless wretches, with whom, for very ignorance, oaths stand in the stead of adjectives." [6]

Most of the freighters were veterans of the Civil War. Camp life continued the rough life of the army, emphasizing similar qualities that carried the force of a code in a masculine community. Courage, or "sand" as the westerners called it, was the most admired of all virtues, though generosity and resourcefulness pressed it for universal praise.

Drivers who consistently violated tenets of the trail code were often a menace to the security of the entire outfit. Pressure from the group soon forced the nonconformist into line, or drove him out. Those who lacked sufficient "sand" drifted into other occupations where frequent accidents, Indian alarms, and capricious weather were less a hazard.

Simplicity of camp life and the infrequency of social contacts often encouraged a spirit of hospitality on the trail. C. E. D. Wood, for many years editor of the Fort Macleod *Gazette*, expressed a commonly accepted view when he testified, "on the prairie the bullwhacker is a most hospitable fellow and more than once I experienced his welcome and rough kindness." [7]

Freighting on the plains was a rugged business. Sometimes filled with moments of tense excitement, it was more often simply monotonous. Hard work, long hours, and primitive conditions marked the driver's life. Novelists and Hollywood writers seem to have found something of romance and color in the teamster's occupation, but for most it was a series of dull assignments, broken only by infrequent visits to the saloons and hurdy-gurdy houses of Benton, Macleod, and Calgary.

From sunrise until evening the caravan of wagons rolled on. At dusk the train halted to make camp in a familiar site known for its good grass and water. Fires were quickly lighted, both for cooking and for smudges to protect both men and animals from the clouds of mosquitoes that descended upon the camp.

Next, the train cook gave the men cups of coffee, strong and hot. This satisfied the crews until the cook, whose incapacity with the mules rather than skill with the frying pan elected him to his office, prepared dinner. The meal that followed was of plain food, generally including bread made of self-raising flour baked in a pan, fat bacon, and beans. Dried apples or peaches and syrup provided sweets for the men. Many travelers who shared the skinners' simple fare found the prairie butter, grease drippings mixed with flour and water, worthy of comment since its flavor and appearance seldom met with their approval.

Dinner completed, the teamsters gathered around the fire for a final smoke and a session of gossip. Conversations often drifted back to Civil War adventures with Federals and Confederates comparing yarns, often from the same battlefields. Others had been on the plains long enough to acquire a fund of Indian tales and frontier stories. Recent visits to Macleod or Benton, with descriptions of saloon fights and other escapades, furnished material for casual gossip around the flickering fires. One British traveler, however, found the quality of conversation of the skinners above his expectations. Nearly all the men, he wrote, were literate and "all discussed local and national politics with a terseness and emphasis that would do credit to a professional politician." [8]

Camp life required certain skills that tenderfeet quickly learned. The newcomers who failed to adjust to these simple requirements endured undue discomfort and suffered the cruel jests of their experienced companions. To prevent unpleasant experiences, the Fort Macleod *Gazette* offered advice to those only recently arrived in the Whoop-Up country.

Prepare for flies, gnats, and mosquitoes, warned the *Gazette*. Take warm clothes against the chill of the plains night and observe weather signs carefully. Since most pilgrims traveled in the company of experienced prairie men, they should "always try to be as useful as they can without continually getting in the way." This could best be accomplished by helping water the animals and picketing the horses for the night in a spot with good grass. Then the newcomer should hustle around, getting wood for a fire and preparing the camp for the night. With these instructions to guide him, any pilgrim would find life on the trail an exciting experience.

Some tenderfeet, however, failed to learn these obvious lessons. Their misadventures became part of the fund of stories exchanged over campfires. Favorite subjects of such yarns were the youthful remittance men from England whose wealthy families sent them to the North American West.

E. H. Maunsell delighted in telling of his experience with two charming and highly educated English youths, fresh from Oxford. These inexperienced gentlemen planned a trip up the trail from Benton to Macleod and purchased a democrat and horses for the journey.

While they were still in Benton, Maunsell met the two Englishmen. Their complete ignorance of the plains appalled him, and led him to offer considerable advice. Patiently he warned them against the danger of losing their horses while on the plains, of the care they must take in picketing their animals for the night, and of the importance of providing them with good grazing. Then he explained that plainsmen always camped near water when possible, not only to obtain water for men and animals but also because buffalo chips for fire could be found near these sites. But to prepare them against the possibility of wet weather on their trip, the rancher urged them to take along a few sticks of cordwood with which to start their fires.

In spite of Maunsell's advice, their journey from Benton to Macleod proved to be a comedy of errors. Douglas Allison, a rancher near Macleod, came upon their camp sometime later. His report of their difficulties provided gossip for Whoop-Up saloons for months.

When he first rode up, the Englishmen were on their knees with a stick of cordwood between them desperately lighting match after match in an effort to start a fire. An astonishing number of used matches lay about them. They had despaired of having a fire while on the plains, but Allison quickly cut kindling for them and soon a roaring fire boiled their tea water.

Later, the rancher described with great glee the amazement of the youthful Oxonians at his primitive achievement. "My word! S'prising" exclaimed the two in their astonishment at the way "these backwoodsmen fellows" did things.

More serious was their mishandling of the horses. The following morning their animals were found nearly strangled as their picket lines had fouled. Placed too close to each other, the two horses had become hopelessly entangled during the night. Fortunately, Allison assisted these latter-day pilgrims to Fort Macleod where they arrived safely. But their mishaps marked them for the remainder of their visit as targets for western humor.[9]

Men who skinned mules or whacked bulls did not occupy a high position in western society. The roughness and simplicity of their lives on the trail and their undisciplined conduct in the towns marked them as vulgarians. Many indeed must have been "hard cases" whose depredations in frontier saloons and pool halls earned a tough reputation for their entire guild.

Many townspeople resented the invasions of the freighters. Their impromptu celebrations often disturbed the peace and cost the community money to repair the damage. Escaping from the monotony of the trail and possessing several weeks' pay, the bullwhackers and muleskinners freely spent their money. "One peculiarity of these prairie mariners is the apparent power exerted over them by the possession of a few dollars of the realm," complained the *Yellowstone Journal*.[10]

Typical of these sprees was one that nearly took Fort Benton apart in May 1876. Unfortunately, two big outfits, the Diamond R and Benton Transportation Company, hit town at the same time. After an evening's drinking bout in the "Extradition," the "Break O' Day," and the "Medicine Lodge," the bullwhackers went on a "big whisky brave," determined to "take possession of the town."

With utter contempt for peace officers, the drunken teamsters marched up and down Front Street, whooping and screaming and kicking in the doors as they passed. Broken windows and damaged property attested to their violent passage.

This was too much for the town's merchants. Fears for the security of their property soon led them to arouse the reluctant sheriff, William Rowe, to his duties. With the aid of several "able-bodied citizens," the sheriff and his deputies soon subdued the rampaging bullwhackers who spent the remainder of their gay night in Benton's jail. Such incidents left Bentonites less than enthusiastic about bullwhacker celebrations.[11]

V

Numerous service industries sprang up to keep the wagons rolling. Late in autumn after the season's freighting, wagonmasters turned out their stock to graze on the range during the winter. But this was the busiest time of the year for the blacksmiths, wheelwrights, and harness makers who overhauled wagons, rebuilt wheels and axles, and repaired worn harnesses.

Slight attention, however, was paid to the upkeep of the trail. Government road building, so important for other western routes, played no role on this international highway. No United States military installations gave convenient excuse for federal appropriations. Some assistance from Chouteau County helped build bridges, but this was on such a limited scale that it gave little aid.

Fortunately, the trail crossed a flat plains country with few physical barriers. Rivers comprised the most serious obstacles, frequently delaying traffic for days. Swollen streams from melting snows in the mountains or flash floods from heavy rains transformed the normally sluggish streams into raging torrents. Crossing the Marias, Milk, or Oldman rivers after they had returned to normal flow required the discovery of new fords, for these capricious streams changed their depth with disconcerting frequency as sand beds took on new contours. Lives were lost and equipment damaged when drivers miscalculated.

Bridges spanned some of the streams during the eighties. Most of these proved temporary, disappearing when spring floods or chinook-loosened ice tore out the footings. At other crossings, crude ferries transported passengers and light freight across the streams. But these were inadequate to handle the heavily loaded wagons of the bulltrains.

Trail hazards filled the region's newspapers with a succession of disaster stories. While no statistics exist to measure the accident rate on this northern trail, a survey of newspaper accounts clearly indicates their frequency and their heavy cost in lives and property.

Runaway teams took a heavy toll. Grim stories of accidents caused by frightened teams appear with disturbing regularity. Frontier editors spared their readers none of the details, as if mortality itself could be held at bay by arousing survivors to the gruesome realities. "His body being mangled and torn into a horrible shapeless mass" was the kind of comment appearing in these nineteenth-century accounts.

Broken arms and legs were commonplace casualties on the trail. Occasionally, drama is evident as witnesses described amputations and surgery under primitive conditions. And sometimes the innocent also suffered. In 1876 a runaway team in Fort Macleod crushed the little six-year-old daughter of William Gladestone.

Not all accidents were as costly as these. John Higinbotham witnessed one during the summer of 1885, while showing the countryside to his father, a visitor from Ontario. As they rode along, one of I. G. Baker's great bulltrains under Milt Emsley forded the Oldman near Fort Macleod.

"Here is something you will not see in the East," Higinbotham assured his father. Just then the heavy chain connecting the train snapped, leaving wagons in the water while the oxen slowly emerged on the other bank.

Casually the wagonmaster walked to an open spot alongside the trail. Here he threw his bullwhip to the ground, carefully deposited his coat, vest, and hat beside it, and kneeling near this impromptu prairie altar cut loose with such a violent and blasphemous collection of oaths that the appalled senior Higinbotham called out, "Drive on at once, or the ground will open and swallow us." [12]

The greatest danger to travelers on the Whoop-Up Trail lay in the capricious weather of the northern plains. Heavy snows in early autumn or in late spring often caught freighters by surprise, causing suffering and occasionally death to men and animals.

Winter travel was extremely hazardous. Cruel storms of sudden ferocity, with blinding snow, harsh winds, and bitter cold, killed more freighters than Indians ever did. Northern plainsmen came to fear these outbursts of nature with a respect born of experience.

Snowblinded, frozen, and lost on the trail — these grim words describe the fate of many. Despite every precaution, even the most experienced plainsmen sometimes got caught. Then, knowledge of plains lore spelled the difference between survival and death.

As experienced a scout as Jerry Potts sometimes ran into trouble. In 1875 an early March blizzard trapped the famous Northwest Mounted Police scout with a party of policemen near the international boundary. After two days and nights seeking shelter in the hollow of a snowdrift, without a fire and subsisting on raw bacon, the party decided to push on before they all froze to death. Through the blinding snowstorm the half-breed led his party. Within a short time Constable Ryan gave out and pleaded with the men to go on without him. This they refused to do, but the exhausted Ryan slowed the party dangerously.

Near Rocky Springs the police found shelter. To their surprise they stumbled on a small trading shack in which a detachment of United States cavalrymen were posted to halt the whisky traffic into Canada. The American troopers rushed out to capture the exhausted Canadians, thinking they were whisky traders giving themselves up in the face of the crippling storm. With the discovery that the distressed party were policemen, the cavalrymen fed and clothed them, cared for their injuries, and finally sent them on their way to Helena.

No other region in the United States imposed such hazards upon the pioneers who conquered it. Bitter cold in winter claimed its victims while intense heat with its accompanying dust storms and myriad of insects made summer travel a chore. But above all, it was the terrors of the winter blizzards that men learned to fear.

On the heels of these storms often came chinooks. Welcomed as a respite from the terrible cold, they impeded travel by reducing the trail to miles of slush and mud. No storytelling session in the Whoop-Up country was complete without some reference to a sudden chinook that raised temperatures fifty degrees in the twinkling of an eye, drying the snow ahead of the runners of the sleds faster than the drivers could get off the trail.

LIFE ON THE TRAIL

Several travelers along the Whoop-Up Trail recorded their experiences. Of these, the Reverend Alexander Sutherland was one of the most observant and reliable. While secretary of the Missionary Society of the Methodist church of Canada he journeyed to the Whoop-Up country in 1879 to study the Wesleyan enterprises at Morleyville, as well as to report on the prospects of further missionary effort in the region.[13]

Sutherland's reactions to the Missouri River, its muddy waters, its Indians, and its scenery, were similar to those of hundreds of travelers. He found the river water too muddy to enjoy as a beverage but, denied its alcoholic substitutes by moral scruple, the clergyman learned to live with it. "A good set of teeth for straining purposes," he observed, "would seem to be indispensable."

To his surprise, the steamboat's crew and passengers did not live up to his expectations of the "Wild West." The West which greeted him seemed so mild that he commented several times upon the "entire absence of that 'roughness' which I had always associated with the belongings of a Missouri 'flat' [boat]." On Sundays he held religious services, "well attended by crew and passengers."

Fort Benton, with its many saloons and gambling halls, more nearly confirmed his image of the West. But the city's commerce impressed Sutherland even more than its sins. The "go ahead" spirit of its businessmen and the magnitude of their enterprise excited him. Several firms, he believed, handled more goods and money than the largest wholesale houses in Toronto.

In Benton the clergyman met David McDougall, brother of the missionary and Whoop-Up trader. McDougall organized the wagon train and took command. With twelve teams comprising their caravan, the party headed north in early July. Four miles west of Benton they forded the Teton River and eight miles farther on pitched their first camp on the trail. To Sutherland every activity provided a new and exciting experience. The arrangement of the wagons in the familiar western corral, into which horses could be driven when needed, struck his fancy. The fact that they carried no oats or hay for their horses puzzled him. Even after long and fatiguing journeys, these native animals existed on grass!

Montana soils did not impress this eastern visitor whose general reactions accorded with the Great American Desert tradition. Soils seemed exceedingly poor in contrast to the rich loams east of the Mississippi. But he guarded his criticisms with frequent observations that vast herds of buffalo had only recently grazed these prairies, hence there must be the basis for a pastoral economy. Absence of timber and scanty rainfall depressed him, as they so frequently did newcomers from forested America, while the alkali character of the soil confirmed his judgment of the inferior quality of the country.

The intense heat of July caused the party considerable discomfort. As far as his eye could reach no shade promised relief; "it seemed at times as if we should absolutely faint away." Even worse, the alkali water of the region failed to relieve his thirst, and with the passage of the second day, parched and cracked lips added to his distress. Soon, mouth and throat became "as dry and sapless as a superannuated sermon." Heat became so intolerable to the clergyman that for two days he ate nothing but three Boston crackers, though the teamsters' appetites seemed unaffected.

These physical discomforts, however, were somewhat moderated after the third day out from Benton. For one thing, the tenderfoot adjusted to the new environment, and he now caught his first glimpse of the Rocky Mountains towering in the distance. From that day on, the party traveled in the shadow of the Rockies, whose beauties are one of the peculiar charms of the western fringes of the Great Plains.

From Pen d'Oreille Springs to the Marias River the train traveled during the night to avoid the burning heat of the July sun. On this river the party found a scow and rope ferry by which they crossed "with considerable ease."

Even more gratifying, they discovered that the little trading post on the far bank offered a well-stocked larder. Most welcomed of its offerings was the unexpected luxury of a pail of ice that the enterprising trader had harvested during the winter months and stored for such occasions.

North of the Marias the trail offered its most barren aspect. Here the wagon trains crossed Big Alkali Flat, a bleak plain offering neither water nor forage for weary animals. The Sutherland party continued traveling at night, but now its progress was slowed by the tendency of the heavy wagons to sink into the light soil.

Most parties pushed through this inhospitable stretch without pausing and this train was no exception. The trip from 18 Mile Coulee across the Flat to Rocky Springs, the next desirable campsite, was a long, trying haul. Extreme fatigue delayed the wagons as dozing drivers lost control of their teams on several occasions, nearly causing serious runaways. Finally at daybreak, they reached Rocky Springs where they spent the day recruiting their horses and refreshing the men.

Rocky Springs, near modern Sweetgrass, was a favorite site. Three separate springs flowed from the hillside into the adjoining valley to form a pleasant stream. Here were grass and water for the largest bulltrains, and this small party had no difficulty in providing for itself. Since it was also the Sabbath, the Reverend Mr. Sutherland used the day's rest to "refresh the spiritual man" with divine services. Renewed in body and spirit, the train crossed the international boundary the following morning.

Like every patriotic son returning to his homeland, Sutherland immediately detected a marked improvement in soils, pasturage, and water "once the train crossed the forty-ninth parallel." Thus the good clergyman testified to that magic alchemy of political boundaries, and the pronounced effect they have upon the traveler. There seems to be slight evidence, however, that the surveyor's chains altered the chemistry of the soil formations or disturbed the ecological balance on either side of this man-made barrier.

Soon the party reached the Milk River, "a beautiful stream."

Here good pasturage and a refreshing cup of tea confirmed Sutherland's warm judgment of his country's West. But evil entered this idyllic garden, not in the form of a serpent, but in the myriad forms of insects. Soon the flies, gnats, and mosquitoes tormented the animals so badly they could not graze, forcing the freighters to build smudge fires for relief from their unwelcome hosts.

For hours the men battled the insects. Smudge fires were kept burning all night and in desperation Sutherland finally resorted to killing the intruders in his tent with a lighted candle. This strenuous encounter led him, as it had countless plains travelers before him, to speculate on the utility of mosquitoes in nature's economy. These speculations proved futile, though the clergyman did conclude that "Darwin's theory of the survival of the fittest is, as applied to mosquitoes, a transparent fraud."

Northward the bulltrain moved across the rolling plains to the Oldman River. After overnight halts at Kipp's Coulee and 15 Mile Butte, the train reached the river only to find it too high to ford. Here the train halted while its leaders took counsel. Fortunately, Nicholas Sheran's coal mines were near by, with their flat-bottom boats, which the New Yorker used to haul his coal across the river. These boats were pressed into service, the goods unloaded from the wagons, ferried across the stream, and reloaded on the other side. It required nearly a day to complete this trans-shipment, but the Oldman was safely crossed and the trail stretched out ahead to Fort Macleod.

VII

Fort Macleod stood out on maps of the Canadian West during the seventies in clear, impressive print. But visitors quickly discovered that the prominence of its name on an empty map gave no indication of its physical size or meager population. Nor did it differ in appearance from other plains towns because it lay north of the forty-ninth parallel. One distinguished British visitor unkindly described it as a "wide, muddy lane, with a row of dirty, half finished wooden shanties flanking each side." [14]

This unfinished appearance struck every traveler. The fact is, old Fort Macleod, built on an island selected by the Northwest Mounted Police, never matured into a permanent settlement. From its founding in 1874 until its desertion a decade later, the island town lived a temporary existence. Spring floods threatened to sweep it into the Oldman annually, while changes in the river's channel sent swirling waters against the tiny island with such force that the town's foundations were gradually washed away. In 1879, when a particularly serious flood threatened the island, most residents reached the conclusion that a new town-site must be found.[15]

Senility thus set in while the town was yet an infant. Since businessmen refused to invest in improving a community of such uncertain habitation, signs of age appeared on the town's face prematurely. For ten years residents debated the advisability of moving to a new site, but with the recession of annual spring floods, they postponed the shift. Through most of its history as the northern terminus of the Whoop-Up Trail, Macleod lived an uncertain existence, an island that during high waters "required swimming to get either on or off." [16]

Despite its primitive accommodations, Fort Macleod earned a reputation of hospitality to freighters and travelers who came its way. Much of this renown lay in the Macleod Hotel. Under the management of Harry "Kamoose" Taylor, it became synonymous with Macleod in many memories.

Taylor's management of the hotel matched his colorful career. Born in England and educated for the ministry, he came into the North American west as a missionary. By 1872, for reasons obscured by time, he abandoned his high calling to turn to the more lucrative business of trading whisky to the Indians. During his two years in this undertaking he won the sobriquet "Kamoose" by stealing an Indian squaw when her family refused to sell her, despite his generous offer of a horse, two pairs of blankets, and some tobacco. After this exploit, the Indian name "Kamoose" or "wife stealer" distinguished him from other more successful traders.[17]

Arrest in 1874 by the Mounted Police ended his career as an Indian trader. But it launched him on a more rewarding one as a hotel owner, for which he seemed fully equipped by temperament, if not by training. His hotel won acclaim throughout the entire West. Nothing south of the boundary in Montana could match it, chiefly because there was only one "Kamoose" Taylor. His amiable spirit, open-handed generosity, and colorful administration won a reputation envied by rival institutions. Travelers stayed with "Kamoose" despite every primitive inconvenience associated with this frontier hotel; they prized their experiences and never forgot them with the passage of time.

When the stagecoach drew up in front of the modest building housing the Macleod, a curious sign welcomed its passengers. Under the name of the hotel hung a large silhouette of the back of a man's head with the cryptic comment "No Jawbone." To eastern visitors these words seemed unduly enigmatic, to westerners they simply meant that "Kamoose" accepted no credit, cash only.

Inside the hotel, the crude accommodations seemed neither better nor worse than many others. But Taylor's rules of conduct quickly attracted the traveler's attention and were soon widely copied throughout the West:

1. Guests will be provided with breakfast and dinner, but must rustle their own lunch.
2. Spiked boots and spurs must be removed at night before retiring.
3. Dogs not allowed in bunks, but may sleep underneath.
4. Towels changed weekly, Insect Powder for sale at the bar.
5. Special rates to "Gospel Grinders."
6. Assaults against the cook are strictly prohibited.
7. Only registered guests allowed the special privilege of sleeping on the Bar Room floor.
8. To attract attention of waiters, shoot a hole through the door panel. Two shots for ice water, three for a deck of cards.

The Captain R. E. Fisk expedition crossing the
northern plains in 1866

*There was a "constant parade of gold-seekers,
freighters, adventurers . . ."*

The Helena–Fort Benton stage at Sun River Crossing in 1885

Piegan lodges

The Whoop-Up country was Blackfoot country

Indians at home

The "stricken rabble" waiting for rations at the government agency

Western civilization transformed Blackfoot society

Tribal leaders at the Blackfoot agency

Deputy Marshal X. Beidler, whose occupation
was "public benefactor"

*Officers of the law on
both sides of the border*

Sheriff Johnny Healy

Commissioner A. G. Irvine   Commissioner James F. Macleod

Northwest Mounted Policemen at Fort Walsh, 1877

*A handful of scarlet-clad Mounties successfully challenged
two centuries of frontier tradition*

Their resplendent uniforms contrasted with the drab plains

Left, Blood Indians meet with a Mountie and Reverend L'Heureaux.
Right, a Mountie scout in the 1870s

*The Northwest Mounted Police Indian policy was "orderly,
well planned, and honorable"*

"Unbending dignity and calculated showmanship"

A wily medicine man harassed two governments for a decade, but the day of the redman was over

Commissioner J. M. Walsh

COURTESY ROYAL CANADIAN
MOUNTED POLICE

Sitting Bull

COURTESY MINNESOTA HISTOR-
ICAL SOCIETY

Fort Walsh Indians in full regalia

COURTESY HISTORICAL SOCIETY
OF MONTANA

9. In case of fire the guests are requested to escape without unnecessary delay.
10. Guests are requested to rise at 6 A.M. This is imperative as the sheets are needed for tablecloths.

All this was in the tradition of the raw West, except that frequent Mounted Police visits kept the Macleod Hotel from violating the laws. Yet police and populace alike grew genuinely fond of the good-natured publican and encouraged his eccentricities as a way of furnishing the little town with colorful publicity.

In physical appearance Fort Macleod resembled countless frontier towns in the American West. But this façade of similarity should not conceal the greater fact that the community life of this town took on a very different character. While western, it was also Canadian, with its settlers consciously seeking to imitate the cultural and political patterns of their Ontario homes.

To create a Canadian community despite the strong pull of regional ties to Fort Benton was not easy. News, for example, came through American sources and possessed a strong American flavor as well as content. Despite the fact that the Fort Benton *Record* published considerable Canadian news, even going so far as to print a digest of debates in the House of Commons, Canadians wanted their own journals. In July 1882, they welcomed the Fort Macleod *Gazette*, edited by Charles Edward Dudley Wood, a former master in Trinity College.

Similarly, they demanded schools. Their concern grew from the desire not only to give their children literacy to prevent their "growing to manhood as ignorant as the Indians themselves," but also to train them in the "glorious traditions of the Empire."

Frequent events reminded Canadians of the magnitude of their problem of cutting the cultural and economic ties emanating from Fort Benton. For many years American patriotic holidays were enthusiastically celebrated in the Canadian village. Washington's and Lincoln's birthdays competed with the Queen's birthday for importance in its hybrid population. As late as June 1883 the *Gazette* observed, "Macleod celebrates both American and Canadian holidays, thus enjoying both sets of national holidays." [18]

These were only superficial evidences of a deeper problem. Of great consequence were social institutions, familiar to the American West but alien to Canada, that came in the wake of the migration up the Whoop-Up Trail. Such was the vigilante society. Whatever its justification because of ineffective government south of the international boundary, Canadians resisted its use in their West as debasing to law and destructive of justice. When a vigilante placard appeared in Macleod in 1883, the *Gazette's* editor indignantly labeled it as "evidently written by some outcast and dead beat from some other country."

Canadian officials saw the problem and worked to create a British community on the northern plains. In his first visit in 1877, Lieutenant Governor Laird expressed the hope that the numerous ex-Americans in the region "will always be found conducting yourselves as becomes worthy subjects of that illustrious Sovereign whom I . . . represent." [19]

Western Canadians succeeded in establishing political, religious, economic, and social institutions peculiar to their own traditions and cultural inheritance. Thus two societies, differing from each other in fundamental aspects, emerged on the northern Great Plains. Westerners, whether Canadians or Americans, built institutions only slightly influenced by the environment around them. National differences prevailed over the sameness of physical environment.

10

Merchant Princes of the Plains

$\mathbb{B}$USINESS enterprise in the Gilded Age is a frequent theme of historical writing. So widespread is this interest and so thorough its influence that the words "Robber Baron" and "Great Tycoon" are the common property of our everyday language, and the careers in accumulation of Vanderbilt, Carnegie, Rockefeller, Fisk, and Drew are part of our folklore. Unfortunately this preoccupation with the achievements of the Lords of Creation leaves untouched the activities of scores of other businessmen who lived by the same principles and in the same hope. This is particularly true of business enterprise along the edge of settlement during the Gilded Age. There, even those who were immensely successful, such as Frederick Weyerhaeuser, are often overlooked. But the fact is, countless able and enterprising businessmen, living by the same tough-minded standards, emulating the same ruthless practices, and exalting similar individualistic ethics, flourished on the Great Plains, the great frontier of post-Civil War expansion. They too created their own dynasties and their own private kingdoms.

They were, of course, clearly motivated by the stimulus of creating a new society in the West. Theirs was the immense satisfaction of building new communities where only the dreary solitudes of the "Great American Desert" witnessed their initial toils. Frontier businessmen thus illustrate with surprising clarity the driving will to create, to win, or to conquer which Professor

Schumpeter discovered in entrepreneurial ambitions elsewhere. They saw themselves as leaders in the last stages of a national epic begun at Jamestown in 1607 and in which they were the latest adventurers conquering a wilderness to leave a heritage of schools and churches, saloons and hurdy-gurdy houses, business establishments and political institutions. Success in the frontier community was easily measured, even if accompanied by personal failure, for its monument was a new city, its tribute the hustle of another thriving community.

The wealth of these men, sons of their age as completely as Vanderbilt or Carnegie, was created in a frontier society and in the environment of the Great Plains. But too often their activities have been viewed as isolated experiences, uniquely shaped by this plains environment or profoundly altered by the alchemy of the physical world about them. True, they seldom accumulated the vast fortunes of the eastern tycoons, but they worshiped at the same altars of success and practiced the same rituals to achieve it.

Visiting Europeans noted little difference in the optimism, the ruthless energy, and the "American brag" of Yankees wherever they found them. "No matter what part of the country one is in," discovered a visiting Britisher in 1876, "there is to be found 'the finest in the world.' This is a stock phrase and a part of his creed he is never tired of quoting." [1] For westerners to speak of their little log-cabin villages as the "finest in the world" annoyed even the most seasoned traveler, who viewed the scene through the hard, clear eyes of realism rather than through the magnifying glass of the boomers' unbounded faith and unlimited desire.

Still more distressing was the American habit of appearing to take credit for the natural wealth of their vast continent. This was a common western vice, but was exceeded by the pride of New Yorkers in Niagara Falls. "Some, again, speak of their country and its great natural beauties as if due to their own individual foresight and exertion, and I doubt not feel complacently satisfied at the compliment they pay the Almighty by flying the American flag over the wonders of His creation," was the way one irritated traveler expressed his feelings.[2]

Similarly, the speculative fever which raged through the West during these years was a national, not a peculiarly regional virus. Securing a quick return from a minimum investment certainly characterized western economic activity. One perceptive English businessman observed that "In the West the ruling idea is to spend the least time and capital. The American does not seem to care about a work being finished. The eaves of a house are not sawn off to a line, or the planks on a bridge are left jutting out on both sides in a ragged edge. 'It's good enough; it don't hurt the bridge.' " [3]

Yet another national quality which visitors found throughout the West was the economic shortsightedness, the "let tomorrow take care of itself" attitude of American enterprise. Fur traders on the northern plains drew bitter criticism from those who witnessed the exploitative character of their traffic. Captain W. F. Butler, the British explorer who spent many months in the region, peppered his reports with scathing denunciations of their ruthless stripping of the country's wealth and their callous treatment of the Indians. The free trader "does not care about the future," wrote the Captain; "the continuance and partial well being of the Indian is of no consequence to him." In fact, Butler was amazed by the single-mindedness, the energy, and the intellectual simplicity with which Americans built their economic empires in the West. "I recollect," he recorded, "a very earnest American once saying that he considered all religious, political, social and historical teaching could be reduced to three subjects — the Sermon on the Mount, the Declaration of American Independence, and the Chicago Republican Platform of 1860." [4]

II

After the Civil War, the virtually untouched northern plains lay fertile and open for economic exploitation. Tiny side-wheel steamboats had already created the vital ties, the essential physical links between this western hinterland and the eastern metropolis so necessary for the transfer of goods and services from the older to the newer America.

Fort Benton, as we have seen, quickly became the economic center of this expansion. Here appeared a group of merchants and financiers whose vaulting ambitions created a commercial empire encompassing half a continent, perhaps more. W. G. Conrad, one of the most successful of its entrepreneurs, later described it as a "business metropolis that had for its active business activities nearly a whole continent, that purchased goods from New Orleans on the south and the Great Slave lakes on the north, almost within the Arctic circle and sold goods all over the world, in St. Louis and New York, in London and St. Petersburg, a business running into many millions of dollars in value annually." Then, with the wistfulness of one who has watched the decline of greatness, he regretfully added, "No such commercial dominion exists today in Montana despite our superior advantages." [5]

With all its pretensions to economic greatness, Benton remained the center of a colonial economy. Behind the initiative and enterprise of Montana businessmen lay the relentless expansion of a dynamic metropolis, lured ever westward by the prospect of profits in colonial exploitation. Here were profits for owners of stock in the burgeoning corporations of New Jersey, for financiers in New York, Montreal, and London, for New England textile manufacturers, for fabricators of Pennsylvania steel, for Connecticut and Kentucky distillers, for inland trading companies and coastal shippers, for wholesalers and commission agents of Chicago, St. Paul, New Orleans, and St. Louis, for railway and river steamboat companies, and for eastern land speculators happy with the prospect of another agrarian El Dorado. The merchant princes of Fort Benton were the final agents for a vast system which provided Canadian and American ranchers, gold-seekers, treaty Indians, and government forces with the products of the looms of Manchester and Hartford, of the forges and furnaces of Sheffield and Pittsburgh, and of the distilleries of Boston and Louisville.

As we have seen, fur traders were first to exploit this region, but their temporary occupation had already run its course. The American Fur Company, symbol of this phase of the Whoop-Up country's history, was a thing of the past. Now free traders, full of greed and lust, harvested the meager crop of furs remaining.

Unhappily, this decline in the fur trade coincided with the playing out of the Montana gold rushes, an equally serious blow to the commercial hopes of the little river town's business community. Thus on the threshold of the 1870s, Benton businessmen faced the somber prospect of the collapse of their extensive trade and the pessimistic admission that their high hopes for the rapid development of the northern plains were premature.

Indeed, this collapse seemed to have struck in 1871 when only six steamboats reached the head of navigation. Declining activity in the gold fields, the completion of the rival system of transportation in the Union Pacific Railway across the central plains, and a disastrously low water level in 1869 paralyzed the Benton commerce. Freight rates on the river fell from ten cents per pound to three, while wagon rates from Benton to Helena skidded from six cents to only one. Numerous businessmen went bankrupt as eastern goods sold at a loss and as gold and greenbacks approached equality in value.[6] When the great depression of 1873 cast its darkening shadow across the plains, steamboating on the upper Missouri seemed a thing of the past and Fort Benton's economic hegemony only a memory.

Yet by 1875, Benton again hummed with activity as the fragile steamboats unloaded their cargoes for the waiting wagon trains. So striking was this recovery that the Fort Benton *Record* exulted in the return of the "palmy days of '67 and '68." [7] Conditions were so good by 1877 that the *Record*'s editor claimed he knew of no business failures in Montana that year. With a nod to easterners who persisted in viewing the West as "wild and woolly," he claimed this unique record was established by the simple expedient of hanging to a tree every businessman on the verge of bankruptcy.[8] This may well be a stimulus to managerial efficiency thus far overlooked by students of the "dismal science."

This revival of trade was all the more impressive since it came while the rest of the country still foundered in the sloughs of depression. As the national economy gradually fought its way up from the lows of depression by 1878, Benton boomed and in 1879 river commerce was better than it had been during the "golden age" of the gold stampedes. In the face of this development, Bentonites were supremely confident their prosperity was permanently secured by their strategic location on the river. With the Peptoptimist spirit again running at full tide, any suggestion that Benton's prosperity was temporary was swept aside.

Revival of the Missouri traffic and the reawakening of Fort Benton rested on economic changes which few contemporaries foresaw and fewer historians have fully recognized. To the north the establishment of law and order by the Northwest Mounted Police created a heavy demand for provisions and supplies, for cash funds and credit facilities which could not be met by the underdeveloped system of communications across the plains from Winnipeg. Soon treaties with Indians required extensive goods and services financed by government expenditures. With the creation of order and the restriction of Indians to reservations, ranchers poured in to use the rich grassland. They too demanded economic services which only the Benton businessmen could adequately provide. Meanwhile, similar developments on the American side of the boundary created further markets.

Government spending in Ottawa as well as in Washington thus offered Benton businessmen an opportunity which they fully exploited. The decade of the 1870s which had begun so miserably and had promised so little ended on a note of unexpected prosperity. This prosperity did not entirely appear, as some have reasoned, from a continually growing population which grew "tired of frontier conditions and demanded more and better things of life which could be procured in the East,"[9] for this ever-increasing demand was largely satisfied through the Utah and Northern extension of the Union Pacific Railway to Corinne, Utah. A more complete explanation is seen in the dramatic expansion of trade into Canada which brought steamboats toiling up the river and sent scores of wagon trains creaking across the plains to Canadian destinations.

III

Control of this extensive commerce rested largely with Benton companies, chief of which were the I. G. Baker and T. C. Power and Brother firms. Keen rivalry marked the growth to power of these great houses during the 1870s as each fought to seize the lion's share of the northwest trade. Though other business firms such as the Carroll, Steell partnership, the Murphy, Neel Company, and the Kleinschmidt Company attained local prominence, the Baker and Power companies dominated the regional trade so completely that their histories are synonymous with the growth of Benton as a transportation hub, a merchandising mart, and a financial center in the years following the Civil War.

In 1864, after business experience in Burlington, Iowa, Connecticut-born Isaac Gilbert Baker traveled up the river to serve as chief clerk for Pierre Chouteau, Jr., at Fort Benton. A year later, however, the ambitious fur trader organized his own company in partnership with his brother George. Thomas C. Power, on the other hand, arrived in Benton in 1867 equipped with a stock of goods and with the hope of a lively trade with the thousands of gold-seekers then passing through the town. He too was joined by a brother, John Power. Both firms quickly prospered and built great empires on the ruins of the American Fur Company.

These brother partnerships were soon joined by equally able young colleagues. In 1873–74, George Baker sold his interest in the Baker firm to the Virginia-born Conrad brothers, William, Charles, and John, who at once became the dynamic personalities in the company, shaping its policy and directing its rapid expansion. Since the Conrads possessed the same economic and political views as the Bakers, they continued the firm without disturbing its dynastic character. This was especially true after I. G. Baker opened offices in St. Louis in 1874. There, the senior partner supervised the purchasing, transporting, and financing of goods and equipment consigned to the firm's Benton headquarters. He also acted as the vital liaison agent between its western and eastern activities. By 1878, this firm shipped $2,500,000 worth of goods through Benton annually and was among the largest taxpayers in Montana. It possessed economic power reaching out along the trails to control the little towns and lonely posts of the northern plains and exercised political influence stretching through Helena to Washington and from Regina to Ottawa.

These were the merchant princes of Benton. Shrewd, energetic, ambitious, they also had important qualities in social background and experience only recently recognized as typical of business leadership in this era. Eastern-born, sons of native-born Americans of British descent, and possessed of superior education for their time, they conform with surprising homogeneity to the composite of business leadership in the 1870s as revealed in recent entrepreneurial studies.[10] The Bakers, Powers, and Conrads undoubtedly possessed much of the initiative, courage, and grit of the heroes of the dime novels of their time, but they obviously do not conform to the folklore image of poor immigrant lads, friendless and without social background, rising from grinding poverty to great wealth through pluck and virtue only.

They were also typical frontier entrepreneurs. Their wide range of business interests and variety of investments were quite in keeping with the freewheeling economy in which they sought their fortunes. Both firms grew strong and wealthy through investments in fur trading, mining, milling, banking, Indian trading, retail and wholesale merchandising, river steamers, wagon freighting, and lucrative government contracts, both Canadian and American.

Both firms made their first profits in a lively trade with the Gros Ventre, Blood, and Blackfoot Indians. Since much of this trade turned on the sale of whisky for robes and pelts, the merchant princes were deeply involved in this dubious business during their early years. Many well-known whisky traders bought their goods on credit from Baker and Power, while several were actual partners in the traffic. At one time or other, Johnny Healy, D. W. Davis, A. B. Hamilton, Abel Farwell, and Moses Solomon were agents or partners of the two firms before the police ended their profitable ventures.

Evidence of direct implication in the whisky trade is difficult to come by. In later years, a certain stigma surrounded a career in the whisky traffic, and men who had made modest fortunes in the trade maintained a discreet silence. But several of the leading citizens of northern Montana and southern Alberta were clearly implicated in this miserable business. Some, even, were national figures such as D. W. Davis, a Baker employee at notorious Fort Whoop-Up, who served as a member of Parliament in Ottawa from 1887 to 1896, and Thomas C. Power, who became a leading figure in the Republican party and Montana's first United States senator in Washington. Others occupied lesser positions of prominence. A. B. Hamilton, I. G. Baker's nephew, was later elected to the Montana legislature, while several of Chouteau County's sheriffs — the most famous, of course, William Rowe and Johnny Healy — were former whisky runners. Still others joined Montana's first families or Alberta's respected pioneers. It was hardly to their interest to publicize their early involvement in the whisky trade.

But the pioneer's urge to tell his story is too great to repress, and many of the lesser fry, having little at stake in such revelations, talked freely. Historical records, too, have a way of exposing the past, even the unpleasant past. Memoirs, diaries, personal letters, as well as official reports in Ottawa and Washington clearly tell the story. Typical of the contemporary evidence is the flat statement of I. G. Baker's guilt in a letter to Montana's territorial delegate, Major Maginnis: "I have seen members of that firm in the very act of selling whisky to Indians." [11]

Both of these firms also came under criticism for the illegal sale of arms and ammunition to Indians. In 1876, the New York

Herald condemned T. C. Power for selling rifles and ammunition to hostile Indians. With Chief Joseph and Sitting Bull on the prowl, army officials were sensitive to the illegal traffic in weapons. General Gibbon warned the T. C. Power Company, "Information from an authentic source has reached me that some 138,000 rounds of small arms ammunition and several cases of breechloading small arms were shipped to you up the Missouri River by the last trip of the *Benton*. In the present state of Indian affairs in this section of the country I desire to impress on your mind the fact that should any portion of these arms and ammunition find its way into the hands of the Indians, you will be held responsible for the consequence by an outraged community." [12]

These and other charges were leveled against the Benton companies, but proof was difficult to assemble and both firms rode out every storm of criticism. Each claimed its trade with the Indians conformed to license privileges granted by the Office of Indian Affairs, including permission to trade specified quantities of arms to the northern tribes.[13] And each denied that its arms trade violated the congressional act of 1873 regulating the sale of arms or ammunition to "uncivilized or hostile Indians."

Whatever the role of the merchant princes in these dubious trades in the early years, by 1875 they vigorously opposed the whisky traffic. Weary of the demoralizing effects of whisky upon the Indian's economic status and shocked by its cost to the traders themselves, the Benton merchants welcomed the shift to a legal trade. Then too, the newly arrived Mounties were a powerful incentive to remain within the law.

IV

Trade with the northern tribes quickly drew the merchant princes across the international boundary into competition with the Hudson's Bay Company. Though the honorable company had long ignored the region between the Missouri and the South Saskatchewan, the intrusion of the Baker and Power traders was keenly resented. I. G. Baker and T. C. Power were not popular names in Winnipeg, Montreal, or London.

Very early in the trading, the Baker and Power firms sought monopoly control over the Indian trade in the Whoop-Up country. In this they were quite in accord with the spirit of their age, and they used the same arguments of efficiency and lower costs to explain their efforts to eliminate wasteful competition.

Initial efforts to control the trade were directed against the numerous free traders, as well as against each other. Until the early 1880s when they divided the region into spheres of influence, the struggle for supremacy was bitter, even violent in the finest traditions of the fur trade. They tried first to control the trading by driving rival traders out of the country and by destroying competition at its source through the Spitzee Cavalry. This crude attempt failed, just as the later effort of the Power firm to represent the frontier fight at Cypress Hills as a brutal slaughter of helpless Indians failed. Power's hope that the Baker traders would be arrested and so eliminated from the trading was not fully realized, but his scheme left the tradition of massacre deeply imbedded in the folk history of the Canadian-American West.

With the failure of these attempts to eliminate rivals, the merchant princes next sought to gain control at a more sensitive point, the exchange in Fort Benton. Here they had greater success, for most of the independent traders had little capital and were vulnerable to pooling arrangements among the buyers. In 1876, the pooling campaign with its private understandings among the buyers successfully eliminated many small competitors. Some of its victims resented their fate. Johnny Healy wrote feelingly of his alleged treatment at the hands of T. C Power: "My relations with T. C. Power in the shipment of robes to Canada has resulted disastrously to me, for the reason that T. C. has gone into the swindling business as it pays better, when a man gets [in] a position to be robbed without having the power to help himself." [14]

Soon the activities of the pool became so transparent that Benton's newspaper felt obliged to protest publicly. "Benton has already suffered enough from Indian rings and corporate monopolies, without having her trade ruined by a robe clique composed of a few temporary residents of the town who have no other interest in the place than to fill their pockets and leave." [15] Official army reports were equally outspoken about conditions at Fort Benton: "There is a community of interest among the capitalists here that enables them to combine and have most things their own way in many respects," wrote Lieutenant Colonel Samuel B. Holabird in 1870.[16]

But now a far more formidable threat to Benton's monopolists made itself felt. Far to the east Winnipeg was a serious rival, using every geographic advantage in its grasp and wielding every political weapon within its power. The Montana town's position on the river, however, gave it important advantages over its Canadian competitor. Moreover, since most of the robes found their final markets in the United States, many traders preferred to ship them through Fort Benton. Shorter by five hundred miles, the Whoop-Up Trail route could lay down freight in Fort Macleod for six to eight cents a pound while its Manitoba rival could do no better than eighteen. Thus Fort Benton outstripped its competitor through the use of its natural line of communications, that spiral staircase ascending from St. Louis.

Unfortunately, Benton's natural advantages were frequently offset by forces over which local merchants had little control. A new tariff schedule in 1876, for example, disrupted the robe trade and was the chief reason for J. J. Healy's troubles, for he was only one of many facing ruin when Congress doubled the rates on imported robes and pelts.[17] By this time, the traditional device of smuggling across the boundary had become too risky for widespread use. The vigilance of the Mounted Police made capture too nearly certain.

To avoid tariff barriers, T. C. Power hit upon a plan which proved the salvation of Benton merchants and nearly gave him the monopoly trade so long his object. His project was simple, yet fully effective. He secured a permit to ship goods from England or eastern Canada through the United States to western Canadian customers under a $100,000 bond deposited in Washington. Power quickly saw that such a scheme was the key to successful competition with the Hudson's Bay Company and at the same time, with an exclusive permit, it would effectively destroy the profits in the Canadian trade of the rival Baker firm.

To this monopolistic end, T. C. Power marshaled his forces in Washington. "I will go to Washington," he wrote Major Maginnis, "and help work it through for we *must* accomplish the shipping in bond arrangement — as it will save us considerable money and unless we can do it we can not cope with the Hudson's Bay company who ship in that way via St. Paul. Work it up Maj[or] and I will see all your expenses paid for it will certainly [be] a big thing for our part of the country." [18]

Power apparently feared, however, that his personal influence was not sufficient to convince Washington officials of the wisdom of his project. He turned, therefore, to the good offices of the ambitious and colorful Johnny Healy, good friend of the territorial delegate and favorite of the Whoop-Up Democrats, to advance his plan. Soon Healy was in correspondence with Maginnis urging an exclusive permit for his friend and pointing out the political wisdom of such assistance. "I have arranged everything with Tom P satisfactory, and if you can do anything for him towards procuring an exclusive permit to ship in bond — the same will be of benefit to me. I understand that I. G. B[aker] is after the same favor — but I must say that you owe him nothing, & for the Wm. Conrads, they are — or would be as willing to sacrifice you, as they were to Jas. Cavanaugh. Tom will call on you and will explain matters fully . . ." [19]

T. C. Power's political maneuvering for monopoly privileges failed. Other Benton firms secured the same permits and free enterprise prevailed, in spite of the exertions of some of the free enterprisers.

By shipping bonded cargoes into the Northwest, Benton merchants undersold the Hudson's Bay Company in its own backyard. Goods shipped via the Missouri River and freighted up the Whoop-Up Trail reached their destination with a saving of 25 per cent in freighting costs. This bonding scheme also provided

Canadian- and British-made goods to suit Canadian consumer tastes, an important factor in competing with rival Canadian firms. By 1876, most cargoes passing through Fort Benton to the Canadian West were bonded shipments from eastern Canada or Britain. Thus the merchant princes launched into international trade in a most unlikely spot on the remote Canadian-American frontier of settlement.

V

To most visitors, the merchandising and warehousing activities of the Benton firms seemed impressive. Extensive warehouses along Front Street provided facilities to protect and trans-ship goods destined for distant markets on the plains. The Kleinschmidt Company created great excitement in 1878 when it constructed the largest warehouse in Benton and built it with concrete. The novelty of concrete construction provoked hot arguments among plainsmen as to its value, durability, and cost. There is no evidence that Bentonites welcomed the new material as a substitute for the timber which the plains country lacked.

Though retail merchandising was only a small part of the commercial empires of the Bakers, Powers, and Conrads, it was a major investment. Supplies for the Indian trade, for farmers, freighters, prospectors, trappers, and ranchers, general merchandise, and luxury services filled their stores in Benton, Fort Macleod, Fort Walsh, and Calgary. T. C. Power's boast that his stores could provide "anything that can be purchased in New York" was close to the truth, for in the same stores with the general merchandise, agricultural implements, and miners' equipment were stocks of fine wines, liquors, and cigars "marvelous for their magnitude," silks, satins, and broadcloth, as well as the services of tailors, bootmakers, milliners, and dressmakers.

Contracts to provide goods and services to the Canadian and American governments were the major source of income for both companies. Politicians on both sides of the international boundary were willing allies in the merchants' schemes to secure lucrative contracts to supply food, clothing, and equipment for military and police forces, to drive in beef for treaty Indians, and to provide supplies for government activities of every kind. The rate of government spending in the West as determined in Washington and Ottawa spelled the difference between success and failure for western businessmen.

Baker and Power played this political game with shrewdness and success. While the Bakers and Conrads were Democrats and the Powers were Republicans, these party distinctions were rather less important than the sound and fury of Montana politics would indicate. Both great dynasties held similar economic views, and used politicians of both parties with equal effectiveness. Major Martin Maginnis was a particularly effective spokesman in Congress for the Montana merchants. S. T. Hauser of Helena, whose advice greatly influenced Maginnis, had numerous investments in the Baker and Power enterprises; hence the Benton men had little difficulty in securing favors from the United States government. This frequently went so far as to call for the shifting of army troops or the redrawing of Indian reservation boundaries to satisfy the desires of the merchant princes of the northern plains.[20]

In Washington, Maginnis served his friends well. He fought any reduction of expenditures to Indians and opposed every effort to consolidate or reform the Indian agencies since "the cutting down and abandonment of any Indian agency will hurt Montana — especially those in close proximity as they spend considerable money." [21] Maginnis' devotion to Montana's welfare did not go unrewarded. His powerful friends secured railroad passes for him, advanced him money, and looked after his political ambitions.[22]

Canadian politicians were equally amenable to the same influence. Lieutenant Governor Edgar Dewdney used his power on behalf of the Baker firm to secure Canadian contracts and favors. In return, he earned handsome investments in Benton enterprises. On one occasion, the Canadian official received fifty shares in the Benton National Bank "to get a deposit by it of $100,000 or $200,000 from the Canadian government." [23] Since the Benton bank received a 1½ per cent rate of exchange on these funds as well as profitable fees for delivering the money to police posts across the boundary, such arrangements were welcomed in Fort Benton.[24]

Even more profitable were contracts with the Canadian government to carry mail into the Northwest and to supply food and equipment for Canadian officials. In 1875, the Baker firm received $122,771 for supplies to the Mounted Police, the following year $122,057. This was nearly one third of the total expenditures by the Canadian government for the force.[25] When the sums spent with other Benton companies and the money left by constables in Baker and Power stores are added to these figures, it is clear that well over half of the money appropriated in Ottawa to police the Northwest Territories ended in the bank accounts of Benton merchants.

More important, both in value and in quantity, were contracts to provide beef and supplies for reservation Indians across the boundary. With the signing of Treaty Seven at Blackfoot Crossing in 1877, I. G. Baker received the contract to supply the Indians with beef. Through the years these beef contracts enriched Benton firms. The Baker Company alone frequently purchased $500,000 worth of cattle to fill their annual obligations. Colonel S. C. Ashby, who knew the Benton companies intimately, believed that the Baker firm owed its success to these government contracts. "I must say," he wrote, "that the great success that came to the Baker people was due largely to the fact that the Canadian Government under Sir John Macdonald decided to send companies of troopers . . . to what is known as the Belly River country." [26]

Canadian businessmen keenly resented this commercial penetration, for it seemed to deny them economic advantages which political control implied. Capital for the development of this new country came from American as well as Canadian centers, while profits were siphoned off by American firms. Assistant Commissioner Irvine of the Northwest Mounted Police expressed this resentment by pointing out that "a large amount of money has been expended, in return for which there is little or nothing to show, our money is merely aiding to build up the town of Benton, U.S.A." [27] Particularly irritating to Canadians was the manner in which I. G. Baker and T. C. Power secured lucrative contracts from Ottawa year after year in preference to Canadian firms.[28]

VI

Freighting was yet another source of income for enterprising Montana investors. Cheaper transportation on the Missouri River was the key to Fort Benton's unique economic position and the merchant princes exploited it fully. They organized their own river steamboat lines, thus reducing their costs and adding further profits through the control of river commerce. T. C. Power, for example, organized the Fort Benton Transportation Company, the famous Benton "Block P" Line, whose little steamers the *Helena, Butte, Benton,* and *Black Hills* were familiar names on the upper river.

This northwest frontier, like so many others on the Great Plains, also relied upon overland transportation systems which imposed heavy costs in pre-railway years. Contemporary estimates indicate that average charges for freight and insurance from the industrial East to frontier towns in the Northwest exceeded twenty-five cents a pound. This high cost of transportation to northern plainsmen is clearly revealed in the fact that annual per capita expenditures in Montana Territory for freighting alone averaged two hundred dollars.[29] One Canadian traveler summarized this burden of transportation costs with the observation, "The expense of bringing anything into or sending anything out of the country by this old-fashioned way is enormous. The prime costs of the articles is a bagatelle. Transport swallows up everything. No wonder that the price of a pound of tea, sugar or salt, is here exactly the same. They weigh the same, and cost the same for carriage." [30]

On top of these heavy charges, businessmen were often deprived of the use of their working capital during the five winter months since they depended upon the seasonal navigation of the river. Seasonal fluctuations in prices further drained northwest capital. This fact was forcefully emphasized each spring, when the high "winter prices" fell dramatically to the much lower level of "summer prices" as river traffic reopened and as the overland trails became passable. Hazardous travel on the river, costly delays due to low water, floods, or navigation difficulties, frequent marine disasters, and a short season made the river traffic both capricious and costly. When the railroads moved westward after the depression of 1873 had run its course, Benton businessmen found their commanding position impossible to maintain.

Wagon freighting to Canadian destinations became a major enterprise during the 1870s. Daily shipments from Benton often exceeded 250 tons, while monthly totals reached impressive figures.[31] Rates in the immediate postwar years averaged about ten cents per pound, but the fierce rivalry among the Baker, Power, Murphy-Neel, and Diamond R outfits and intense competition from numerous independent freighters reduced charges to an average of six cents.

Wagon trains returning from British North America first carried furs and buffalo robes. As this trade declined, Benton freighters faced serious losses in income as the prospect of deadheading their empty wagons back to Benton seemed inescapable. Happily, the enterprise of Nicholas Sheran, a New York Irishman and Civil War veteran, solved their problem, for Sheran, who entered the Whoop-Up country in search of gold, found coal near modern Lethbridge. There as a squatter on Dominion land he developed a coal mining industry which provided fuel for Benton, Fort Macleod, Fort Walsh, and Calgary and laid the foundations on which Sir Alexander T. Galt, with British capital, built the great industries of southern Alberta some years later.[32]

Again T. C. Power was the pioneer. In November 1875 this energetic merchant imported coal from British North America at a cost of $25 per ton. To critics who protested at this high cost, Power pointed out that even at this price it was more economical than dry cottonwood at $8 a cord.[33]

Whoop-Up coal answered many needs. Freighters found in it additional profits and it solved for Benton residents their chronic fuel shortage. Shipping charges, however, were kept high by the freighting companies. Prices at Sheran's mines never exceeded $5 a ton, but Benton consumers seldom paid less than $20 and sometimes as much as $30. Still, Whoop-Up coal was cheaper to burn than the inferior Missouri River coal or native cottonwood. Most of this cost, as the editor of the Fort Benton *Record* indignantly pointed out, represented profits of $11 to $16 a ton — "a clean profit, for it kept wagons from returning empty-handed or dead-headed." [34]

Since control over transportation was the foundation of Benton's economic power, every effort to devise other routes met with resistance from her leading citizens. Benton's politicians and professional orators chose to ignore the weakness of the inland port's supremacy in an age of railroads, but the Conrads and Powers were never so foolish. As late as 1882 the *Record*'s editor proudly boasted that "no future combinations or discriminations can vitally affect or injure our busy, enterprising little city of 1500 people at the head of the navigable Missouri river, and without a rival. Benton is too well established, too far advanced, ever to fear a rival on the Missouri river or elsewhere in northern Montana." [35]

While optimists whistled bravely in the gathering dark, the empire builders foresaw disaster. To prevent it, they drew elaborate railroad building plans, schemed with politicians, and organized railway companies. But all in vain, for every scheme faltered and every dream vanished. As early as 1876, T. C. Power and a group of Benton businessmen planned a narrow gauge railway to Helena. This scheme, based on an act of the Montana legislature in February 1876 authorizing contributions by counties, secured considerable support and widespread publicity. The great river freighting company, S. B. Coulson of Yankton, agreed to build the railroad if secured by $700,000 in twenty-year, 7 per cent bonds. In spite of every exertion, however, the Benton planners could raise only $80,000 and the scheme collapsed.[36]

Again in 1882 the Northern Pacific Railway raised high hopes by surveying a branch line from Billings to Fort Benton, but the project never passed the survey stage.[37] In the same year, the Conrads and Powers, backed by Minneapolis capital, incorporated the Fort Benton, Barker, and Yellowstone Railroad Company, but it too failed to materialize.[38]

Profits from the trade with Canada and northern Montana attracted investment from many quarters. Much of the capital for Benton firms came through the integrated financial empire erected throughout Montana by S. T. Hauser and his associates; the Hauser enterprises received their aid from St. Louis, New York, and Montreal. Both Power and Baker secured much of their financial strength from these ties. Their Diamond R competitor, on the other hand, was backed chiefly through A. H. Wilder of St. Paul.

Demands for capital frequently exceeded available resources. W. G. Conrad often urged greater financial assistance from Hauser, while other Benton firms also felt the pinch during periods of cautious investment.[39] So urgent were the requirements for additional capital during years of expansion that one of the first books published in western Canada emphasized the need: "a little capital is an excellent lubricator for the wheels of life, especially in the North-West." [40]

Insurance posed a particularly serious problem to frontier businessmen. Since local financiers lacked sufficient capital to underwrite insurance companies, the merchant princes were forced to turn to eastern companies, often at heavy cost. The United States Insurance Company of St. Louis, for example, insured T. C. Power's stock of goods for $35 per thousand, a rate substantially higher than that in Missouri. Later, Power secured more favorable rates from the National Fire Insurance Company of New York and reduced his insurance costs to $7.50 a thousand.[41] But high insurance rates were a heavy burden to Benton merchants during most of the period to 1885 and led to frequent protests in the local newspaper. "There seems to be little enterprise about the insurance agents of this Territory," complained the *Record* in 1876. "The property owners of Benton are compelled to effect insurance directly with eastern companies, which costs considerable unnecessary trouble and expense." [42]

An important indication of the maturing of the economy centered at Fort Benton was the founding of the Benton National Bank in 1879. Backed by S. T. Hauser, the Conrads and Powers organized a financial house which at once proved its value to the Canadian-American Northwest and the Benton bank found more opportunities to invest its surplus at 2 per cent per month than it could satisfy with its limited resources. The Bank of Northern Montana was soon organized by competing merchants to take up the slack, but profits in the Hauser bank remained high. By 1882 they reached 33 per cent on capital invested and the bank's stock had increased in value in three short years from a par of $100 to a gratifying $150.[43]

Financial ties reached north into Canada as effectively as they stretched out from Helena, St. Paul, or New York. The Benton merchants annually furnished through their bank the funds with which the Canadian government paid the police and treaty Indians. Financial relations were so intimate that the region must certainly be regarded as an economic entity. Canadian and American currency circulated freely on both sides of the international boundary, and not until 1881 did Chouteau County officials feel it necessary to refuse Canadian currency in payment of taxes and license fees.[44]

VII

Dramatic economic changes in the early 1880s drastically altered the character of Fort Benton's economic role in the Whoop-Up country. Isolated in a four-hundred-mile gap between the Canadian Pacific and the Northern Pacific railways, the little village slowly died of commercial malnutrition. The coming of the railways doomed the great empires built upon the river traffic. In July 1883 the last important shipments left Fort Benton for Fort Macleod; by August a twenty-year era had ended. Business was so quiet that even the normally optimistic *Record* admitted that "not even a dog fight relieved the monotony."

These sweeping changes forced the merchant princes to revise their policies. Some invested in the expanding range cattle industry on both sides of the boundary or in the Treasure State's mining industry. Other capital found investment in flour milling, lumbering, and meat packing. The sinking of the *Red Cloud* in 1882 marked the end of the I. G. Baker Company's interest in river steamboating and in 1891 the Conrads sold their Benton holdings to a Great Falls firm.

North of the boundary, the Conrads and Powers sold their stores to the Hudson's Bay Company. Thus the great company absorbed its American competitors just as it had swallowed up all its previous rivals. This assimilation was effected smoothly and without excitement except in Fort Macleod where the chief clerk for I. G. Baker, John Black, refused to transfer his allegiance to the old enemy. Undaunted, he established a rival store directly across the street from the Hudson's Bay Company building. With humorous contempt for the ancient monopoly's familiar slogan, "The Governor and Company of Adventurers of England trading into Hudson Bay, *Pro Pelle Cutem*," he prominently displayed a sign of his own design: "John Black, Adventurer and Trader, Groceries and Guff, Pro Belly Catch'em." [45]

So ended the regime of the merchant princes. "The railroad that reached us in 1888 changed all the channels of business," wrote W. G. Conrad years later, "and many who had ardently prayed for it and longed for it, were ruined by its advent, because they were unable to adjust themselves to the new conditions it brought. The coming of the railroads annihilated time and distance . . . but at the same time it wiped out our independent trade dominion and annexed the country to the commercial territory of the great eastern merchant princes." [46]

In a few years, little but a memory remained of Benton's economic glory. After 1885, the little village dozed in the bright sunshine of the plains and dreamed of the hustle and enterprise that had once been Benton.

11

Graziers and Grangers

AGRICULTURAL activity in the Whoop-Up country began surprisingly early. Some years before cattlemen or grangers occupied the grasslands stretching westward from the Red River valley, farmers were harvesting crops along the Dearborn, Sun, Teton, and Missouri rivers at the foot of the Rockies.

Gold was again the reason. The rush of miners into Montana created a heavy demand for farm products of all kinds. High prices at the gold fields led many ex-farmers to see that a more certain profit lay in farming than in mining.

Led by William Sparks, Robert Vaughn, and R. S. Ford, farmers occupied the narrow, sheltered "flood plains" of the rivers, combining land cultivation with modest stock-raising, to build a prosperous agricultural community in the sixties and seventies. A wide variety of fruits, vegetables, cereal and forage crops, as well as dairy products, left their farms for nearby markets.

Pioneers in the Sun River valley benefited greatly by the earlier experience of the Indian agency farm. As we have already seen, the government farm failed, but the successful cultivation of wheat, oats, barley, and vegetables proved that this northern climate was not too severe for crop production as many had feared. Failures were equally instructive. Flash floods destroyed crops with discouraging frequency, while droughts, early frosts, and grasshoppers proved to be serious hazards.

Farmers devised safeguards against floods by constructing

dikes and prevented the loss of their crops during droughts by digging irrigation ditches. They reduced the losses from early frosts by developing early maturing crops. Against grasshopper infestations, however, the only protection was a firm faith that next year's crop would succeed. "My object in selling," wrote one discouraged farmer to J. H. McNight, "is to pay my debts and try something that grasshoppers can't eat." [1]

High prices for butter, fresh milk, and eggs encouraged diversified farming. Easy wealth in the gold fields, Fort Benton's mercantile prosperity, and army quartermaster purchases kept egg prices above fifty cents a dozen and butter prices at forty to fifty cents a pound. One newly arrived pilgrim, unaccustomed to the high prices of the frontier, refused to purchase butter for her family, "for I knew I would have tasted the 40 cents for a week after the butter was gone." [2]

Visitors to the region frequently expressed surprise at the extensive dairying and buttermaking on this remote frontier. Charles Bull, pioneer farmer in the Sun River valley, introduced "modern appliances" in dairying in the early seventies with a much-admired cooling system that reduced milk temperatures rapidly while preventing "dust and disagreeable flavors" from spoiling the milk. [3]

During the same years, Fort Benton boasted the services of the Excelsior Dairy. Daily milk deliveries at 6 A.M. and again at 6 P.M. kept Benton housewives and business establishments well provided, but the informal containers and low quality of the milk provoked some protests. For those who preferred a stronger beverage, John Hunsberger built a brewery, securing sufficient barley from local farmers to meet his production needs. [4]

Until the late eighties when the river town lost its mercantile character and became a farming center, demands for food were not wholly met by local production. During the boom years, eggs and butter were imported from the Middle West, but the long river trip without adequate refrigeration left them inferior to the locally produced dairy products. Curiously, Benton suffered no shortage of turkeys for its Thanksgiving celebrations. Moses

Solomon on the Marias River alone produced four thousand birds for the 1880 holiday.

Sheep growers occupied the foothills country before the surrounding plains were settled. Good grass, water, and shelter attracted them to the region and within a few years a thriving industry existed on both sides of the boundary.

The industry moved into the Whoop-Up country from the West Coast. Drives of several thousand sheep from Washington and Oregon brought the "woollies" into the region, and later drives from Utah and as far as southern California enlarged the flocks.

From the beginning, sheep and cattle grazed the same ranges. Other western states, especially Colorado and Wyoming, suffered fierce range wars between cattlemen and sheepherders, but in the Whoop-Up country they lived in peace.

Encouraged by good profits, sheepherders rapidly expanded their flocks. These profits were chiefly the result of low production costs. Free grass on the public domain, low labor charges for herding and shearing, and careless preparation of the wool for market kept costs low, thus ensuring profits despite relatively low prices on eastern markets. Montana sheepmen attributed their prosperity to the protective tariff act of 1870. This was important, but low costs explain their success in displacing eastern wool producers. Grazing conditions in the Whoop-Up country resembled those of the great sheep stations of the Australian Outback, and the same factors of cheap production contributed to the industry's expansion in Montana.

Sheep were better fitted than cattle for the intense cold of northern winters and survived without the heavy losses that were taken for granted in the range cattle industry. When properly cared for, the flocks often lived through the winters without any losses. Many sheepmen constructed rough log shelters covered with hay to protect the sheep and provided feed during the severe winter weather.

Within a few years, sheep owners turned to better breeds to improve the quantity and quality of their wool clip. They imported improved Merinos with heavier fleeces from Vermont, as well as the increasingly popular Shropshires and Southdowns. Paris Gibson and Company of Fort Benton pioneered in introducing these breeds into Montana.[5]

By 1880, Fort Benton was the leading wool market in Montana. Informal methods of wool buying, however, often sent badly sacked, wet, and dirty wool to Boston purchasers. David Hilger recalled that T. C. Power instructed his "Block P" steamboat captains to unload their wool cargoes at Bismarck during the night. Then, before Northern Pacific shipping agents arrived to check the wool for shipment, his men "threw sand over the bottom part of the sacks where the water had drained." These shipments often brought thirty cents a pound to the growers, but by 1900 wool in similar condition, thought Hilger, "would scarcely be entitled to a bid at any figure."[6]

North of the forty-ninth parallel, a similar expansion of the wool industry followed the Montana lead. There too, sheep growing was combined with cattle raising. Professor Macoun believed that this union of the two industries promised the most profitable investment for Alberta settlers. The universality of the practice indicated that the settlers agreed. By 1881, they were sending their wool down the Whoop-Up Trail to Fort Benton for shipment to eastern brokers.

II

Cattlemen were first to occupy the benchlands and plains of the Whoop-Up country. Their use of these northern grasslands was anticipated by the extensive grazing activities of Fort Benton's freighting companies. In the sixties, "Diamond R," I. G. Baker and Company, and T. C. Power and Brother placed thousands of work oxen on the open ranges during the winter. In the spring, when wagonmasters rounded up the oxen their excellent condition was convincing proof that the region was well suited for the range cattle industry.

Demands for beef in the gold fields prompted the beginning of cattle raising in this district. Farmers owned most of these herds and their production was small, but in 1869 Conrad Kohrs began driving cattle from Deer Lodge valley onto the Sun River range. By Texas standards his holdings were small but in Montana the Sun River herd of one thousand cattle was regarded as the "finest as well as the largest" in the territory.[7]

Other stockmen were slow to follow Kohrs' lead. For another ten years settlement stayed in the river valleys. Not until the range cattle industry pushed north across the Missouri River to escape the crowded ranges of the central plains did this area become a province of the Cattle Kingdom. Then it took on the character of the range cattle empire so often and colorfully described in historical and fictional writings.[8]

The region north of the Missouri River was Indian country and the federal government was slow to push back the reservation. As late as 1876, the Fort Benton *Record* reported that northern Montana's great resources remained unused because of the Indian barrier. Destroy the buffalo, urged the *Record,* and the Indians will also disappear.

For fifteen years following the Civil War, Fort Benton's spokesmen continued their demands to free the grasslands for the cattlemen. "Here is a country containing thousands upon thousands of square miles of the most fertile agricultural lands, the most desirable stock ranges, and rich deposits of mineral wealth of unknown extent. This vast area of undeveloped wealth has ever been the home of the buffalo and the haunt of savage men. Civilization dare not venture there . . ."[9]

Not the presence of Indians but the absence of a railroad delayed the cattlemen's occupation. As long as local markets remained the only outlet, the Indians were unmolested. Once railroads opened the profitable markets of the East, an obliging government reduced the reservations.

Conrad Kohrs and other pioneer stockmen drove their cattle to the Union Pacific, eight hundred miles south of their Sun River ranges. This long and hazardous trip across Indian country and through a region of numerous natural barriers was too long and too dangerous for extensive use. Similarly, others used the trail through eastern Montana to the Northern Pacific Railroad at Bismarck, but Indians made this trail unsafe until the late seventies.

The westward building of the Northern Pacific unlocked the riches of the Whoop-Up plains. By 1881, northern stockmen could drive their cattle to Glendive and the rapid expansion of the industry began. Soon stock cattle from Oregon and Washington came pouring in, as well as herds from the central plains of Wyoming and Nebraska. Occasionally, a herd came all the way from Texas. By 1883, "pilgrims" or "states' cattle" came in from Iowa, Illinois, or Wisconsin to stock the ranges. The unrestrained speculation of the "beef boom" had hit the Whoop-Up country, and within three years cattlemen complained that many of their ranges were already overcrowded.

This expansion transformed the Whoop-Up country from an unoccupied wilderness to a thriving agricultural community. For a brief time, the boomers had their day as the magic "beef bonanza" formula of quick profits prevailed. Free grass, cheap labor costs, natural reproduction of untended cattle on the open range, and ample capital pouring in from eastern and British investors — all this only repeated what had been going on for more than a decade on the central plains. This speculative mania swept Fort Benton so completely that one critic observed he had never seen anything like it — "even the steers have got calves this year." [10]

Chouteau County's growth during the cattlemen's invasion astonished many observers, hardened though they were to overnight development of frontier communities. Within three years the population trebled and more than a million dollars poured into range cattle investments annually. By 1884, the county ranked third in the production of beef in Montana with its 120,000 head of cattle, worth an estimated $4,195,000.[11]

Great cattle companies, not individual ranchers, were responsible for this achievement. The famous Marquis de Mores correctly argued in 1884 that it was "foolhardy to engage in cattle raising with less than $100,000." [12] A survey of ownership in Montana that year confirmed his judgment by revealing that ten companies owned more than 90 per cent of the livestock in the territory.[13]

Many of the major companies centered at Fort Benton were owned by local investors. The capital accumulation described in the previous chapter made large funds available for investments in cattle.

The outstanding example of this trend was the formation of the Benton and St. Louis Cattle Company by the partners of the I. G. Baker Company. Popularly known as the Circle outfit, this company began with a capitalization of $500,000 in 1882. Two years later it possessed the largest herd in Montana and shipped more than $100,000 worth of steers to market. During its twenty years before reincorporation as the Conrad Circle Company, stockholders received more than $980,000 in dividends.[14]

Stuart, Kohrs and Company was equally successful. With a capital of $400,000 furnished by S. T. Hauser, Conrad Kohrs, and Granville Stuart, this company paid a dividend of $34,000 in 1883 while reinvesting another $38,000 of its profits in further expansion.[15]

Texas longhorns, mostly drawn from nearby regions, formed the bulk of the herds in northern Montana despite their well-known inadequacies as beef producers. In the eighties, influenced by editorials in stock journals and prompted by growing consumer resistance, especially in Britain, to the tough, stringy steaks of the "uncouth, mongrel Texas steers," stockmen began importing blooded cattle from the Middle West, from Scotland, and from the British-owned ranches of the Bow River valley. As early as 1871, Conrad Kohrs purchased shorthorn bulls in Iowa for his Sun River range, a practice which he continued through many years. During the eighties, T. C. Power and the Conrads also brought in Angus and Hereford bulls for their ranges.[16]

The import of costly blooded stock gradually forced cattlemen to shift from an open to a fenced range. This transition was greatly hastened by the disasters of the famous winter of 1886–

87. Sheltered river valleys with their wild hay fields and proximity to the mountain forests made conversion to the new era of fences and winter feeding less painful in this region than elsewhere in the Cattle Kingdom.

Cattle companies had their "home ranges," recognized more by custom than by legal right. These were located along the numerous streams that flowed onto the plains from the nearby mountains, for water was the key to successful ranching. Cattlemen secured their ranch lands through the familiar system of land claims under the Homestead Act, pre-emption acts, and Desert Land Act of 1877. By 1881, three fourths of the river bottom lands of northern Montana were held as "desert" claims by cattlemen.

Charges of "land grabbing" by "cattle barons" were heard less frequently in this region than elsewhere. At this early date, grangers had little interest in such a remote region and farmer spokesmen concentrated their attacks on cattlemen farther south. Since most of the herds were locally owned, the absentee owner, favorite target of critics, was missing.

Cowboys on the northern ranges, like their counterparts on the central and southern plains, attracted considerable comment. Now regarded as mounted knights of the plains, living lives of high adventure, they then enjoyed a rather indifferent reputation. Like artisans in other western industries, their work called for skills acquired through experience and, like the stagecoach driver, the bullwhacker, and the gold miner, they developed a way of life peculiar to their kind.

Few resembled the modern version of the movies. Most were hard-working hands whose tasks were more often monotonous than exciting, and better described as menial than lordly. The stockman perhaps could view himself in the "patriarchal tradition" in which a man's wealth was computed by his livestock and his word was law throughout his grazing realm; but the cowboy's true status was revealed by his rough food, primitive lodgings, and low pay.

Stockmen complained that too many cowboys were "counterfeits," equipped with "sombrero, cartridge belt, and gun" and drifting from one region to another. John R. Craig, well known on both sides of the boundary as manager of the Oxley ranch, judged that "first class cowboys are not plentiful. There are as many grades in this as in any other calling."[17]

Visitors to the northern plains recorded varied impressions of the cowboys. A. Staveley Hill found them of a "very picturesque and workmanlike appearance," while his fellow Briton William Shepherd observed that unlike southern areas where the "cowboy is equivalent to desperado, in the north the men on the ranges are as good as any class of Americans."[18]

Across the boundary, Northwest Mounted Police officers viewed the cowboys, north or south, with a fine impartiality. "It is well to bear in mind," the commissioner cautioned Sir John Macdonald, "that the American 'cowboy' or horse thief, is a desperado of the worst description, who holds the life of a man as cheaply as that of an animal, being always well mounted and armed."[19]

III

Land use during these years was strikingly similar on both sides of the forty-ninth parallel. Ranching in southern Alberta and Saskatchewan was an extension of the Montana industry. Cattle from American ranges stocked the Canadian plains and American cattlemen furnished the experience. In its physical aspects, the Canadian industry closely resembled the American.

Enthusiastic Canadian publicists predicted that the cattle business north of the international boundary would surpass the Montana development. Frequent comparisons argued that the Bow River district was vastly superior to the ranges of northern Montana. Better grass, more water, and the absence of "badlands" convinced Alexander Begg of the "superior grazing properties of the country." Western Canada, he argued, was to become the chief stock-raising country in North America. "In a few years it will be difficult," he wrote in 1882, "to find a vacant range in Wyoming, Nebraska or Montana suitable or capable of sustaining 5,000 head of cattle. The Dominion of Canada, on the other hand, has 'limitless' ranges waiting to be taken up and occupied." [20]

Within two years his optimistic prophecies began their fulfillment. Large cattle outfits — the Cochrane, Walrond, Oxley, Northwest, Benton and St. Louis, and Powder River companies — began stocking Canadian ranges, largely with cattle from the United States.

Successful cattle raising by individual ranchers began many years earlier. John McDougall, Whoop-Up's famous missionary, drove in the first herd from Montana in 1872 and others soon followed suit. Most of these early stockmen were Americans who drifted across the boundary or former policemen who, having resigned from the Northwest Mounted Police, turned to ranching in the Fort Macleod vicinity.

Limited markets delayed large-scale enterprises for another ten years. Early ranchers supplied beef contracts for the police and the Indians and shipped the hides to Fort Benton. Jack Lauder made the first drive to Winnipeg with a herd of 400 in 1882. The Fort Macleod *Gazette* hailed his achievement as the "real commencement of our cattle trade," but this was premature.[21] Not until the Canadian Pacific railway reached Medicine Hat in 1883 were eastern markets made available to Alberta ranchers.

As in Montana, large companies stocked the Canadian ranges. In 1881, the Cochrane Ranch drove in nearly 7000 head from Oregon and Montana and in the following year the company brought in another 5000. This second drive ended disastrously, for the cattle reached the ranges late in autumn in poor condition. An early winter with severe snowstorms decimated the herd and served as a harbinger of the catastrophe of 1886–87. Many ranchers heeded the warning and began cutting hay for winter feeding.

Montana experience prompted the Dominion government to design a different system of land leasing. Though grazing lands were leased for only one cent an acre, the government restricted the number of cattle that could be placed on the lease, hoping thus to prevent the overstocking and destruction of the grasses characteristic of the American industry. Large leases, frequently reaching 100,000 acres, were granted to the companies.

Government policy excited considerable opposition, particularly from land speculators, since it appeared to lock up this new country against the farmers. As the railway moved west, increasing agitation against the leasing system forced the Macdonald government to modify its policy. "Men before bulls" became the effective slogan of enthusiasts who looked to the development of the plains by wheat growers rather than monopolistic cattlemen. "Few people outside of those actually living in the country realize what an injury these immence tracts of country, given over to the control of comparatively few men will be to this District," complained the Fort Macleod *Gazette*.[22]

Conflicts soon broke out between the large leaseholders and the squatters. Northwest Mounted Policemen found themselves enforcing unpopular laws against the grangers who moved onto the "unoccupied" lands. By 1883, Prime Minister Macdonald, sensitive to the mounting criticism, ordered the Department of Interior to reduce the number of large leases and to cancel those on lands not yet occupied.[23]

The greatest blow to the continuing expansion of the range cattle industry in Canada came late in 1885 when the government announced a 20 per cent tariff on all cattle imported from the United States. This ended the large drives of Montana cattle onto Alberta ranges and sped the transformation to a fenced-range industry. "The impost of this duty now means the strangling of a young industry at the very time it needs encouragement," complained William Carter to the prime minister. Carter had leased extensive grazing rights for 10,000 cattle owned by Conrad Kohrs. The cattle did not reach the boundary before the September 1 deadline and he faced a $72,000 customs duty on the herd.[24] Events of this kind prompted the *Gazette* to protest the effect of a tariff on Alberta's growth: "The great reason why this duty should be done away with is that it is preventing wealth from coming into our country. We all know that for every head of stock we get in, we are richer by $30 at the expense of Montana . . ."[25]

The 20 per cent tariff on American cattle had far-reaching effects upon the Canadian industry. By slowing down the movement across the boundary, it forced Canadian ranchers to turn to eastern Canada and Britain for their stock. Consequently Angus and Herefords replaced the inferior range cattle more quickly in Alberta than in Montana.

The tariff also encouraged American cattlemen to allow their herds to "drift" across the boundary from overcrowded Montana ranges. This practice reached such proportions that Mounted Police constables were busy patrolling the boundary to keep out foreign cattle. One year they impounded 1200 of Conrad Kohrs' cattle and compelled the prominent Montana cattleman to travel to Ottawa to pay for their release.[26]

Other American cattlemen avoided police action by leasing land on both sides of the boundary and running their cattle onto Alberta ranges despite the tariff laws. The overstocking of Montana ranges in the eighties led them to place large numbers of cattle on their Canadian leases. This practice, especially by the Conrad Circle outfit, drew frequent complaints from Canadian cattlemen.

Registry of the same brands on both sides of the boundary had a further advantage. Stockmen could sell their cattle on whichever side of the line offered the best price without paying customs duties. Not until 1901 were American owners forced to brand their Canadian stock differently so that officers could detect the presence of "estrayed" American cattle on the Candian ranges.[27]

Ranching in Alberta took on a different character from that south of the boundary. The transfer of the industry from American ranges determined that the care of the stock, the dress and speech of the cowboys, and the use of the range closely resembled the earlier experience. But the extraregional ties with British traditions infused the Canadian development with a distinct spirit. Ranching in Alberta produced an interesting synthesis of the codes of Victorian England's upper classes with those of the

Great Plains frontier. As Professor Thomas has pointed out, "in such communities the body is American but the spirit is English." [28]

"Gentlemen ranchers" startled visiting American cowboys with their customs. Ranch houses with interiors decorated like English country houses, formal hunts with the etiquette of the English squirearchy strictly enforced, polo playing, and formal dress for dinner seemed strange to those schooled in the crudities of life on the open range south of the boundary. Lionel Brooke, owner of the "Chinook" Ranch, earned the sobriquet "Window Pane Chief" with his ever-present monocle, and W. E. Smith was universally called the "Gentlemen Cowboy" from his practice of appearing at every community dance in formal dress. [29]

To protests that the customs of England's gentle countryside seemed pretentious in these surroundings, British cattlemen explained that they adhered to old country customs to avoid "reverting to savagery." Preserving the amenities gave the early Canadian ranches an atmosphere of gracious living and provided employment for the otherwise unused talents of many of the "remittance men."

IV

Cattlemen on both sides of the boundary faced similar problems in establishing their industry and they turned to similar solutions. During the initial years, Indian depredations posed a serious problem. With the buffalo rapidly disappearing, hungry Indians turned to cattle herds to supplement their government rations. They slaughtered thousands of steers in the same fashion they had earlier killed the buffalo. From 1879 to 1881, pioneer stockmen were forced to retreat from many of the northern ranges to the safety of the more settled areas along the Sun, Teton, and Missouri rivers.

Both governments acted to moderate the suffering among their Indians. Army quartermasters joined Indian agents in providing additional rations to feed the Piegans and Bloods on the reservations while Canadian officials secured special appropriations to purchase flour and meat for their Treaty Seven annuitants. These emergency measures prevented a general uprising, but the Indians remained restless in their poverty.

Newspapers exaggerated these difficulties by picturing the Indians as hostiles. Canadian officials did little to discourage these reports. "I don't propose to make light of them for I think it better that the people should have the 'brazen side of the shield' at present exhibited to them and then they won't grumble at the large expenditures that the new system involves," Indian Commissioner E. B. Dewdney wrote Sir John Macdonald.[30]

Americans also exaggerated the crisis in the Whoop-Up country, though for other reasons. Montanans complained that the Northwest Mounted Police force was too small to prevent Canadian Indians from raiding their herds. "As it is," protested the Fort Benton *Record*, "the police are making no pretence at protecting anyone but themselves, and are in hourly danger of an attack from overwhelming numbers of redskins."[31] Commissioner A. G. Irvine dismissed these complaints as "motivated by the wish to retain expenditure of Canadian money in Montana."[32]

His judgment was only partially correct. Police officials played for time in the Northwest, for their numbers were inadequate to coerce the Indians. In their view, the West was not yet ready for settlement and cattlemen who entered the country must accept losses to the Indians as part of the risk of their premature entry. When the railway reached the West, they looked forward to altering their policy, but not before. "In a year or two with the Railway in the centre of the Continent we shall be in a position to dictate to the Indians. We are not so now, and any outbreak occurring this year or next would be disastrous," Dewdney warned Ottawa officials.[33] Ironically, the Indians and their métis allies waited until the railway reached their land before they launched their rebellion against Dominion authority. Then it was too late.

Canadian officials hoped to purchase peace through gifts of food and clothing. Cattlemen were not as patient. Heavy losses led many on both sides of the border to urge direct action against the Indians. In Fort Benton, the *Record* urged cattlemen to settle matters in the approved frontier style with gun and rope. "Our stockmen must . . . kill a few of these Indians," concluded the editor.[34]

Canadian stockmen shared these views. The "meager punishments" given to Indians convicted of killing their cattle irritated ranchers and led to complaints that the police were worthless in protecting their property. "These Indians must be kept on their reserves," warned the Fort Macleod *Gazette*; "else the indignant stockmen will some day catch the red rascals and make such an example of them, that the noble red man will think h—l's apoppin . . ." A month later, the Canadian editor predicted that one day soon the body of a dead Indian would be found on the range; next the charred remains of a ranch house and a dead cattleman; and then the fighting would be general. "If we are obliged to fight these Indians to stop their depredations, let the entertainment commence." Losses of horses to raiding American Piegans brought the warning that "it would go hard on any Indian who attempts to hold down the opposite end of a rope over the limb of a tree." [35]

The failure of Canadian and American officials to halt these depredations prompted cattlemen to organize to protect their herds. Efforts to form a territorial association were launched as early as 1873, but no permanent organization survived. The crisis of 1879, however, forced stockmen to act in unison or be driven from their ranges. Leading cattlemen gathered in Helena in February to form the Montana Stock Growers' Association. Little was accomplished until its reorganization in 1884; even then its powers were never as great as those of its model, the Wyoming Stock Growers' Association.

Local associations carried the burden of cooperative effort during the early years. The Sun River and Shonkin Stock associations were the first permanent groups through which cattlemen regulated their brands and range use and supervised roundups. These associations tried to eliminate confusion and fraud over vents and brands; to prevent conflicts over mavericks and unclaimed strays; and to improve the quality of the herds by buying blooded bulls. In 1881, the Sun River Association purchased one hundred Hereford bulls for its ranges, and others followed its lead.

Small ranchers, many of whom owned dairy cows, believed these associations were tools of the large cattle owners. They feared the organizations would rewrite the estray laws to the disadvantage of small owners. Their opposition, combined with the restraining influences of the territory's other industries, prevented a domination of political and economic life comparable to that exercised by the Wyoming association.

During 1880 and 1881, stockmen in the Shonkin, Teton, and Benton areas organized temporary "protective associations" to patrol their ranges with armed riders. The "Chouteau and Meagher County Protective Association" authorized Sheriff Healy to deputize its members to accompany him on expeditions to halt Indian raiding parties. The association paid his expenses and posted rewards for the apprehension of anyone guilty of selling whisky to the Indians or of setting prairie fires. Cattlemen particularly resented the half-breed settlements along the Milk and Missouri rivers where whisky smugglers, horse thieves, and cattle rustlers found a hospitable refuge.[36]

Sheriff Healy pursued the Indians with his customary vigor. Soon, fears that his aggressive tactics would excite a general Indian uprising led to a disbanding of the temporary association. In September 1881, the Sun River cattlemen announced their refusal to participate in the organization and in the following March the Stock Growers' Associations of Chouteau and Meagher counties withdrew their support.

Effective organization became imperative as local associations failed to meet the needs of the cattlemen. Their great herds grazed over ranges too extensive for local control; the necessity of stricter regulation of brands on the overcrowded ranges and the growing complexity of roundups also argued for closer cooperation. In 1884, therefore, cattlemen gathered in Hauser's offices in Helena to reorganize the Montana Stock Growers' Association. The consolidation of the older group with the newer but more powerful Eastern Montana Stock Growers' Association made it a territorial power. With Granville Stuart as its president, the new organization successfully sponsored so much special legislation in the Assembly of 1885 that it won the title "Cowboy Legislature."

Canadian cattlemen closely followed the Montana example in organizing their industry. The first well-regulated roundup in the Pincher Creek district under the local association in 1882 foreshadowed the creation of a general organization the following year. When the cattlemen formed their South Western Stock Association in April, they adopted without significant alteration the rules of the Montana society. The extent of their dependence upon American precedents is suggested by the *Gazette*'s notice on May 24, 1883: "A special meeting is to be called to consider the round-up and other laws when received from Montana." [37]

Close cooperation between the two associations solved many common problems. Joint efforts to control diseases, regulate brands, and capture rustlers created a keen sense of unity along the boundary. Lax law enforcement south of the forty-ninth parallel, however, cooled Canadian enthusiasm for cooperation. The South Western Stock Association urged Montana cattlemen to secure territorial legislation similar to that in the Northwest Territories.

Considerable ill-feeling developed in Canada as American officials failed to recover stolen horses and cattle. This was in marked contrast to the success of the Mounted Police in restoring stolen stock to their American owners. Extensive rustling and horse stealing by gangs which moved from one side of the boundary to the other, finding refuge in the Missouri River badlands or in the Cypress Hills or Wood Mountain districts created a reign of lawlessness. These gangsters proved a more serious threat to the cattlemen's welfare than Indian depredations and led eventually to vigilante action by eastern Montana cattlemen.

Ranching lingered in this region as the major industry for

many years after farmers displaced it on the central plains. Enthusiasts on both sides of the boundary urged grangers to exploit the wheat-growing potentialities of the area. Optimists, like Professor Macoun, launched a campaign to educate middle western farmers to the suitability of the land for grain growing. Lack of rainfall, they announced, was no longer a problem since "aridity vanishes before the first efforts of husbandry." [38] Even those who had no direct interest in agricultural development accepted this attractive doctrine. General Gibbon reported that the necessity for irrigation lessened each year as the farmer "by his labors, produces those climatic changes which are known to follow his footsteps." [39]

More cautious observers warned homesteaders against trying to farm a region fit only for grazing. "The reports as to the magnificent agricultural future of Montana . . . are highly misleading," warned the Fort Benton *Record*. Across the border, Professor Henry Y. Hind denounced Professor Macoun as a "charlatan" and predicted that agricultural settlement in the dry belt would lead only to "great misery" for the settlers.

Few homesteaders arrived during these years, not because farmers heeded these pessimistic predictions but because there were still good lands to be claimed on the central plains. When these were exhausted, they turned eagerly to the Whoop-Up country, putting aside their fears of early frosts and aridity under the influence of persuasive propaganda from railway and land companies. By the turn of the century they began to arrive, vanguard of the last great land rush in North American history.

12

Sitting Bull and the Queen

JUNE 25, 1876, was a bleak day in American military history. Citizens of the republic read with dismay accounts of the tragedy on the Little Big Horn where the powerful Sioux and their allies joined forces to upset the American government's carefully planned campaign "to whip them into submission."

From that day to this, historians have lavished undue attention upon "Custer's Massacre." With almost pathological interest they have pursued the phantoms of alleged white survivors, often forgetting that hundreds of Indian survivors remained to create a series of incidents more significant than a military engagement, and more fraught with danger than a massacre.

"Custer's Massacre," grossly exaggerated and badly named, was only a minor episode in western history. Events which followed it were of greater importance, both to whites and reds. And among these was the flight of the Sioux north into Canada. This invasion by American Indians precipitated a crisis in the recently acquired territories of the Dominion, imposed a burden upon the newly formed Mounted Police that sorely tried their organization, threw a chill over Canadian-American relations, and forced the Canadian government to take diplomatic steps which, though faltering, led inevitably to a new chapter in Imperial relations.

During the months following the battle on the Little Big Horn, the wrath of American military power harassed Sitting Bull without pause. Relentlessly, General Terry's forces pursued the victorious Indians, scattering their forces and smashing their power. In vain Sitting Bull pleaded for an "old-fashioned" peace, with the soldiers retiring to winter quarters while the Indians recruited their strength for further campaigns in the spring.

Late into winter the blue-clad troopers hunted the fleeing warriors. Under this ruthless pressure several Sioux chieftains and many of their people sought peace on the reservations, but not Sitting Bull. His passionate hatred of the Long Knives, his stern determination to avoid the ignominy of agency life, and his prestige as a successful leader among his people drove him on. Surrender would destroy everything he lived for.

In October and again in December, Colonel Nelson A. Miles' forces dealt crippling blows to the Sioux, destroying tons of their dried meat and supplies, capturing their ponies, and leaving them destitute in the face of winter's ravages. Three major engagements and eight minor skirmishes broke the once powerful Sioux. "Indians left pools of blood in the snow where they fought, on the ice where they crossed the river and for five miles up the valley in their retreat," reported Colonel Miles after defeating Crazy Horse's Oglalas.[1]

Three hundred miles to the north, Mounted Police officers viewed with growing concern these death struggles of Indian power, while in Ottawa grave fears prompted the Mackenzie government to warn western officers of the probable consequences of American policy.

As early as May 1876, cabinet officials alerted the Mounted Police to American plans to destroy the Sioux. Confidential reports from south of the boundary led the Canadian government to speculate that the proposed three-pronged attack against the Sioux might easily result in their "being driven for shelter into the Territories, and using Canadian soil as a base for predatory and hostile operations."[2] Even before the American army launched its final assaults, Canadian officials feared they would reap a harvest of troubles where Americans had sowed.

During June 1876, Mounted Police patrols guarded the international boundary. From their lonely posts, the policemen kept a "strict watch" on Sioux movements below the boundary. With unconcealed admiration, the Fort Benton *Record* hailed these activities. "The Mounted Police don't scare worth a cent. Parties of two and three men are scouting along the line looking for Sitting Bull." [3]

Information from spies in Sitting Bull's camp confirmed Canadian fears. Daily councils discussed possible courses open to the beleaguered Indians. Two paths seemed most reasonable to chiefs determined to avoid surrender. Sitting Bull explained them in clear terms to his followers. "We can go nowhere without seeing the head of an American. Our land is small, it is like an island. We have two ways to go — to the land of the Great Mother, or to the land of the Spaniards." [4]

Thus warned of Sioux intentions, Mounted Police officers tried to keep the fugitives under constant surveillance. This proved impossible, however, and rumors of impending attacks swept the northern plains.

Difficulties in following the elusive Sioux led to a pooling of news. Canadian police officials and American army officers created an unofficial, but effective, liaison to exchange information. Major Guido Ilges at Fort Benton and Superintendent James M. Walsh at Fort Walsh were in frequent, though private correspondence. By comparing their reports, the two officers successfully tracked down many rumors, preventing costly mistakes on both sides of the boundary.

Estimates of Sitting Bull's intentions were not always correct. Late in September, Major Ilges informed Walsh that the Sioux appeared to be concentrating near Fort Peck, apparently intending to surrender. On the basis of this report, Walsh wrote Ottawa advising the secretary of state that Indian troubles in the United States were at an end. With the Sioux tired of war and headed for their agencies, sixty Mounted Policemen could easily maintain the peace in the Fort Walsh region. [5]

American officers shared this appraisal. General Alfred H. Terry advised General Philip H. Sheridan in Chicago that the Sioux were entirely destitute, without food or ammunition and incapable of causing further trouble. With a continuation of the firm policy of disarming and dismounting the hostiles before allowing them food, the field commander saw no future for Sitting Bull but surrender or starvation.[6]

But the wily medicine man had other plans for his people. North of the forty-ninth parallel lay a sanctuary, virtually untouched by the rapacious white man and policed by a merest handful of troopers. In the Queen's domain still roamed great buffalo herds, and there the harassed tribes could sleep at night, secure in the knowledge that the Long Knives could not follow them across the border. Nor had Sitting Bull forgotten the stories of times past when his people were allies of the Great White Father across the seas. Somehow he had been succeeded by a squaw, but no matter, the Sioux remained allies of the British. Now they would find peace and food, security and friendship by restoring a half-forgotten alliance.

During November, scouts brought in news that the Sioux were streaming northward instead of toward their agencies. This forced Walsh to revise his plans and to send out patrols to meet the refugees. In December they came. Oglalas, Hunkpapas, Sans Arcs, Miniconjou, Two Kettles, and Blackfoot Sioux, powerful tribes of plains warriors unlike anything the police had yet faced — tall, bronzed men whose warlike appearance impressed Mounted Police officers and whose great numbers explained in part their victories over blue-coated armies. Nearly three thousand bitter, hungry Indians came during the first invasions. Others were hard on their heels.

II

Superintendent Walsh faced a crucial assignment. With a handful of men he must police warriors who had defied entire American armies. But more important, his every act created a precedent shaping an uncertain future. Mistakes at this point could touch off an Indian war destroying everything the police had accomplished during their three years on the plains.

Fortunately, Major Walsh possessed unusual skill in Indian

negotiations. With dignity and pageantry, so dear to Indian temperaments, he firmly met the great Sioux chiefs in council. Little Knife, Long Dog, Black Moon, The Man Who Crawls — these were among the famous chiefs the policeman faced in this first experience with the hostiles.

Without hesitation, Walsh made his position clear. Did they know they were now in the Queen's country? When the chiefs replied yes, the major challenged them with their purpose for coming into a British territory. Did they intend to remain during the winter, only to return with spring to renew their war on the Americans? No, said the Indians, they wished only peace for their weary people. Would the major implore the Great White Mother to have pity on them? [7]

Then the shrewd chiefs introduced a theme that was to plague Canadian officials for years. Though they did not sense its importance immediately, it later complicated negotiations between Washington and Ottawa. We were driven from our homes, said the chiefs, but we remembered that our grandfathers told us they could find peace in the Great Mother's land and we recalled we are British.

My Queen, replied the policeman, will never allow you to make war from her lands. You must not use Canadian soil as a base from which to raid Americans. If you do, warned Walsh, you can never return. To this the Indians hastily consented, knowing very well that the future could take care of itself.

Then Walsh permitted the starving Indians to barter with local traders. Among other things, they secured sufficient ammunition to hunt buffalo for their families.

This was only the beginning. In March, Four Horns, head chief of the Tetons, and Medicine Bear, chief of the Yanktons, brought their tribes across the boundary. Again Walsh insisted they must promise to obey the laws of the country and never use British soil for adventures against American citizens. And again he heard the same complaints, the same abuse of the Long Knives and the same pledges of loyalty to the Great White Mother. "They claim that the Sioux are British Indians," reported Walsh, "that 65 years ago was the first their fathers knew of being under the Americans. Why the White Father gave them and their country to the Americans they could not tell."[8]

On May 7, 1877, the long-awaited news reached Fort Walsh that Sitting Bull had entered Canada. With keen interest, mixed with some concern, police officers greeted the famous refugee. And the Sioux medicine man, dramatic actor that he was, did not disappoint them. With bitterness he denounced the Americans and professed his devotion to the Queen. Keen resentment marked every statement and a passionate spirit of revenge motivated his lengthy speeches. "Sitting Bull is of a revengeful disposition," Assistant Commissioner A. G. Irvine telegraphed Ottawa. "If he could get the necessary support he would recross the line and make war on the Americans."[9]

Major Walsh greeted Sitting Bull with the same advice he had given the others. But his interview with Sitting Bull was filled with unexpected tension and drama. After the usual Indian oratory, an incident of great importance in shaping Sioux conduct suddenly took place.

Three Assiniboins rode into the camp, trailing horses that they had obviously stolen. Immediately, Major Walsh challenged White Dog and his two companions about the animals. With unconcealed truculence White Dog sneered at the red-coated officers. Thinking his position secure in the presence of hundreds of armed Sioux, only recently engaged in killing white men, the Assiniboin flouted police authority. Without hesitating, Walsh threatened to throw White Dog into irons and take him to Fort Walsh unless he told his story.

This turn of events greatly excited the Sioux, whose experience with law enforcement was limited. Few of them had ever seen the laws enforced, and fewer still had witnessed such courage in the face of overwhelming odds. Walsh, however, could only warn White Dog against any further suspicious conduct, since there were no witnesses to prove his guilt.

White Dog's humiliation visibly impressed the assembled Indians. But it also incensed the Assiniboin, who had lost face before his cousins. As he turned to leave, therefore, the angry Indian muttered that he would see Walsh again. The superintendent overheard this impertinence and compelled the crestfallen Indian to apologize publicly or go with him to the fort.

This singular act astonished the American Indians. Though the proud Sitting Bull could hardly have foreseen it, one day he too would suffer humiliation and disgrace at the hands of the scarlet-jacketed officers when his ambitions exceeded his legal privileges. White Dog was an individual before the law, but so was Sitting Bull, or any other man in the Canadian West, white or red.

High-ranking police officers shared an understandable curiosity to meet their notorious visitor. When news reached the police, therefore, that Sitting Bull held three American prisoners, Assistant Commissioner Irvine hurried to his camp. The three Americans, led by Father Martin Marty, a Benedictine priest whose good works among the Indians in Dakota were widely known on the northwest frontier, had come north to urge Sitting Bull to return to his native land. But for solemn promises to the police to protect white men in his camp, Sitting Bull would have put the men to death. Instead, they joined Irvine in a series of councils with the chiefs, entreating them to return.

Sitting Bull warmly welcomed the assistant commissioner to his camp. Irvine found that Sioux warriors were "of immense height and very muscular," and was "particularly struck" with Sitting Bull's appearance. The medicine man seemed to be of short stature but of "wonderful capacity," with a pleasant face, a mouth showing great determination, and a fine high forehead.[10] In an age when character could be read on a man's face, Sitting Bull awed his guests.

With appropriate formalities and many speeches, Irvine smoked the calumet. Around the council stood warrior guards, armed with United States carbines and displaying Yankee scalps from the ill-fated Seventh Cavalry at their belts.

Two lengthy sessions followed. In each, Sitting Bull expressed his pleasure for the protection afforded by the Queen. In turn, his chiefs Sweet Bird, Spotted Eagle, and Pretty Bear proclaimed their loyalty to the Great White Mother, while at the same time swearing eternal hatred for their enemies across the boundary.

Most of the sessions seemed tedious. But Sitting Bull, too much an actor to let such an opportunity escape him, dramatically denounced the Catholic priest who had come to plead with him.

"You told me you came as the messenger of God," said the medicine man. "What you told me was not good for me. Look up, you will see God. I don't believe the Americans ever saw God, and that is the reason they don't listen to me. You know as a messenger of God that they tried to kill me. Why did you wait until half my people were killed before you came?"

"After hearing all this talk and what these British officers say," calmly replied the priest, "I would think you were better on British soil. If you wish to come back, I pledge you my life that your lives and liberties will be safe. You will not be killed or made prisoners."

"What would I return for?" asked Sitting Bull. "To have my horses and arms taken away? What have the Americans to give me? They have no lands. Once I was rich, plenty of money, but the Americans stole it all in the Black Hills. I have come to remain with the White Mother's children." [11]

But more moving to Irvine was his private conversation with Sitting Bull on May 31. Late that night the Sioux leader slipped into his tent to tell him of the great happiness of the Indians that they could sleep soundly. Then the Indian poured out his grievances and described his recent experiences. In great detail he told Irvine of his bloody encounters, especially with Custer at Little Big Horn, and claimed that for twelve days his scouts had shadowed the cavalrymen who rode unwittingly into a trap prepared for their destruction. [12]

III

Sitting Bull's flight into Canada touched off an international incident. From Fort Walsh on the periphery of empire to London at its heart, politicians suddenly faced the problem of what to do with a savage medicine man and his ragged followers. Decisions could not be delayed indefinitely, for a terrible Indian war seemed imminent.

Canadian Indians resented the intrusion of thousands of hungry Sioux. Their assault on the buffalo herds made food gathering more difficult for the native tribes. Moreover, the Sioux were traditional enemies whose constant wars had left a heritage of hatred among their neighbors.

Native chiefs complained to Mounted Police officers. Why should they be driven from their hunting grounds to accommodate these invaders? They had obeyed the Great Mother's laws, was this their reward? No, the police must protect them. Crowfoot, powerful chief of the Blackfeet, immediately offered his warriors to aid the police in driving the Sioux back to their own land.

There was an even greater danger, though less immediate. Sitting Bull had already used his powerful medicine to unite Indians south of the boundary. Suppose he now turned his talents to the erection of a greater alliance encompassing Indians on both sides of the boundary from the fringes of settlement to the Rockies. Rumors of such an alliance appeared again and again, and Canadian officials could not afford to ignore them. Such an international alliance of redmen would sweep everything before it and delay settlement of the Northwest Territories indefinitely.

No government policy guided western officials in this crisis. As early as March, Commissioner Macleod warned Lieutenant Governor David Laird of the dangers of temporizing. With unmistakable clarity he urged the government to announce a policy for these alien Indians. In their present demoralized state, the police held the whip hand and could deal with them far more easily than if they were "allowed time to become rich and powerful." [13] Delay could be costly!

Laird fully shared these fears. Western officials faced an immediate problem and they sought Ottawa's wisdom in solving it. To aid eastern politicians in understanding its complexity, the lieutenant governor carefully analyzed every aspect. If the Sioux remained in Canada, they would inevitably place too great a strain upon food resources. This in turn would lead to conflict with the native Indians, whom by treaty the government was pledged to support.

More important to politicians sensitive to balanced budgets was Laird's depressing picture of growing expenses. If the Sioux stayed, provision for their welfare must be made, requiring land, agricultural implements, seeds, educational facilities, and maintenance. All this promised a larger budget for the Mackenzie cabinet to defend in the House of Commons.

In sum, he urged that the cabinet instruct the Mounted Police to inform the refugees that their stay in Canada was temporary. The government must pursue a policy of accomplishing their return by peaceful means, for "their continued residence in our territory will be a constant source of trouble and expense and will, I fear, seriously retard the prosperity of the country." This was another convincing argument to a government that had come to power in the wake of the Pacific Railway scandals of 1873. Liberals had pledged to develop the West and they could not permit Sitting Bull and his savages to embarrass their program.

Laird also urged Ottawa authorities to take immediate steps through diplomatic channels to ensure Sitting Bull's removal to the United States. The Privy Council, he wrote, should request the governor general to communicate with the American government through the British minister in Washington, inquiring under what conditions the Sioux could return. Moreover, the Americans should be advised to make every effort to persuade the Indians to return to their own land.[14]

This was a logical suggestion. But it opened five years of prolonged and tedious negotiations that sorely tried the patience of British and American diplomats and on occasion hindered the growing sense of accord developing between London and Washington. And it created a spirit of frustration in Ottawa that burdened two cabinets.

Dispatches from Colonel Macleod reinforced Laird's suggestions. But Macleod, in a letter to the prime minister himself, introduced a new note of warning which the government could not ignore. The Sioux would be a constant source of anxiety and trouble along the international boundary, predicted Macleod, and "it would be impossible for the police to keep them in check over such an extended frontier." [15] This frank admission clearly stated the real problem. What could the police do with thousands of hostile Indians, too powerful to be coerced and too hungry to be denied?

These warnings brought action in Ottawa. On June 1, 1877, the Privy Council formally recommended Laird's proposal to the governor general, Lord Dufferin. Through the British minister in Washington, the privy counselors urged that the American government act quickly to secure the return of the refugee Sioux. "Any delay in so important a matter," warned their report, "may be attended with serious embarrassments to both the Governments of the United States and Canada."

In Washington, however, British diplomats greeted the affair without enthusiasm. In fact, Francis R. Plunkett, British chargé d'affaires, received the message with frank pessimism. American officials had little stomach for Sitting Bull. To suggest they welcome him back was like asking a man to invite the return of devils he had just cast out. With more accuracy than he could have imagined, Plunkett predicted that this question would lead "to a lengthy and unsatisfactory correspondence with the State Department." [16] Moreover, officials in Ottawa soon came to feel that British diplomats, whether in London or in Washington, really had little interest in continental problems, particularly those involving a savage tribe along an unpopulated frontier in the heartland of North America.

Though convinced he already knew American reactions, Plunkett presented his request to Secretary of State William M. Evarts on June 20, 1877. As he had foretold, his message touched off prolonged negotiations. Five years later, the two governments were still exchanging notes on Sitting Bull.

One month after presenting his note, the British diplomat inquired what steps had been taken to solve the problem. He probed a sensitive point when he raised this issue with American authorities. Without hesitation Evarts made it clear that his government regarded the Dominion remiss in its duties as a responsible neighbor. But since Canada had already admitted these Indians as refugees, they must now be regarded as political offenders seeking asylum. Under this definition, the United States government had no legal right to demand their extradition.

Obviously, Evarts sought a rational excuse for American disinterest in the return of Sitting Bull. He pursued his argument with another legalism. Canada certainly would not tolerate the passage of American forces across her territory to subdue the Indians. Therefore, it was the Dominion's responsibility to drive them back into the arms of American forces. The American government was helpless under present conditions.

While Plunkett had anticipated a negative answer, he was considerably shaken by the spirited American reaction. Force might not be the proper answer at all, he replied. A humane and prudent policy with favorable terms might regain Sitting Bull's loyalty. He sensed, moreover, that Evarts had baited a trap, and he hurried to render it harmless. If the American definition of political refugee held, the Canadian government could hardly object to the presence of thousands of Sioux whom they had welcomed with food and protection. They were not political refugees, argued the Britisher, since they were wards, not citizens of the United States. He had answered one legalism with another.

To this response Evarts, and F. W. Seward who had joined him, reacted vigorously. Seward rejected the proposition that the United States hold out inducements for Sitting Bull's return. The American government was only too happy to be rid of the savages. Canadians must not expect the Americans to make serious efforts seeking their return, for they were criminals under American law. Their murders and depredations would cause many of them to be shot if they were captured by the American army.

Because of this agitation, wrote Plunkett to the home government, "I contented myself with saying that I hoped he would consider the question carefully and dispassionately." No matter how glad the United States authorities might be to get rid of troublesome Indians, warned Plunkett, the gain would be more than offset by the danger of bringing on serious complications with Her Majesty's government.[17]

Diplomacy had accomplished little. Americans remained determined to keep Sitting Bull across the boundary, while Canadians seemed all the more anxious to unload their unwelcome burden. Under these conditions, stalemate faced every diplomatic move.

Washington officials shared Ottawa's confusion over the Sioux question. Advice poured in from every quarter, but the problem remained. In the West, military commanders urged a firm policy, going so far as to insist with General Miles that an American army march to the international boundary to demand the return of the Indians for punishment and incarceration.

American military leaders felt a keen resentment that the Sioux had escaped at the moment of victory. Frustrated by the escape of Sitting Bull's forces and embittered by a Canadian policy that welcomed savages whose weapons were stained with the blood of their comrades, they urged a drastic policy. From their myopic western viewpoint the British empire looked weak and impotent, represented by only a small force of policemen. Washington diplomats, however, were too close to salt water to afford such a judgment.

General Sherman, in his blunt and forthright manner, sharply criticized British policy. English authorities, he wrote the secretary of war, must decide at once to adopt the refugees as their own Indians or they must force them to return before they recovered their strength. If the Sioux rebuilt their power, warned the general of the army, the whole northern frontier would again be aflame. Such a condition, Sherman grimly pointed out, "will surely be equivalent to an act of hostility, which I am sure the English authorities do not intend."

Quietly, Seward gave a copy of Sherman's letter to Plunkett

for transmission to London. There his blunt advice convinced British officials that this was no trifling matter. And they winced under Sherman's prediction that Canadian policy in the West threatened to create the same anarchy along the forty-ninth parallel "as long existed on our Mexican border." [18] British diplomats were not accustomed to their strength being compared with Mexican weakness.

Similar advice reached Washington from civil authorities. James Wickes Taylor, writing from his strategic post in the Winnipeg consulate, warned the State Department that Sioux warriors were rearming with weapons that could later be used against American troops. With a touch of unaccustomed severity, the genial Taylor reported that Sioux braves traded United States government equipment, including horses and mules, for ammunition. Canadian officials treated these as spoils of war, not as stolen property.

Even more disturbing, chaos could develop along the boundary at any moment. The Mounted Police, wrote Taylor, are not adequate "to prevent or punish outrages." [19] Again, State Department officials discreetly handed Taylor's dispatch to British diplomats.

Late in July the American secretary of state countered with a request of his own to British officials. Numerous dispatches from authorities in the West, said Evarts, have charged Canadian traders with providing the Sioux with arms and ammunition. Surely the Canadian government does not willingly countenance these acts "which increase the power of the Indians to indulge their propensities for murder and plunder." [20]

Here were inflammable issues and diplomats began to move cautiously. But newspaper editors, seldom famous for their restraint in diplomatic matters, played them to the full. Indictments of Anglo-Canadian policy appeared in western papers, and eastern journals reprinted them with approval.

Powerful voices emerged both in Canada and in the United States, however, to defend Canadian policy. Humanitarians in both nations rushed into print, for the Indian had now replaced

the Negro as the North American symbol of injustice and ine-
quality.

Wendell Phillips, veteran crusader for Negro freedom, released
an open letter to Lord Dufferin, governor general of Canada,
pleading with the Canadian government to hold fast to its enlightened course. Refuge to victims of political misrule was England's pride for centuries, argued the distinguished Bostonian.
Now only British power and British justice stood between this
"friendless and hunted race," and the "greed and neglect of a
powerful and grasping people." [21]

IV

Diplomatic stalemate in Washington distressed the Mackenzie
government in Ottawa. By August, growing concern prompted
the Canadian cabinet to take an unusual step, one that had
repercussions in all three capitals. With a view to cutting the
Gordian knot, the cabinet sent David Mills, minister of interior,
to Washington to consult informally and unofficially with American authorities.

Mills first visited Plunkett, who briefed him on the current
status of negotiations between Washington and London. Thus
prepared, the Canadian next called upon the State Department
where his unofficial status created some confusion. Seward quickly made it clear that American diplomats were not anxious to
talk about Sitting Bull. The proper official in Washington to
visit was the secretary of interior, Carl Schurz.

When Mills reached Schurz, the American whisked the startled
Canadian off to the White House for a brief visit with President
Hayes. There, the Americans found Mills' views so interesting
that they arranged a lengthy conference with him on the following day.

Their conversations on August 9 revealed the striking con-
trasts between Canadian and American attitudes toward the
western Indians. They enabled the Canadian cabinet member,
moreover, to present his government's views to the highest ranking American officials, for with him sat the President of the

United States, the secretary of interior, and the secretary of war.

Schurz opened the conference with the flat assertion that the United States could do nothing about Sitting Bull. His Sioux had retired across the Canadian boundary under arms. They were political offenders — the phrase must have revived memories from 1848 — and his government could not demand their return under existing extradition laws.

No good could possibly come from such a viewpoint, replied the Canadian envoy. Legalism hindered rather than helped. It must be worth some effort to conciliate the Indians, inducing them to return to their reservations where they would be under the supervision of American authorities. From the Indian point of view, Mills gently reminded the great humanitarian, these hostilities were begun by the United States and not by the tribes. Stories of dishonest agents and of adventurous and lawless gold-seekers who violated treaty obligations were too common for Mills to mention, but the American officials saw the point.

In the face of these opinions, Schurz shifted his ground. Would the Canadian government be prepared, he asked, to disarm the Indians if they rejected diplomatic overtures?

This question touched off an analysis of America's Indian policy by the visiting Canadian. When he had finished, in fact, he realized he had delivered a rather complete lecture, urging a humane and liberal policy toward the red men. They need not be disarmed, for taking their weapons deprived them of their livelihood through hunting. Moreover, it humiliated them, thus exciting rather than quieting their resentments.

A true course for the American government to follow was a bold one. Indian good will and obedience could easily be won, not by force or guile, but by giving superior arms to the chiefs, dressing them in showy uniforms, and awarding them impressive medals. These devices, as inexpensive as they were, comprised a recognition for the headmen that captured their imaginations and won their loyalties.

Far from resenting this impromptu lecture, President Hayes

stated that he understood the Canadian position. But was it really possible "to buy up Sitting Bull and the leaders of the Sioux?"

To this presidential question, Mills had a ready answer. Yes, if accompanied with justice. The United States government had constantly used its power in the West, not on behalf of the aggrieved but on behalf of the trespassers. This left no course open to the Indians except to make war in self-defense. The Sioux desired peace and had no intention of resuming hostilities, but they must be assured of justice before returning to American jurisdiction.

This indictment stirred Schurz into asking a basic question that had faced American officials since Independence: "How do you keep your whites in order?" [22]

With this question, Schurz probed the heart of the problem. He also exposed Mills' advice as a counsel of perfection. Canadian officials and Canadian public opinion insisted on viewing the Indian problem in the United States as similar to their own. But such a view was based on a fallacy. Conditions in the Canadian West were different from those south of the forty-ninth parallel and a policy suitable for the one might be impractical for the other.

From the Red River to British Columbia the Canadian West was still the Great Lone Land. Only a handful of traders competed with the natives for nature's wealth. To the south, however, thousands of gold-seekers, ranchers, farmers, and adventurers exploited the region's resources. The American government, as the secretary of war hastened to point out, lacked the power to restrain them, however ruthless they might become in their pursuit of happiness. Indeed, it is difficult to imagine an American government in the nineteenth century with such despotic powers. Reservations were the only solution, and Indians on reservations needed no horses or guns. Government beef provided their meat and sedentary agriculture promised economic security.

David Mills returned to Ottawa confident that his mission

had prodded American officials to action. While his optimism exceeded reality, his efforts did pry loose a promise to appoint a commission to negotiate with Sitting Bull. That the commission would delay its activities for months, and then execute its task halfheartedly, was beyond the Canadian's knowledge at that moment.

But the directness of Canadian action in Washington fluttered the Imperial dovecotes in London. Clearly, David Mills' informal mission short-circuited the normal channels of Imperial diplomacy to create a "dangerous precedent." Plunkett showed at once his distress and irritation at the Canadian move. Mills' arrival, he complained to Ottawa, was so unexpected that it embarrassed the legation and violated the "ordinary forms of diplomatic etiquette."

Far more important, the Canadian cabinet had established an unacceptable precedent. The British diplomat, therefore, urged London to remind Ottawa of proper diplomatic procedure. Later it might well prove "most inconvenient" to have the regular course of diplomatic representation interfered with in this summary manner. Moreover, such steps, if they must be taken at all, should be initiated by the governor general or his deputy, and not merely by an "individual of the Cabinet." [23]

Soon official correspondence from London reprimanded Canadian officials for their brashness. On September 6, 1877, Lord Carnarvon protested strongly on behalf of the home government to the governor general that Canadians must recognize the importance of adhering to procedures that have been recognized "as convenient and desirable." Canadian cabinet ministers should remember that "Imperial considerations" are always involved in such matters and they should consult His Majesty's legation in Washington before deciding to confer on "local matters" with American authorities. [24]

A month later, the Canadian cabinet admitted its mistake. Through the Privy Council, the Mackenzie government advised the governor general that "the Government of Canada acquiesce in the views expressed by His Lordship." [25]

But the matter was not so easily disposed of. Canadian politicians were struggling with a problem whose solution could be accommodated within Imperial organization only with undue difficulty. In economic relations with the United States, they had already adopted the device of sending unofficial emissaries to prepare the way for commercial treaties.[26] Now they found the British machinery too cumbersome and too indirect to represent their interests in continental problems, or "local matters" in Lord Carnarvon's unhappy phrase. Some Canadian nationalists also feared that the Imperial diplomats pursued Canada's interests only after those of the United Kingdom had been served.

Nationalism and expediency had prompted an important move. Though immediately repudiated, it comprised, as Plunkett correctly saw, a disturbing precedent. Sitting Bull, concerned only with securing food and protection for his people, unwittingly released forces that were deeply buried in Canada's growth to nationhood.

Two years later, the Macdonald government defended the principles implied by the Mackenzie government's venture in diplomacy. Arguing for a quasi-diplomatic post of high commissioner for Canada in London, Macdonald, Samuel L. Tilley, and Charles Tupper pointed out that "Canada has ceased to occupy the position of an ordinary possession of the Crown . . . Her Central Government is becoming even more responsible than the Imperial Government for the maintenance of international relations towards the United States, a subject which will yearly require greater prudence and care, as the populations of the two countries extend along, and mingle across the vast frontier line three thousand miles in length." [27]

Sir John and his colleagues thus argued that Canada's westward movement into the "vast regions lying between Lake Superior and the Rocky Mountains" had profoundly altered Imperial relations. These influences, similar to those prompted by America's westward movement, accelerated the movement to national self-reliance and diplomatic individuality.

V

Sitting Bull had become a pawn in international politics. Not because the nations sought his alliance, but because they wanted to avoid it. The world watched the amusing spectacle of a diplomatic scalp dance, with the nations' spokesmen outwardly expressing grave concern for the welfare of the Sioux, but inwardly praying that they would somehow vanish from the earth.

To officials in Ottawa, the Sioux medicine man assumed more menacing aspects with each passing month. Dispatches flowed westward, ordering Mounted Police officers to exert every effort to convince Sioux chiefs that the President of the United States and his cabinet were "upright men, willing and anxious to do justice to the Indians." [28]

But with the perversity so common to international politics, many Americans believed that Canadian policy followed an opposite course. Some suspected police officers of seeking personal publicity and glory in their successful handling of Sitting Bull. Others professed to see an elaborate plot by the Hudson's Bay Company to protect its declining power by populating the West with hostile savages. Their furs and robes would enrich company coffers while their numbers would hold the farmers at bay for many years, in this way perpetuating company control despite its political reverses. The Indians, in turn, would become faithful servants of the company, since they would be kept in debt.

Canadian half-breeds further complicated matters. Sitting Bull's promises aggravated their resentment against government policy. Frequent rumors linked their discontent with Sioux power in a grand alliance that alarmed observers. Ominously, the name of Louis Riel, leader of the Manitoba rebellion of 1869, figured conspicuously in these reports.

In Ottawa, Canadian policy turned to a more resolute course. American intransigence annoyed the Mackenzie government. The conversations in Washington convinced Mills that Sitting Bull would become a source of serious contention with the neighboring republic. He immediately wrote Macleod of his fears that American policy would only create further problems in the West.

Unreasonable demands upon the Sioux, he warned the commissioner, might destroy the forthcoming commission's usefulness. In such case, the United States would certainly insist that Canada assume the "ordinary responsibility of one nation to another" by demanding reparations for any crimes committed south of the forty-ninth parallel by Sitting Bull's people.

Canada stood in the position of an injured bystander in the whole affair. American misrule of her Indians, the consistent record of injustice and breaches of faith, the heartless frauds perpetrated by Indian agents, and the trespasses of adventurers upon Indian reserves accounted for the flight of the Sioux into Canada. "We claim no right to interfere with the domestic concerns of the United States," Mills informed Macleod, "but when the misgovernment of any portion of that population is notoriously such as to give rise to civil war on our border, to force a portion of that population upon our territory, and to impose upon us additional expense, we certainly have a right to remonstrate . . ." [29]

These were severe judgments, but politicians in Ottawa were sorely troubled. Unless the United States genuinely sought measures to correct the "abuses of the government of its Indian population," western Canada threatened to become the scene of bloody Indian hostilities. Events over which Canadians had no control menaced every effort in Ottawa to devise a humane and enlightened Indian policy. On top of frustrations in domestic policy, these incidents also threatened to launch the Dominion upon an unchartered sea of diplomatic troubles with its southern neighbor.

To forestall such a crisis and to protect the Canadian government from "unreasonable demands" by Washington, Mills ordered the police to gather "all possible information" regarding American violations of Indian treaties. Another curious byproduct, therefore, of Sitting Bull's sojourn in Canada is the excellent collection of documents dealing with American Indian policy in the Canadian archives.

In Washington, meanwhile, the Hayes administration turned to the task of forming the promised commission to visit Sitting Bull.

13

Border Line Diplomacy

OFFICIALS in Washington fulfilled their promises to Ottawa promptly, but with little enthusiasm. Two days after the conversations with David Mills, the Hayes cabinet approved the project, but only after lengthy debate and with grave misgivings. And three days later, cabinet members still argued over procedures to adopt and disagreed over the personnel to carry out the mission.

Numerous problems immediately appeared. Neither the War Department nor the Interior Department wanted the responsibility of sponsoring the mission. Both protested a lack of funds for such an enterprise, and both denied any obligation for the "peace commission," arguing it should properly rest with the State Department since it was in effect a diplomatic mission.

On August 14, after a two-hour conference, the cabinet worked out a compromise. They appointed Brigadier General Alfred H. Terry, Department of Dakota commander, as head of the commission, while Secretary Schurz agreed to appoint a civilian employee of his department as the second member.

American officials authorized the commission in an atmosphere of frank pessimism. Publicly, as well as privately, they emphasized the fear of armed invasion of American territory by Sitting Bull's Sioux rather than the hope of securing his return. The Washington *National Republican* undoubtedly expressed the true feelings of the administration when it observed, "it would be pleasing to this government if the proposition did not succeed, as Sitting Bull is not a denizen to be desired by any country." [1]

Actually, the Americans possessed so little faith in the commission's prospects that they planned further steps. The Canadian government, cabinet members believed, should either disarm the hostiles and force them to return to the United States or send them "somewhere to the far north, away from the American frontier." Both proposals later figured in negotiations with the British Foreign Office. [2]

Canadians welcomed the news from Washington with high hopes. At once the Mackenzie government sent dispatches to the Mounted Police arranging for the commission's work in western Canada. Officials instructed the police to expect the commission about August 25, an unduly optimistic estimate that indicated both their miscalculation of American intentions and their ignorance of western geography. They ordered the police to cooperate fully with the Americans, mounting a suitable escort, arranging the conference with Sitting Bull, and providing for their welfare while in the Northwest Territories. Officers should make every effort to induce the Sioux to change their minds, but undue pressure must not be applied to the Indians. Persuasion, not compulsion, promised the best results. [3]

Secret instructions, not to be revealed to the American commissioners under any conditions, accompanied these orders to Colonel Macleod. Secretary Mills directed the Mounty commissioner to deliver an ultimatum to the Sioux, threatening to permit the American army to pursue them across the international boundary into Canadian territory should they be guilty of any hostile raids into the United States. This was an important move; one that acknowledged the government's serious view of the Sitting Bull crisis in the West. [4]

These preparations in Canada contrasted markedly with the confusion in Washington. Repeatedly, the British chargé d'affaires called on the State Department, urging action and protesting "the unnecessary procrastination." On each visit, State Department officials assured Plunkett that their government sought every measure to speed the commission on its way, but unavoidable delays intervened. First, General Terry was sick; then General McNeill of St. Louis, the second member of the commission, fell ill and retired from the assignment. With this, the government turned to General Walker of Connecticut, but he refused to serve. Finally, A. G. Lawrence, a Rhode Islander of limited diplomatic experience in South America, agreed to join the commission.

The delays continued. With the commissioners selected, the Americans faced Plunkett with the surprising news that they had no funds for the mission and nothing could be accomplished until the following year. The British diplomat dryly observed that he understood the State Department always possessed funds for diplomatic missions as part of its function. But we do not regard this a diplomatic mission, replied F. W. Seward. In view of the conflicting interests of the United States and Canada, mildly warned the Briton, it was a diplomatic mission, and one of some importance.

In despair, Plunkett finally blamed the impasse on Canadian meddling in diplomatic matters. The American State Department, he pointedly wrote the deputy governor general in Ottawa, had little enthusiasm for a project growing out of "a private arrangement with another department." If the mission had been ordered through the normal channels of Imperial diplomacy, with proper attention to accepted precedents, many of these difficulties would never have appeared.[5]

This charge against the Canadians was ill-founded and unfair. American intransigence grew from entirely different motives. The *National Republican*, with its close cabinet contacts, came closer to the truth when it warned that "If the matter is not arranged very soon, the Canadian government might very properly entertain the opinion that the great parade made over this affair at three different cabinet meetings was but a sham."[6]

At this juncture, Sitting Bull added to the confusion by vanishing. With the elusiveness that so often marked his movements, the medicine man dropped out of sight along the international border. Neither the American army nor the Mounted Police could locate his camp.

At once rumors swept both nations of impending attacks upon American settlements by the Sioux. General Miles warned Washington that the hostiles had crossed the boundary into the United States and mistakenly claimed that war had broken out between the Indians and the Canadian police. In this atmosphere of rumor and uncertainty, the American government found opportunity for further delay. Nothing could be done, Seward informed Plunkett, until the governments learned whether Sitting Bull roamed Canada or the United States.

To this argument, the British diplomat advanced a logical counter proposal. He urged Seward to have "double instructions" issued to General Terry, one set to be used if the Sioux proved to be in Canada, the other to be valid if they turned up in the United States. "The road to be followed was the same in either case for a couple of thousand miles," he assured the American, "and long before it was necessary for General Terry to know whether he was to use the sword or the pen, the telegraph would convey to him all he might learn as to Sitting Bull's position." [7]

Another fear now appeared in American circles. General Terry, as well as his superiors, voiced concern at the prospect of a treacherous attack by Sitting Bull upon an undefended commission. Therefore, they proposed that a powerful escort accompany them into Canada.[8] This suggestion disturbed Canadian officials who saw no evidence of such treachery and believed that a large escort would alarm the Indians.

In early September, the Mounted Police located Sitting Bull on Canadian soil near Wood Mountain. This eliminated the final objections and on September 6, 1877, Secretary of War George W. McCrary and Secretary of Interior Carl Schurz jointly issued instructions to the newly formed commission. While the Canadian government received copies of the orders, they were not disclosed to the public. Amid great newspaper speculation, therefore, the commissioners organized their mission on September 11 in St. Paul.

The instructions ordered General Terry to offer presidential pardon to the former hostiles. He was further authorized to promise them reservations and cattle, but only on the condition that they surrender their firearms and their horses at the international boundary.

The secretaries made it clear to the commissioners, however, that the United States government was no longer responsible for Sitting Bull. He had taken refuge on British soil where he had been rearmed despite the responsibility of the British government, under recognized principles of international law, to protect her neighbor against acts of armed hostility by the refugees. Because of the obvious difficulties in dealing with a savage population, and because the American government wanted to do everything in its power "to prevent any interruption of the relations of good neighborhood," Washington was willing to take this unprecedented step of negotiating with "an Indian chief who occupies the position of a fugitive enemy and criminal." [9]

When the commissioners met in St. Paul, they asked for a modification in their orders. To require the Indians to surrender their horses and to dismount before reaching their reservations would be impracticable. Such a requirement would defeat the purpose of the mission. Secretary McCrary consented to this change and the commissioners departed for Fort Benton via Omaha, Ogden, Helena, and Fort Shaw.

II

These innumerable delays placed the commission in the West at a most unfortunate time. When General Terry and his group reached Montana, Chief Joseph and his Nez Perce were engaged in their heroic march, fated to end at the Bear Paw Mountains only a few miles south of the refugee Sioux. Chief Joseph's successes against General Howard fired Sioux imaginations, while his adroit escape from the Big Hole country after attacks by General Gibbon rekindled the fires of hope in many Sioux hearts. If the two peoples could join forces, perhaps the blue-coated armies could be held at bay indefinitely. White Bird, refugee

Nez Perce who had crossed the boundary to join the Sioux, talked war to Sitting Bull and pleaded for a joint campaign.

But the wily Sioux leader remained aloof. "This is your fight, not mine," he was reported to have told White Bird. "You must not expect that any of my warriors will go across the border to help you." [10]

American commanders pursuing Chief Joseph watched Sitting Bull warily. His intervention in the Nez Perce war would change the entire picture, prolonging the campaign and jeopardizing the army's position in northern Montana. General Miles informed Washington that Chief Joseph delayed surrendering in the hope of assistance from the north. American generals, therefore, exerted every effort to prevent this union. [11]

These events stranded the commissioners in Fort Shaw. Their escort was out chasing Chief Joseph, and Sitting Bull had not yet consented to meet them. Superintendent Walsh's patient diplomacy finally exacted a reluctant agreement to confer with the Americans. But no sooner had Sitting Bull acquiesced than Nez Perce refugees, wounded and stricken, appeared in Sioux camps. It was only with great difficulty that Major Walsh induced the excited Sioux chiefs to travel with him to Fort Walsh for the interview. Even then, they stopped frequently during the trip to smoke and to reconsider their decision. Not until Colonel Macleod joined the party and assured them that they would be protected from the Americans did the chiefs move on to Fort Walsh. There they camped around the post, but the medicine man's tepee stood alone near the north wall of the tiny fort. [12]

News of Sitting Bull's agreement to meet with General Terry reached the commissioners in Fort Benton. On the tenth of October, they headed north on the well-marked trail to Fort Walsh. Newspaper correspondents accompanied them to the conference. These writers sent vivid accounts of the rendezvous at the border and of the events that followed. The New York *Herald*, fresh from its journalistic triumphs with Henry M. Stanley in darkest Africa and Boss Tweed's confessions from darkest New York

City, turned to Sitting Bull to provide the sensational news. Jerome Stillson, the *Herald* reporter, carried out his assignment with great enthusiasm, filling the paper's columns with colorful accounts of scarlet-clad Mounties, copper-tinted savages, and the familiar United States cavalry. Here was a formula that could sell newspapers, and the *Herald* made it work.

When General Terry's cavalcade reached the forty-ninth parallel, the Mounted Police were there to greet them. Colonel Macleod, "clad in his scarlet uniform, at the head of a small but brilliant retinue," crossed the boundary into the United States, dismounted and warmly greeted the Americans.

Soon an escort of Mounted Police lancers advanced across the plains to accompany the commissioners to Fort Walsh. As they approached, wrote Stillson, "their red uniforms and the red and white pennants affixed to their lances contrasted beautifully with the monotonous dun color of the plains around them." [13]

On the following morning, a dispatch from Major Walsh informed the party that Sitting Bull had agreed to meet them inside the fort. With this welcome news, General Terry ordered the commission to move with all possible speed to reach Fort Walsh before the medicine man changed his mind. The party even suffered "dry camps" in their haste to reach the conference.

On October 17, 1877, the commission met Sitting Bull in what the New York *Herald* described as "one of the most extraordinary scenes in the intercourse of white men with American savages." Careful preparations smoothed the way for a full understanding by the Indians of the President's message. Three interpreters, an American, a Canadian, and an Indian representative, met during the morning to discuss the message and to have it fully explained. When the conclave gathered that afternoon, no misunderstandings marred communication between whites and reds.

In the largest room at Fort Walsh the stage was set. Tables for the commission and their newspaper correspondents and buffalo robes for the Indians comprised the room's meager furnishings. But the dramatic scene that followed required few stage properties to give it color. After the Americans and the Mounted Police were seated, the Indians stalked in. With great exaggeration, Stillson informed his readers, "Now for the first time was visible to white men since the beginning of the late Indian wars the most noted Indian of the period." Somehow, the reporter forgot that the Mounted Police officers sitting beside him had been in conversation with the medicine man many times since Custer's defeat at the Little Big Horn. But it was a tense moment for the Americans, and the Indians added to their discomfort by deliberately ignoring the bluecoats, striding across the room to shake hands ostentatiously with the Canadians. This was only the first of several studied insults to humiliate the Americans.

General Terry then read his message to the solemn chiefs. From the outset, it was apparent they had not come to listen to the Great White Father's message. And as they made their short speeches in response, it became obvious that their only purpose was to embarrass the American officers.[14]

"For sixty-four years you have kept me and my people and treated us bad," said Sitting Bull, the first Indian to speak. "I would like to know why you came here . . . This house is a medicine house. You came here to tell us lies, but we don't want to hear them. Don't you say two more words. Go back home where you came from. This country is mine, and I intend to stay here and to raise this country full of grown people."

Then with biting sarcasm, the angry medicine man urged the commissioners to be on their way, but not to worry about their safety since his warriors would not harm them. "Take it easy going back," said Sitting Bull as he again shook hands with the Canadian officers.

Speeches by The-One-Who-Runs-The-Ree, Flying Bird, and the Crow repeated Sitting Bull's rejection of the American offer. But the most dramatic moment of the conference came with the unprecedented speech by a squaw, The-One-Who-Speaks-Once, wife of Chief Man-Who-Scatters-the-Bear. This procedure of allowing a squaw to speak in a council was the greatest indignity the Indians could heap upon the Long Knives. Her message was equally offensive and direct. "I wanted to raise my children over there, but you did not give me time to breed."

Then the Indians arose as if to leave. General Terry, however, addressed one final question to the chiefs. "Shall I say to the President that you refuse the offers made to you?"

"I could tell you more," responded Sitting Bull, "but that is all I have to tell you. If we told you more — why, you would not pay any attention to it. That is all I have to say. This part of the country does not belong to your people. You belong on the other side; this side belongs to us." With this the council broke up.

At once, Colonel Macleod called the chiefs into another council to speak to them privately. He impressed upon them the gravity of the decision they had just made and pointed out that though they claimed to be British Indians, the Canadian government did not regard them as such. It considered them American Indians who had taken temporary refuge in the Queen's country. He warned them that their only hope lay in the buffalo which would soon be gone. They could expect nothing from the government except protection, and that only as long as they behaved themselves. They must not cross the boundary on raids or with hostile intent; if they did, they forfeited the Queen's protection.

They gladly adhered to these conditions, Macleod wrote Terry in his summary of the interview. But Macleod did not reveal to the American the most important phase of these conversations. In compliance with his secret orders, the commissioner told the Sioux that if they crossed the international boundary on raiding parties, "that wall which I spoke to you about the other day will be broken down and the Americans may be permitted to cross the line as well as we can." [15]

At the same time, Macleod carried out another secret order. To build the Canadian case against American criticisms and demands, he now requested the chiefs to formulate their grievances against the American government. But he failed to elicit any specific information. "They always deal in generalities," complained the commissioner to Ottawa. "It is almost impossible to procure from Indians any distinct statement of facts." [16]

Sitting Bull's rejection of the American offer surprised no one. But the commissioners were able to report that he was no longer a threat to the American frontier. He would remain in Canada, they believed, partly because he feared General Miles' troops and partly because he knew that the reopening of hostilities would make him "the enemy of both governments."

General Terry's commission suggested another reason for Sitting Bull's refusal to return. His hatred for the Americans was so great, they wrote, that it gave him pleasure to obstruct American plans. Whether this was true or not, it revealed the atmosphere of suspicion that marked the conference.

The future of Sitting Bull's people, the report predicted, appeared to be similar to that of their fellow Sioux who fled north into Canada during the outbreaks of 1862. In time they would become so attached to their new land that they would regard it a permanent home. This forecast ignored the announced intention of the Canadian government to return the Sioux to their American reservations as soon as possible.

One danger seemed apparent to the commission. Sitting Bull's following came from many Siouan tribes and their presence along the boundary disturbed their fellow tribesmen on the reservations. So long as they roamed as free Indians, they would attract others who would fall under the medicine man's "evil counsel and advice." Thus there might be continued disaffection and limited acts of hostility.

In concluding their report, the commissioners turned to a delicate subject. Canadian authorities, they pointed out, should comply with the rules of international law requiring the internment of insurgent forces driven into neutral territory. It seemed their obligation, therefore, to disarm the Sioux and relocate them in the interior north, far from the troubled boundary.

Montana citizens showed little disappointment that the Terry commission failed. Most, in fact, seemed glad that "the old savage, imbued with the blood of Custer and his companions, decided to remain on British soil." [17] But many also realized that the Sioux were still buffalo Indians, and the buffalo ranged on both sides of the boundary. The Sioux would return, and with them further trouble.

Some newspapers regarded the mission's failure as an indictment of American Indian policy. The New York *Herald*, which had followed Sitting Bull more closely than any other eastern newspaper, viewed it as another failure in Indian relations. This was further proof that until "radical changes" transformed American policy, there could be no peace between the red man and the white. But the *Herald* summed it up to the satisfaction of its western, as well as its eastern, readers with the comment, "We wish the Great Mother joy of her new subjects." [18]

III

Four years of turmoil along the forty-ninth parallel followed the failure of the peace mission in 1877. As westerners had predicted, Sioux braves ignored the boundary in their search for buffalo, playing a game of cat and mouse with American military authorities who could chase them to the boundary, but no farther. Newspapers exaggerated these buffalo hunts into a border war of raids and alarms. At the same time, Sitting Bull's emissaries quietly visited the tribes south of the border, stirring them into restless discontent. Through it all, the three governments continued their diplomatic efforts to solve the Sioux refugee problem.

Sitting Bull, on the other hand, basked in the limelight of international publicity, becoming one of the most famous figures of his age. But to officials responsible for peace along the international boundary, he was the symbol of trouble, both great and small.

Sitting Bull's disdainful refusal of American offers discouraged Canadian officials. But it taught them valuable lessons which they now put to good use. Further negotiations with the Indians, they cautioned the police, must be conducted behind the shield of strictest secrecy. Lurid publicity during the recent negotiations defeated their plans; it must not happen again. Secretary Mills also ordered Macleod to deal with Sitting Bull as if acting on his own responsibility rather than under instructions from Ottawa. The medicine man already thought too highly of himself. He must not learn the gratifying news that three governments debated his future.[19]

Canadian maneuvers to dislodge the Sioux now concentrated on two objectives. They must convince Sitting Bull of the wisdom of returning to his old home and they must persuade the American government to devise a formula to attract him. To achieve the former, Mounted Police officers marshaled every argument to break down the stubborn wills of the embittered chiefs. Their own reserves in the United States promised more security; better soils and climate farther south assured greater comfort; American annuities guaranteed supplies after the buffalo disappeared; and the President's good will and liberality pledged adequate supervision to prevent further fraud or guile. At Ottawa's suggestion, Colonel Macleod even proposed that Sitting Bull visit the Great White Father in Washington accompanied by a Canadian commissioner.

Through British diplomats in the American capital, Canadians worked to convert their opposite numbers to a generous policy toward the refugees. Sir Edward Thornton, now returned to his long-time post as British minister, urged State Department officials to take further steps. He informed Secretary Evarts, moreover, that the Canadian government could no longer "undertake the responsibility of restraining them, should they be turbulent, or attack the United States settlers on the American side of the border."[20] This policy, though born of necessity, irritated American opinion and created considerable ill-feeling against Canadians, particularly in the West.

In London and Ottawa, meanwhile, politicians worried that the American government hoped other tribes would flee into western Canada, thus solving its Indian problem without further cost. Statements by responsible Americans seemed to confirm this idea and Thornton was instructed to warn Washington that the Dominion could not sustain the burden of further Indian refugees in her territories.[21]

On top of these considerable problems, minor irritants embarrassed both governments. While British diplomats argued in Washington that the Sioux were only "refugees seeking temporary asylum," the Ottawa *Free Press* published a report that Colonel Macleod had administered the oath of allegiance to them and had appointed Sitting Bull their head chief.

American newspapers picked up the story immediately. This Mounted Police move promised to solve the American problem, once and for all. Sitting Bull was now a British citizen who could not return to the United States. Embarrassed Canadian officials at once denied the story and privately denounced the correspondent whose "mendacious statement" so damaged their case in Washington.

Another incident imposing additional duties on both governments occurred in November 1877. Since the battle on the Little Big Horn, Americans had vainly sought survivors of the Seventh Cavalry. But when Baptiste Shane, interpreter for the Terry mission returned to the States, he informed a reporter that the long search was over. He had seen and talked to one, a Corporal Martin Ryan of Company C, now a prisoner in the Sioux camp where he had been forced to marry Spotted Eagle's daughter.

Here was melodramatic news that touched American sentiments. A brave hero of the massacre lived, but his fate was worse than death. Newspapers loudly demanded his release and public spokesmen called for governmental action to rescue this hero from the savages. How could army morale be sustained if brave soldiers were abandoned to the savage enemy?

Slowly the machinery of government moved into action. From General Terry's headquarters on the Missouri, the request for Corporal Ryan's release reached the secretary of war in Washington. The War Department then passed the message to the State Department which, in turn, handed a note to Sir Edward Thornton. Sir Edward sent it to Lord Dufferin in Ottawa, who forwarded it to the cabinet for action. Finally, Colonel Macleod, only three hundred miles north of General Terry's headquarters, received the message that had traveled over six thousand miles.

Commissioner Macleod at once launched a thorough investigation. Police inspected Sioux camps and Lieutenant Colonel Irvine searched Spotted Eagle's tepees, but no trace of Corporal Ryan could be found. In fact, the police could discover no daughter, for Spotted Eagle's only child was a fifteen-year-old boy. When all the evidence was in, Mounted Police officers labeled the story a hoax and sent their report on its circuitous route to General Terry. But some romantics, determined to have a survivor, perpetuated the legend.[22]

Tensions along the international boundary mounted during 1878 and 1879. White settlers in Montana regarded Sitting Bull a constant menace, for hunting parties south of the boundary often turned aside to plunder wagon trains, to loot isolated ranches and occasionally to murder unprotected travelers. Indian agents also appealed to Washington for military protection against intrusions upon their reservations.

These raids strained good relations between the two neighbors, in their capitals as well as in the West. Frequent rumors of Sioux invasions kept American nerves on edge, though Mounted Police officers denied that the Indians planned the mass attacks prophesied by frontier newspapers.

Authorities on both sides of the boundary came to recognize these rumors as dangerous exaggerations causing ill-will between the two nations. Many false stories of red invasions from the north were deliberate falsifications by Fort Benton citizens, "interested in the establishment of a military post in the neighborhood of Fort Benton." [23] This was an old game on the frontier and unscrupulous boomers continued to use it until the Indians were finally gone.

Neither Canadian nor American military commanders could afford to ignore the explosive situation along the boundary. In 1878, therefore, the Mounted Police moved their headquarters from Fort Macleod to Fort Walsh, thus transferring their strength into the troubled area.

Similarly, American authorities altered their policy along the so-called "unguarded frontier." During 1878, they sought a Canadian pledge to disarm and intern the Indians should they attempt an invasion of American territory. General Miles publicly urged the Mounted Police to remove the savages from the boundary before April 10, 1878, to avoid a serious clash.

In the following spring, General Miles deployed his forces along the boundary to prevent Sioux parties from crossing into the United States. This assignment, General Terry cautioned Miles, would be "difficult and delicate." He must force the Sioux back into Canada "rather by a display of force than by actual conflict." [24] This Miles succeeded in doing, but much to the distress of Canadian officials, he also cut off the Indians from their supply of buffalo and added to Canada's problem of keeping the hungry Sioux in check. The logical fulfillment of this new policy came with the construction of Fort Assiniboine on the Milk River north of the Bear Paw Mountains. From this northern post, the army policed the boundary and kept the Sioux necromancer in his adopted land.

Many Americans questioned the ability of the Mounted Police to restrain the Sioux. Sitting Bull's powers were now at their zenith and hunger made his followers restless. The Fort Benton *Record* spoke for many when it observed: "the fact remains that the Sioux are no more under the control of the Mounted Police than they are held in check by the civil and military agents of the American government." [25]

American commanders did not share this lack of confidence. When Major Walsh visited General Miles in July 1879 to assure him that the Indians would commit no further depredations south of the border, Miles welcomed this news as a guarantee of peace. "I regarded this as the best results that could have been attained," he wrote General Terry, "and the assurance worthy of confidence." [26]

Dramatic confirmation of this confidence came during the troubled summer of 1879. Sitting Bull, increasingly restive and belligerent as the buffalo disappeared, turned his young men to frequent horse-stealing expeditions against American ranchers. When Major Walsh curtly warned him that these raids must cease, Sitting Bull showed resentment, but accepted the reprimand.

Some time later, however, the medicine man reappeared at the Wood Mountain post, defiant and reinforced by a large following of chiefs and warriors. Without preliminaries, Sitting Bull demanded supplies and provisions from the police for his starving people. To this request Walsh turned a deaf ear, denouncing the medicine man as a nuisance and threatening him with imprisonment if the horse stealing continued. Sitting Bull and his people were American Indians; if they wanted food they must go south to the Long Knives.

This was blunt talk; the kind never before used with the feared Sioux leader. Sitting Bull immediately showed his resentment and warned the policeman that no white man talked that way to Sitting Bull. With this, Walsh lost his temper and loosed a volley of vituperation that stunned the listening Indians. "No man," shouted Sitting Bull, "can treat me like this."

Here was the direct challenge that so many predicted. But when it came, Walsh acted decisively, warning Sitting Bull that no one could bluff or threaten the police. To this, the Indian cried out in anger and reached for the weapon at his belt. Before he could act, however, Walsh seized him by the arm and breech-clout and threw him out the door. To the horror of the watching Indians, the irate Mountie then kicked Sitting Bull as he sought to regain his feet.

For a few minutes, this humiliation seemed fated to touch off a fight. The Indians knew they could kill the handful of policemen facing them, but they also knew that this victory would destroy them by opening the floodgates of American power to the south. General Miles' command only waited for a word from the police to move north and destroy the Sioux, once and for all.[27]

IV

Though not immediately apparent, Sitting Bull's power was now on the wane. Publicly disgraced before his followers, the proud medicine man no longer commanded the respect and loyalty once his due.

Even more important, the Conservative government, newly returned to power under Sir John A. Macdonald, adopted a firmer policy. During the early months of 1879, Macdonald carefully studied the western problems inherited from the retiring Liberals.

Two developments pushed his government into this new policy. In the West, Mounted Police officers increasingly emphasized the dangers inherent in shielding the Sioux refugees. With complete candor, Major Walsh wrote Lieutenant Colonel Irvine that the present policy allowed the Sioux to recruit their strength and replenish their arms and ammunition. This, in turn, could lead Canada "into complications, which she cannot afford, and never should permit."

Growing disillusionment with Sitting Bull also changed their perspective. Though the police at first believed and respected him, now they recognized his craftiness and guile. Moreover, they came to see that Sioux "hatred is not against Americans, but against the white men generally." [28] Irvine passed Walsh's comments on to Ottawa for study.

There the prime minister carefully analyzed these dispatches from the West. His conclusions, outlined in a memorandum to Lord Lorne, now the governor general, recognized the growing risk of collision between Canadian and American Indians over a dwindling food supply. The Sioux, wrote Macdonald, comprised a "marauding element . . . antagonistic to the peace of the country." Food supplies on the plains could not last more than five years at a maximum, and during that time the American government could be led to devise a more lenient policy toward the refugees.[29]

But American impatience upset Macdonald's timetable. From March onward, the American government presented a series of notes to the British minister protesting the Sioux incursions from Canada. On March 27, Evarts informed Thornton that the "gravity of the situation" required immediate precautions to avert a general Indian war. To this warning the British acted promptly. Within a week a telegram from the governor general directed Assistant Commissioner Irvine, acting commander of the police, to order Sitting Bull "to act peaceably towards allies of the Queen" or Canadian protection would be removed.[30]

Later the same month, Secretary of State Evarts again interviewed Thornton to urge firm action by the Canadian government. When Thornton pleaded that the Dominion did not possess sufficient strength in the West to restrain the Sioux, Evarts suggested that the government invite Sitting Bull to Ottawa for a conference where he could easily be arrested and confined. This proposal did not appeal to the British government.

Evarts also complained that the Sioux had not been disarmed or interned despite their hostile intentions toward the United States. In view of this failure, the American government held Her Majesty's government responsible for any mischief the Indians committed south of the border.

Inadvertently, the American secretary had touched a tender spot in British memory, for the historical parallel of American failure to end the arming and training of Fenian troops following the Civil War immediately came to mind. Thornton reminded Evarts that the United States had been duly warned about the Fenians, yet had done nothing to halt their depredations across the boundary. These Fenian raids had carried "death and destruction into Canada," yet the American government had disavowed any responsibility and had refused to compensate those Canadians who suffered loss of property and kin.

But Evarts brushed aside this painful reference with the observation that the Fenian raids were now a matter of history. No question had been raised about compensation during the negotiations framing the Treaty of Washington, the American pointed out, and none would be discussed now. But Evarts' history was as poor as his argument was weak. Compensations for Fenian raids had been an important issue in 1870 and Thornton knew it. Sensing the strength of his position, he referred frequently to the Fenian experience.

Finally, Evarts answered the Fenian argument with a hypothetical situation. The two cases might be similar "if United States troops were to cross the border into Canada." Then, quite obviously, "the Imperial Government would bombard New York, and send troops to Canada for her protection." Why, asked the secretary, should Britain not send troops to the Canadian West to prevent a hostile expedition from being organized against the United States?

During the remainder of this important thirty-minute conversation, the two diplomats turned to other phases of the problem. Thornton made it clear that his government refused to accept the responsibility for a political refugee, driven from the United States by the misrule of American politicians. Evarts, on the other hand, remained cool to any suggestion that the United States should devise a lenient formula for Sitting Bull's return. The American government remained interested only in a scheme to disarm and intern the Sioux on Canadian soil. [31]

Throughout the prolonged negotiations over Sitting Bull, both British and American diplomats showed every disposition to avoid ill-feeling or undue tension. Admittedly, if either sought trouble, Sitting Bull could have offered ample excuse. But Anglo-American relations were heading toward a happier day and tensions along the remote forty-ninth parallel were handled in the larger context of the growing community of interest between the two powers. And when diplomats of either nation, whether by accident or design, failed to demonstrate a conciliatory spirit, Canadians rushed in to smooth ruffled feelings. Geographic position forced Canadians to promote understanding between the two nations.

Though diplomats demonstrated a spirit of moderation, public opinion was not as generous. American newspapers frequently denounced Anglo-Canadian policy in the West, and Canadian editors replied in kind. Congressman J. Floyd King of Louisiana joined the public clamor in April by introducing a resolution in the House of Representatives requesting the President to inform the Congress of the military preparations being made to thwart the anticipated invasion from British America.[32]

As a climax to this growing dissatisfaction with Canadian policy, the American secretary of state handed the British minister a stiff note on May 28, 1879. In it, the American government summarized its grievances against Ottawa and urged immediate steps to remedy them.

Evarts also introduced new themes in the old controversy. For the first time the American government now formally insisted that the Sioux were British Indians. "In the most formal manner possible to their savage state," argued Evarts, they had renounced their rights in the United States and had rejected American terms of security, subsistence, and peace to receive asylum and residence in Canada. Moreover, no act of Her Majesty's government had denied this "rudely asserted right to British protection." The American government, therefore, "conceives that it is bound now to regard the Indians of Sitting Bull's command as British Indians."

In addition, his government now regarded Sitting Bull a "menace to American security." Evarts made it clear that the Sioux constituted a threat to the domestic peace of the western territories. Every effort, therefore, would be made by American military authorities in the West to resist intrusions by the Sioux.

Finally, the American government could no longer tolerate Canada's protection of marauding Indians. We cannot countenance, wrote Evarts, any line of argument "by which these savages may quit and resume allegiance or protection at will" by merely passing from one side of a line traced through a wilderness to the other.[33]

This was such a vigorous statement of American grievances that Thornton accepted it without comment. But in Ottawa, it brought immediate results. With complete secrecy, the prime minister employed half-breed spies to keep the Sioux camps under constant surveillance. Macdonald preferred these dusky agents to policemen since this procedure avoided giving the American government "further excuse" for placing the full responsibility for Sitting Bull's conduct on the Canadian government.[34]

Next, the prime minister sternly rejected Sioux pleas for land and subsistence. In June, he ordered western officials to make it unmistakably clear that the Canadian government could not afford to assist the refugees. Nor could the government encourage them to have any hope of a permanent residence in the Dominion.

In addition, Macdonald directed the new Indian commissioner, Edgar B. Dewdney, to inform Sitting Bull he must make immediate overtures to American authorities. The Sioux were foreign Indians who must return to their homes or starve.[35]

In July, Thornton verbally informed Evarts of the steps taken by the Canadian government. In September, he gave the Americans the formal documents relating to the new "starve or get out" policy. While this did not end the flow of notes from Washington concerning Sitting Bull, it materially reduced their number and sense of urgency.

Another phase of the campaign to persuade Sitting Bull to leave Canada appeared in the form of unofficial missions to the medicine man. One of these came in September 1879 when Father Martin Marty of Grand Forks, Dakota Territory, tried a second time to convince the Sioux to return.

Father Marty believed this second mission would succeed where his previous attempt had failed, chiefly because the Sioux now suffered intense hunger. This was his major weapon, but it had no force against the Indians, who believed there would be buffalo as long as there were Indians.[36]

The priest failed to persuade the Indians, but he passed on two important suggestions to Canadian officials. Ottawa should demand from Washington, he believed, a restoration of the "traditional, tacit understanding" by which Indians followed the buffalo wherever they roamed, ignoring the international boundary. Also, treaty payments due the Sioux for their lands in the United States should be given to their true guardians, the Canadian government, thus enabling them to buy lands, cattle, seed, and equipment to establish the refugees as farmers and ranchers.

The next move in Macdonald's plan to force Sitting Bull out of the Northwest Territories lay in Washington. He hoped through British diplomats to lead the American government to drop its "unconditional surrender" policy announced in 1877. In September, the Canadian cabinet outlined the strategy to be used.

First, the American government should grant the right of chase across the boundary to Indians of both countries. Second, the Americans should halt their practice of burning the grass along the boundary to keep the buffalo south of the forty-ninth parallel. Finally, the Americans must relax their policy of seizing all the Indians' horses and chattels when they surrendered. But when these proposals reached London, Lord Salisbury in the Foreign Office refused to act, arguing that no "advantageous result" could come from approaching the Americans at this time,[37] and the Foreign Office instructed Sir Edward Thornton not to press the matter.

V

Hunger quietly did its work. By July 1880 the exodus began as the once proud Sioux, now broken and poverty stricken, moved south. But not Sitting Bull, for he stubbornly claimed that the sight of an American still made him sick.

Secret delegations continued to seek his ear, but few of them did more than confirm his distrust of American promises. As late as January 1881, J. B. Hubbell wrote Territorial Delegate Martin Maginnis that the medicine man could perhaps be won if a mission could be sent "without the aid of newspaper reporters."[38] Later, Bill Nye commented wryly on Sitting Bull's love of publicity. In a mock farewell address, the western humorist put these words into the Indian's mouth: "I desire also to thank the members of the press throughout the country for the aid and encouragement extended by them all. Whenever I sent a special to any paper, stating that I had once more surrendered, it was greedily paid for and published. By this means I have inaugurated a system of cooperative and attractive surrenders that has been the envy and admiration of the civilized world."[39]

The most promising mission came in October 1880. Then Sitting Bull pledged to the American agent, E. H. Allison, that he would surrender soon, but delayed because his friend, Major Walsh, was in England. Sitting Bull claimed that before his departure in July the policeman had promised to visit the Great White Father in Washington. He could not surrender until the superintendent's advice reached him.[40] American reports of Allison's conversations emphasized Major Walsh's role in Sitting Bull's decision. "Whether on Canadian soil or immediately south of the line, Sitting Bull . . . appears to be under the control or influence of that Canadian official," wrote General Miles.[41]

Dispatches to Ottawa from Superintendent L. N. F. Crozier and Indian Commissioner Dewdney seemed to confirm these judgments. Crozier argued, in fact, that Walsh delayed rather than facilitated Sitting Bull's surrender and expressed the opinion that knowledge of this incident by American officials would be very embarrassing.[42]

Superintendent Walsh vigorously denied these allegations. On the contrary, argued the colorful policeman, through patient negotiation and steady persuasion, he had convinced Sitting Bull of the folly of starving in Canada when food and shelter waited across the boundary. Under his unceasing pressure, Sitting Bull had gradually weakened until by April 1880 he had told those of his followers who wanted to return to do so, and in May the medicine man had finally expressed his willingness to shake hands with the Americans.[43]

Undoubtedly Sitting Bull misunderstood Major Walsh's proposals. But in Ottawa, cabinet officials were disturbed by Walsh's conduct. The policeman had exceeded his orders, and Macdonald scrawled a note to Fred White on Dewdney's dispatch of October 23: "Write Col Irvine or the officer nearest Sitting Bull that Walsh is not to return to Fort Walsh and has no authority to go to Washington."

During the winter of 1880, the police began their last and successful campaign to force Sitting Bull out of Canada. Superintendent Crozier systematically undermined the medicine man's prestige with his fellow Indians by ignoring him in councils, by turning to other headmen for advice, and by consulting with all the Indians on important matters. In this manner, the police broke Sitting Bull's power, reducing him to a wandering mendicant.

In June 1881, Dewdney reported to the prime minister that Sitting Bull was harmless. His followers had returned to their American homes, his family and friends were poverty-stricken, and the surrounding half-breeds and Canadian Indians spoke openly of destroying their old enemy.[44]

This was the end. On July 19, 1881, to the accompaniment of great newspaper publicity, Sitting Bull surrendered at Fort Buford, and a chapter in border line diplomacy was closed. Immediately, everyone who had dealt with the problem claimed credit for the achievement. Mounted Police officers filled their reports with self-congratulation, while United States Army officers hailed another American victory. At Wood Mountain, trader J. L. Legare wrote his friends in Winnipeg that he was responsible for the return of the Sioux. Others would take the credit, "but it belongs to me alone," he wrote. "My influence made them give up the bad opinions they had against the Americans."[45]

Whoever was responsible, officials in both countries welcomed this action of the old medicine man. Attitudes on both sides of the boundary were summarized by the editor of the Fort Benton *Record* when he wrote: "It is to be hoped that we are forever rid of these Sioux, who, since they crossed over to the Canadian soil have behaved themselves well, comparatively speaking; still, they have been a source of endless trouble and anxiety."[46]

But Americans were not rid of the medicine man for another decade. In December 1890 he was shot for resisting arrest for his "ghost dance" activities. Then, and then only, did he disappear from the front pages, though not from troubled memories.

14

Manifest Destiny Looks North

WESTWARD expansion is a basic and persistent theme in North American history. The Canadian and American people looked to the West for their national fulfillment and both claimed a landed heritage before they were nations possessing a sense of unity.

In the republic the fusion of the national spirit and westward expansion expressed itself in that sense of inevitability labeled "manifest destiny." In Canada the achievement of political unity in 1867 and a growing sense of nationhood prompted a similar conviction of western destiny that looked to the annexation of the Hudson's Bay Company territories.

Spread-eagle oratory emphasized the manifest destiny of the United States to control North America from the isthmus of Panama to the Arctic. To ambitious expansionists the limits of American power should coincide with continental boundaries. "The American mind," observed a western editor in 1857, "poured out of the narrow bowl of an Eastern horizon, spreads over the wide expanse of western scenery, like water spilled upon a table — uncontained, indefinite, diffusive." [1] He badly mixed his figures of speech, but his readers understood.

Similar political and cultural institutions north of the Rio Grande seemed to cement the unity suggested by the geographical integrity of the continent. "A geography merely political has little significance," wrote James W. Taylor to the Canadian nationalist Thomas D'Arcy McGee, "especially when close communications by water and rail and a community of language, ideas and interests suggest, and even constrain unity of plan and harmony of action." [2] Where dissimilarity existed, as in the striking case of French-Catholic Quebec, the continentalists ignored it.

Continentalism promised the "room for growth" that expansionists believed essential. This *Lebensraum* concept argued that failure to expand into underdeveloped regions would constitute a serious check upon the "natural" growth of American "democratic" institutions. "We need 'ample room and verge enough' for this majestic development," claimed Minnesota's golden-voiced Ignatius Donnelly. "Nothing less than a continent can suffice as the basis and foundation for that nation in whose destiny is involved the destiny of mankind. Let us build broad and wide those foundations; let them abut only on the everlasting seas." [3]

Expansionists lived in an emotional atmosphere that distorted their political judgments. They greeted every symptom of disaffection in the neighboring provinces as a harbinger of annexation and they viewed every passing disturbance as evidence of a universal demand for entry into the American republic. Self-deluded by their enthusiasms, they easily convinced themselves that Canada was ready to fall into American hands.

A universal conviction of the superiority of American institutions strongly reinforced the argument for the inevitability of political union. This spirit, born of a vigorous and youthful nationalism, exalted republicanism at the expense of the monarchical system north of the boundary.

Faith in the superiority of their institutions led many Americans to conclude that it was part of a national mission to banish undemocratic and aristocratic rule from the continent. In the new world, how could monarchy exist cheek by jowl with freedom? "The Dominion has become an intolerable nuisance," warned an American senator. "With a Royal Scion at its head, with its standing army, with its royal institutions," it was a threat to free government![4]

Economic ambitions also aroused interest in the political fate of the unoccupied plains north of the forty-ninth parallel. America's westward march was essentially an agricultural imperialism seeking new lands for old. This "peaceful penetration" by farmers armed only with "the steam engine, printing press and patent reapers and mowers" promised to conquer the potentially wealthy plains of the Saskatchewan region.[5] Oregon and Texas were constant reminders of the success of this method of acquisition.

Business and commercial leaders joined agriculturalists in looking northwest. American metropolitan centers viewed the Canadian-American plains as a vast hinterland to be developed with American capital. Behind the politicians' bombast was the vision of a commercial empire stretching from the forty-sixth to the sixtieth parallel and reaching from the Great Lakes to the Rockies.

John L. Scripps, editor of the *Daily Democratic Press*, assumed the role of spokesman for Chicago's interest in developing this region. Through his newspaper and on the lecture platform he urged his fellow-citizens to recognize the opportunities that awaited their energies. Chicago, he claimed, stood as the "inevitable gateway" to the Northwest. In the glowing language of the boomer, he predicted that "railroads will, ere long, penetrate the old solitudes. Agriculture, mining and manufactures will supercede the pursuits of the chase . . . Think of manufacturing away up there on Athabasca River, sending down vulcanized fabrics made from bituminous fountains, and competing with the Indian Rubber and gutta percha water-proof clothing of Horace H. Day & Co. of New York!"[6]

The enthusiastic editor believed that American civilization would reach its "noblest triumphs" in the Saskatchewan valley. Economic growth would be matched by freedom's expansion. "The blighting hoof of slavery shall never touch its green sward, but freedom of body and mind shall there have its highest realization . . ."[7]

Before these roseate dreams could be realized certain things must be done. First, the Hudson's Bay Company monopoly in Rupert's Land should be destroyed "in the interests of humanity." This "giant monopoly" must be driven out so that the "whole country could be thrown open to settlement."[8] Peaceful penetration by land-hungry farmers would then solve the political problem, for the region was already "maturing like ripe fruit in autumn to fall into our expectant lap." Even if annexation failed, the newly developed country would contribute to Chicago's economic greatness.

Strategic position gave St. Paul similar dreams of a northwest empire. For many years the Minnesota capital was the center of a keen interest in the Canadian plains and the home of a small but noisy group of annexationists.[9]

Many St. Paulites turned their attention to the development of the Northwest out of fear that the Great American Desert blocked a westward expansion south of the forty-ninth parallel. The editor of the St. Paul *Advertiser* urged his readers to realize that a "practically inexhaustible" agricultural empire lay to the northwest. "None of the states lying west of the Mississippi," he argued, "are backed up by similar resources . . . Iowa looks out upon the *mauvaise terres* of Nebraska; Missouri has Kansas, but western Kansas is a sandy plain, which extends westward to the Rocky Mountains in the first installment of the Great American Desert."[10]

Hopes of exploiting this northwestern hinterland were shattered by a series of events over which the St. Paul empire builders had no control. In 1857 a serious depression paralyzed Minnesota's economy and five years later the Sioux outbreak forced frontiersmen to retreat to the safety of older settlements. From 1861 onward, the Civil War drained the energies of the North Star State, preventing further expansion. Though discouraged by these setbacks, they kept their dreams alive, waiting for better days. These seemed to come when the war's end released dynamic forces of expansion and brought the Radical Republicans to power in Washington.

II

Following the Civil War the American people were in an expansionist mood. Conscious of a military strength that made their nation one of the most powerful in the world, many confidently expected the acquisition of nearby territories. Led by a small but vigorous faction in the Congress, these expansionists dreamed of the revival of the manifest destiny spirit of the forties and fifties. Senator Zachariah Chandler of Michigan, always ready to indulge in verbal heroics, warned the world of American power: "the United States today have more men that have actually been in battle under fire than all the rest of the world put together, more experienced soldiers and more experienced officers." [11] Expansionist orators carefully avoided any estimate of how many of these citizen soldiers would willingly rejoin the army to underwrite their imperial adventures. Wendell Phillips feared that with this new strength the "old farming and reading republic would give place to a strong military, and perhaps predatory state." [12]

This was an era of bad feelings in Anglo-American relations, and nearby Canada bore the brunt of American ill-will. British diplomacy during the war aroused the latent dislike of British power to active hostility. Americans resented Britain's friendliness to the Confederate cause, particularly the construction in English ports of the *Alabama* and other Confederate raiders. They also recalled Confederate raids on Vermont from Canadian soil.

Annexationists used these resentments as weapons in their struggle to win British North America by linking the "*Alabama* claims" to their desire for Canada. "We simply say to Great Britain," announced Senator Chandler, " 'Give us a quit claim deed to this continent and we will forgive you the debt, and nothing short of that.' " [13] Since this claim rested on the preposterous argument that Britain must pay one half of the total expense of the Civil War as an indemnity for the depredations of English-built raiders, it won support from only a handful of Radical Republicans and expansionists.

More convincing to many Americans was the argument that

Britain should cede her North American colonies as a guarantee of peace. "England might be willing to transfer the region west of Canada in settlement of every outstanding question between the two countries," wrote James W. Taylor to Secretary of the Treasury Hugh McCulloch.[14] Napoleon, he argued, had ceded Louisiana to the United States to remove any possibility of Franco-American conflict; perhaps British statesmen would be as wise. Expansionists ignored the fact that the Canadians were not Britain's "to give away," had British statesmen been so foolish.

Much of the agitation in Washington came from the maneuvers of Republican extremists to capture control of their party. Annexation was an emotional issue with which they challenged executive control of foreign affairs; control properly belonged, they believed, with congressional committees. Their fervent appeals to annexationist sentiment before the election of 1866 and their subsequent failure to act following their victory suggest that they used the issue to capture votes by exploiting the anti-British sentiment of the postwar years. Their strategy also won important Irish support.[15]

They played a dangerous game. Foreign policy, when used as a tool by ambitious politicians to advance the cause of party, invites risks that statesmen carefully avoid. Radical Republicans sought power at any price; they endangered Anglo-American relations, frightened their neighbors to the north, and aroused a warlike spirit in all three nations.

For a short time some talked of war with Britain and the fruits of conquest that would follow a glorious victory. But annexationists overplayed their hand when they advocated hastening the union by direct action. Few Americans were in a mood to pay in either blood or treasure for any or all of British North America. A war-weary people were not favorable to another costly conflict. "Comprehensive national policy would seem to sanction the acquisition and incorporation into our Federal Union of the several adjacent continental and insular communities as speedily as it can be done," admitted President Johnson in his last annual message to Congress. But he hastened to point out that this must be accomplished "peaceably, lawfully and without violation of national justice, faith or honor." [16]

Postwar America was too deeply involved in domestic issues to take seriously the many proposals to annex neighboring areas. President Grant's pet scheme to annex the Dominican Republic failed not only through the President's ineptitude, but for want of public support as well. Even more revealing were the stubborn debates over the purchase of Alaska, despite the eagerness of Russia to be rid of it and the modest price required to add it to the American realm. The burdensome problems of Reconstruction, the dynamic industrial expansion of the economy, and the rapid settlement of the plains and mountain states fully absorbed the energies of the American people. Annexation of Canada was only a minor theme in the Gilded Age, but its advocates made up with noise what they lacked in public support.

Two small but energetic factions joined forces to sponsor annexation. In the East, railroad financiers led by Jay Cooke looked to the economic unification of the Canadian and American Wests. Their chief activity was to provide financial support to a western clique centered in St. Paul, but representing the ambitions of Detroit and Chicago as well. Spokesmen for these groups in Washington included Senators Zachariah Chandler and Jacob Howard of Michigan and Alexander Ramsey of Minnesota. Editorial support for their schemes came as a matter of course in the columns of the expansionist New York *Herald* and Chicago *Tribune*. Then too, they could always count on verbal support from the Irish Fenians who welcomed every scheme designed to weaken the British empire.

Behind the scenes James Wickes Taylor organized the forces of annexation and provided the ammunition for their campaign. Taylor, a typical publicist during the Gilded Age, dedicated himself to the mission of securing the Saskatchewan country for American exploitation. With an eloquence born of extensive knowledge of the region, he preached the gospel of manifest destiny. With prophetic insight he foretold the potential greatness of the economic empire that lay sleeping across the boundary. Through Taylor's leadership the two factions joined forces, for he labored as enthusiastically for Jay Cooke as he did for Senator Ramsey.

Taylor first attracted public attention to his schemes with his famous "Plan of Union" in 1866. Employed by Secretary McCulloch as a special agent for the Treasury Department, he prepared an extensive report on commercial relations with British America. To this economic study, he added an unsolicited plan for the annexation of the Canadian provinces.[17]

In elaborate detail Taylor outlined the steps necessary for political union. His program rested on the voluntary cooperation of Canadians, for he made it clear from the outset that this must be a peaceful acquisition. Once provincial governments requested admission, his plan provided machinery through which they could take their places as full-fledged states alongside their older sisters in the American Union.

Taylor's "Plan of Union" was primarily a propaganda document designed to convert Canadians to the values of an American connection. Economic inducements were Taylor's chief lure in this effort to win Canadian support: his scheme called for the assumption of provincial debts, the construction of a navigable St. Lawrence seaway system, and the building of sorely needed internal improvements throughout the provinces — canals, roads, and railways.

West of the 105th meridian, the plan looked to the creation of territorial governments with laws similar to those of the Territory of Montana. It promised an immediate survey of the new territories for settlement, and the putting aside of land for education along the familiar American pattern. Five per cent of the revenues from public land sales was to be devoted to the construction of roads, telegraph lines, and other public improvements. To the Hudson's Bay Company for its title to the land, Taylor recommended the liberal sum of $10,000,000. Obviously, he hoped to make the offer sufficiently attractive to win support in Canada as well as in the United States.

Taylor's scheme received only passing notice throughout the republic. A handful of annexationists loudly praised it and the expansionist press endorsed it, but most congressmen and most newspapers ignored it. Congressman N. P. Banks quickly followed it up by submitting a bill written by Taylor establishing conditions for the admission of the "States of Nova Scotia, New Brunswick, Canada East and Canada West," and for the organization of three territorial governments in the West. General Banks sought to attract Irish votes in his constituency with an anti-British gesture, but Taylor and the annexationists acted in good faith. They saw that the impending confederation of the Canadian provinces would strike a fatal blow to their hopes and they hastened to head it off by offering an attractive alternative.[18]

In December 1867 and again in January 1868 Senator Ramsey introduced resolutions calling for the cession by treaty of British America west of longitude 90°. The people in this region, he argued, preferred union with the republic rather than with the newly organized Dominion.[19] All these efforts met the same fate; they quietly died in committee.

The annexationist junto used every opportunity to keep their cause in the political foreground. The protectionist tariff policy of the postwar administrations presented an opportunity to use an economic weapon against Canada and they seized it eagerly. In 1864 the ten-year reciprocity agreement with Canada expired and protectionist Republicans refused to renew it. Political-minded annexationists joined in defeating any further reciprocity arrangement in the belief that isolation from American markets would force Canada to seek admission into the American system. Their arguments offended Canadians and their policy prompted a closer economic alliance with Britain.

Debates over the purchase of Alaska four years later brought another opportunity to advance their cause. They welcomed the acquisition of the Russian territory as a fulfillment of manifest destiny and as a prelude to the absorption of the British Northwest. The United States, they argued, must possess a "compact" national area; it could not tolerate the separation of its terri-

tories by a wedge of British sovereignty. Moreover, Alaska out-
flanked British possessions and would eventually force their in-
clusion in the American Union.

Congressman William Munger of Ohio professed to see the
acquisition of Alaska as a phase of America's emergence as a
great power and of Britain's decline. "England's star has passed
its zenith," predicted the Ohioan. "Russia will one day, and that
at no distant period, control England's Asiatic possessions. When
that happens, as a natural consequence the United States will
take possession of the Bahamas and all the British West Indies
islands; and Canada will fall into our lap like a ripe apple."

Warming to his global prophecies, the congressman continued.
"Spanish possessions on this continent must be ours; and the two
great Powers on earth will be Russia and the United States." [20]
Ignatius Donnelly hastened to add that American political institutions were uniquely fitted for this imperial destiny, especially
for "that great and most valuable region, Western British America, which may be fairly esteemed the largest and finest region
of agricultural lands now left unsettled on the continent." [21]

American expansionists aroused keen resentment in Canada.
Manifest destiny, caustically commented the Montreal *Gazette*,
is the "divine right of the great Yankee nation to meddle in the
affairs of every other community and to propagate democracy
as Islamism was propagated by the followers of Mahomet." [22]

Ironically, if the annexationists accomplished anything with
their noisy agitation, it was to hasten the political union of the
Canadian provinces and to make certain their absorption of the
Hudson's Bay territories. Confederation destroyed any possibility of annexation; subsequent plans to link British America to
the republic possessed only the shadow and never the substance
of reality.

III

During the sixties Canadians became impatient to create a
transcontinental state. Their westward expansion waited, however, upon the solution of the political unification of Britain's

North American provinces. The legislative union of Quebec and Ontario before 1867 was too weak to achieve this empire building. Confederation freed Canadian statesmen to negotiate with the British government and the Hudson's Bay Company for the annexation of Rupert's Land and the Northwest Territories. At the Quebec conference in 1864, in which the political formula for confederation was designed, the "Fathers of Confederation" made it clear that they anticipated the addition of western territories to the Dominion as a logical sequence to their efforts. When the first Parliament of the new Dominion assembled, many of its members regarded this expansion as the most important question facing them.[23]

Dynamic forces similar to those at work south of the boundary led the Dominion to expand its boundaries. "The dream of the patriot and the speculation of the political philosopher had been of the destiny that should unite these British people in one nationality from one ocean to the other," observed William McDougall to his colleagues in the House of Commons.[24] His speech was only one of many that expressed the burning zeal of the rising national spirit that soon produced the "Canada First" and "National Policy" movements. Its corollary was a demand to round out the continental limits of the new nation.

Westward expansion seemed as much a Divine mandate to Canadians as to Americans, though northern politicians couched their ambitions in less provocative language. "Who cannot see that Providence has entrusted us the building up of a great northern people, fit to cope with our neighbors of the United States, and to advance step by step with them in the march of civilization?" asked George Brown in his influential Toronto *Globe*.[25]

Whether prompted by a spirit of British imperialism or by Canadian nationalism, Canadians were increasingly aware of their "duty" to establish British institutions in the West. A deep conviction of the superiority of British constitutional practices to the republican institutions of their neighbors spurred them to action. Slogans such as "British justice," "British orderliness," and "the Empire" carried the same emotional impact as their counterparts in the American experience. To "save British America for the British Americans" became as potent a drive among Canadians as any Manifest Destiny ambition south of the international boundary.[26]

To the architects of Canadian nationalism, the Dominion could achieve its nationhood only by claiming the West. In 1867, Canadian nationalists foresaw similar opportunities for expansion to those facing the American republic in 1789. "Already it is the second power on this continent and should careful and moderate views animate our statesmen and the struggles of hostile and intemperate factions continue to be a part of the policy of our southern neighbors, rending the various sections asunder, there is no reason that in time it may not be the first of American Powers." [27]

Economic ambitions strengthened these political hopes. Faced with a dwindling supply of good land, Ontario farmers looked eagerly across the barren Pre-Cambrian Shield to the rich lands of the West. Montreal and Toronto bankers, manufacturers, and commercial interests saw in the region an opportunity for profitable expansion. Behind both groups stood Britain's capitalists, eager to invest their money in frontier adventures, though preferably under the security of the Union Jack.[28]

Fear of American imperialism hastened westward expansion. With the cheers of his colleagues in the Legislative Assembly ringing in his ears, Alexander T. Galt challenged Canadians to their "manifest destiny" by demonstrating that their economic expansion and political allegiance could not be dictated by a foreign power. His was but a single voice in a great chorus raised on behalf of Canada's western ambitions.

Others warned that unless they moved quickly to claim their western heritage, Americans would. Many viewed Yankee expansion as a menace to the empire "on which the sun never sets." The United States, cautioned E. W. Watkin after his thirtieth visit to the republic, "become, year by year less English and more Cosmopolitan; less conservative and more socialist; less peaceful and more aggressive." [29]

Postwar annexationist sentiment in the United States forced British officials to consider measures necessary to protect the West against "American encroachment." Several actions seemed imperative. They should make clear that British power protected the West north of the forty-ninth parallel and they should transfer the Hudson's Bay title to the new Canadian government as soon as possible. They must also build a safe line of communications to link Manitoba and the West to the older provinces. The projected "Dawson route" north of the Great Lakes promised to solve the communications problem, at least temporarily until a railway could be built.

Still other officials believed that Britain must look to the defenses of the region in the event of a war prompted by American aggressions. The half-breeds, though a "semibarbarous race," would give a good account of themselves in defending their homes. The defense of the West, however, rested largely upon the Indians, Britain's traditional allies in her frontier wars with the republic. "From their hatred for the Americans," and their devotion to the Hudson's Bay Company, they would undoubtedly be "trustworthy allies." [30]

A series of provocative events brought Anglo-Canadian fears into focus. Widely publicized Fenian preparations to invade British North America kept Canadians in a state of tension following the Civil War. For five years, fears of border raids by lawless bands of Irish-Americans troubled Canadian-American relations and created an atmosphere of international ill-will. The complacency of the American government in allowing the Irish brotherhood to store arms along the boundary and to proclaim openly their military objective of capturing Canada aroused suspicion that the Fenians played a larger game for American annexationists.

At the same time, a proposal by a group of Anglo-American capitalists to purchase Hudson's Bay Company land for agricultural settlement brought immediate protests from Canadian officials. They believed that this would open the way for American farmers who "will utterly disregard the authority of the Company, will endeavor to establish a government and tribunals of their own and as similar bodies have done elsewhere on this continent, assert their political independence." [31]

James W. Taylor's confident prediction in his "Plan of Union" that gold-seekers from Montana would Americanize the Saskatchewan region aroused officials to the need for "speedy action." The Milk River valley seemed particularly vulnerable to this penetration since it was part of the Missouri River drainage and, though north of the forty-ninth parallel, was not included in the grant by Charles II to the company. [32]

After lengthy negotiations, the company agreed to transfer its holdings on December 1, 1869, and most Canadians believed that this would solve their problems in the West. This expectation was shattered by news that the métis of the Red River valley had rebelled against Dominion rule under the leadership of the young half-breed Louis Riel. In the face of this development, the Canadian government refused to accept title until peace could be restored.

IV

For a brief moment, the political destiny of western Canada seemed in question. Led by the messianic Riel, the half-breeds challenged the Dominion's sovereignty over their valley. Sick with fear that their lands were in danger and that their way of life was imperiled by the transfer, they halted the newly appointed lieutenant governor at the boundary and refused to allow him to set up the new government. Instead, a provisional government under Riel ruled the country for eight troubled months.

Ottawa officials were largely responsible for this outbreak. Dominion land surveyors ran their chains to conform to a rectangular survey, thus creating the impression that the new government would destroy the half-breed system of land holding. Métis plots were similar to those along the St. Lawrence — elongated strips of land stretching from narrow waterfronts along the Red River to community pastures. The ten thousand half-breeds in the valley lived a precarious existence, combining a subsistence agriculture with hunting. Their plots were poorly suited to the cereal crop farming of Ontario farmers. Moreover, these carefree, seminomadic people had not bothered to secure legal titles to their modest holdings.

In the background, disgruntled Hudson's Bay Company employees quietly supported the métis. They, too, felt a deep dissatisfaction with the agreement that had transferred the West to the Dominion. They believed the company had betrayed them in its failure to provide for their financial security from the £300,000 it received for Rupert's Land. Their loyalty to the new government was lukewarm at best.

Church officials also viewed the transfer with grave doubts. They feared that the church with its unique position among the métis would suffer irreparable loss of prestige and power. When Quebec had earlier joined the Dominion, the church's position was protected by special legislation, but the Catholic community on the Red River faced absorption into the Dominion without similar guarantees.

A small but extremely vigorous pro-American group in Winnipeg also stirred resentment against the terms of union. Their ambition to maneuver the colony into annexation added to the political confusion created by métis dissatisfaction. Similarly, Fenians gathered about the provisional government to promote their ambitions. "General" William E. B. O'Donaghue, "General" John O'Neil, "Colonel" J. J. Donnelly, and other assorted generals and colonels assembled to use the rebellion to divide the British empire.

In St. Paul the rebellion appeared to be the opportunity for which the annexationists had anxiously waited, and they hastened to take full advantage of the confusion. Through General Oscar Malmros, American consul in Winnipeg, they received information of Red River events and kept in touch with Riel. Soon Malmros dropped all pretense of neutrality and, taking advantage of his quasi-diplomatic status, supported Riel to the limits of his power. To his friends in St. Paul the ardent annexationist appealed for financial support. "I am convinced," he wrote Senator Ramsey, "that $100,000 would make the annexation movement a success." [33] The indiscreet consul overplayed his hand, however, and soon retired in haste from the Canadian community.

Riel's government was besieged by self-seeking groups of many kinds desiring to use the inexperienced leader to promote their own designs. Annexationists and Fenians tried to direct his thoughts toward a pro-American policy, but they failed as he grew wary of their purposes and rejected their counsel.

Meanwhile, the Dominion government acted to repair the damage. Persuasive Donald A. Smith hurried to the valley to smooth over the troubles and Colonel Wolseley marched west with fifteen hundred British regulars and Canadian militiamen to coerce the métis if diplomacy failed.

The Dominion's strategy succeeded and the rebellion collapsed. Riel fled to the United States for refuge and the Manitoba Act of 1870 formed a new province with safeguards for the métis community and their church. [34]

Minnesota annexationists made numerous blunders in their campaign to win the Canadian West. Their policies rested on a basic miscalculation. They believed that the new Canadian federation would collapse along regional lines of economic and political interest. In this, they repeated the mistake made by foreign observers about the infant American republic in 1789. Both North American governments possessed sufficient vitality and statesmanship to weather the storms of their first years.

They also counted on strong support from the railway builders of the Northwest. Through James W. Taylor they were in close communication with Jay Cooke of the Northern Pacific and with George L. Becker of the St. Paul and Pacific, but the railway magnates viewed annexation as a politically dangerous scheme not worth the risks. "My own judgment," Becker wrote Taylor, "is that settlement and development of that region is far more likely to be encouraged and promoted through the Canadian officials, than by a successful rebellion of half-breeds." [35]

Northern Pacific officials shared these views. When "General" O'Donaghue's Fenians attempted a filibustering expedition across the boundary from Pembina in 1871, President A. B. Nettleton expressed pleasure that it had failed. "We are much gratified," he wrote Taylor, "at the prompt extinguishment of this new Fenian nuisance, and congratulate you on the prompt measure adopted by yourself to prevent a fresh cause of complaint on the part of our friends across the border." [36]

The enthusiasm of Minnesota's politicians for political annexation was not shared by eastern capitalists. The railway builders believed that commercial dominion could be achieved without the risks of political intervention and they failed to support their western friends at the decisive moment.

Annexationists exaggerated the hostility of Manitoba church officials toward the union with Canada. They believed that the church and the Canadian government would not be able to find a compromise formula. Actually, the Catholic hierarchy probably feared the influx of American settlers in the event of annexation as much as they feared control from Protestant Ontario. The American system tolerated no legal privileges in religion, education, and language comparable to those enjoyed in Quebec or written into the Manitoba Act.

They also underestimated the ability of the Canadian government to work out the necessary political compromises to satisfy the métis. Politically astute Sir John A. Macdonald outmaneuvered them at every turn, accomplishing through diplomacy what they believed impossible.

The most serious threat to Canadian development of the western plains was the economic penetration from American centers. Political annexation was never a real possibility after 1867, for British America was no Mexico, weak and defenseless. It was part of a great world empire and the verbal heroics of the annexationists must be measured against the reality of British power.

James W. Taylor proposed economic absorption through a northern railway system. His bold scheme sought to link the Saskatchewan country to St. Paul with an international railway from Montreal to the Pacific Coast via the Minnesota capital. His hopes were summed up in the prediction: "the Saskatchewan will be brought within our limits and within the grasp of our system of communications." [37]

Taylor's plans for a Pacific railway along the boundary attracted international support. Financiers and politicians in both countries expressed interest in his project. Lieutenant Governor Adams G. Archibald of Manitoba, anxious to secure railroads for his new province, supported Taylor's program with the argument that such a railroad "passing several times from the territory of one nation to that of the other would . . . do much to connect the two countries commercially and develop . . . a strong feeling to promote a healthy commercial intercourse between the two countries." [38]

Economic nationalism defeated these plans for an international railroad. With extensive government support Jay Cooke pushed his Northern Pacific across the plains hoping to seize the commerce of both the Canadian and American Wests. Since few men expected that more than one transcontinental railroad would be built north of the fortieth parallel, Northern Pacific builders played for international stakes. "The Government which first inaugurates this enterprise with such resources as to exclude a rival work, commands the trade, the colonization, the destiny of the Northwest — a vast interior of this continent from latitude 44 to 54," reported a special committee of the Congress on the Northern Pacific railroad.[39] Moreover, since the authoritative British explorer Captain John Palliser had already pronounced the Canadian West incapable of supporting a railroad through its vast deserts, American planners viewed their railroad as the "central agency in utilizing the empire of the North-West." [40]

Taylor became Jay Cooke's willing ally in the plans to create an economic dominion. With untiring energy and skill he served his Philadelphia masters. To President Nettleton he confessed that he accepted the Winnipeg consulate in 1870 to forward Northern Pacific ambitions. For several years, railway officials paid the consul to serve their ends, particularly to use his great influence with the lieutenant governor and with the Manitoba legislative assembly. Taylor wrote optimistically to his Northern Pacific friends, "My relations to Gov. Archibald are very satisfactory. I shall be consulted with regard to the Railroad system of Northwest British America and I am sanguine that it may be adjusted on an international basis, entirely in accord with the interests of the Northern Pacific." [41]

Canadian capitalists and politicians quickly sensed the dangers in Jay Cooke's railroad schemes. Economic penetration, not military or political action, was their greatest fear and a single railway system controlled by American capital would undo their political victory in the West. "A common danger threatens British and Spanish Possessions in America," Sir Alexander T. Galt warned Prime Minister Macdonald, "through the preponderance of the United States. The danger is not one of violence, as the people of the United States are not favorable to such a course. It consists in the establishment of such a state of commercial dependance upon them, as will centre there all the national interests of the adjoining countries and then gradually draw them into the Union." [42]

V

No region along the Canadian-American boundary illustrated this danger more forcibly than the Whoop-Up country. Fort Benton's enterprising capitalists dominated the economic life of the region, integrating it so completely that the boundary for many years was only a line on a map. Though established as the boundary by an Anglo-American convention in 1818, the forty-ninth parallel remained unmarked until 1874. For another decade it was hardly more than a row of stone markers across the plains. Not until the Canadian Pacific Railway entered the region in 1883 did the boundary line really indicate a division in the economic and cultural life of the Whoop-Up country.

Canadians deplored the economic domination of their plains by the I. G. Baker and T. C. Power firms whose extensive enterprises north of the boundary confirmed the view that Canadian resources were "merely aiding to build up the town of Benton." [43] Behind these resentments, shrewdly observed the Fort Benton *River Press*, lay the greater fear that through the energy and ability of Benton's entrepreneurs, lasting economic ties were being forged to St. Louis and Chicago rather than to the St. Lawrence system centered at Montreal.[44]

Some observers hoped that the Saskatchewan River could be used as a "natural outlet" for the Whoop-Up country. Professor Macoun believed that the navigation of the South Saskatchewan would free the western plains from Benton's economic control. "When its navigation is an accomplished fact," he predicted, "all supplies for the police and Indians can be taken within less than thirty miles of Fort Walsh at Cypress Hills and those for Fort Macleod, landed at the Forks of the Bow and Belly Rivers within two short days' journey of the Fort." [45] But when steamboats were launched on the South Saskatchewan, the experiment failed; only a railroad could break Fort Benton's grip.

To many Canadians this economic regionalism in the Whoop-Up country seemed a forerunner of political assimilation. There is little evidence, in public or private records, that any Montana group other than the Fenians actively supported annexationist views. Nothing comparable to St. Paul's ambitious junto developed in Fort Benton despite the similar roles of the two cities in the economic growth of the Canadian communities to their north.

Montana newspapers generally ignored annexation. Fort Benton's editors opposed it, though they were spokesmen for the city which appeared most likely to gain by the political absorption of the Canadian West. The Fort Benton *Record*, though edited by a nephew of James W. Taylor, argued that Canadians were loyal to Britain and that there was "no great enthusiasm" for it in the United States. The huge debt of the new Dominion was too heavy a burden to impose upon American taxpayers and the bitter religious bigotries and social tensions between Protestant Ontario and Catholic Quebec were undesirable additions to American life. If annexation were ever to have a serious hearing in the United States, it would have to be sponsored by Canadians, not by ambitious American politicians.[46]

Undoubtedly there were those in the region who favored annexation, but few argued publicly for it or raised a hand to promote it. When Louis Riel rode out of Fort Benton for Saskatchewan to lead the unhappy métis people in their last bid for freedom in 1885, Colonel J. J. Donnelly poured Fenian encouragement in his ear. But no American support developed to assist the métis leader in the Saskatchewan Rebellion as had followed him north from St. Paul fifteen years earlier.

The idea of annexing Canada to the American republic lingered as a will-o'-the-wisp, attracting attention through succeeding years. When thousands of American farmers streamed across the boundary at the turn of the century to take out Alberta or Saskatchewan homesteads, some observers briefly revived the old dream of the "Americanization" of western Canada. Again, some Canadians feared it as the "peaceful penetration" they had so often predicted. As late as 1903 a leading American journal referred to the movement as a prelude to annexation and observed that "it has long seemed the part of a manifest destiny that this union should come." [47]

Canadian determination to destroy the north-south economic axis symbolized by the Whoop-Up Trail led to the building of the Canadian Pacific Railway. With eastern Canada aroused to the political and economic stakes, the infant Dominion undertook this tremendous project. Against fearful odds, financial as well as geographical, Canadian nationalism drove the steel across the plains to supplant the vital ties that bound the Whoop-Up country to Fort Benton. With this achievement, Canada's "manifest destiny" to develop the northwestern plains prevailed.

15

The Parting of the Ways

WHEN the Canadian Pacific Railway reached Medicine Hat in 1883, the close ties between the American and Canadian areas were broken. Montreal's system of communications prevailed north of the forty-ninth parallel, while Chicago, St. Paul, and Fort Benton were virtually eliminated from the Canadian trade. Winnipeg emerged as the new sub-metropolis, the focus of western expansion north of the boundary.

The regional divorce was as nearly complete as modern nationalism can devise and the surveyor's line across the plains took on the reality of an international boundary. Identification with the larger national communities was achieved as much through the routine functioning of government — registry of property transactions, incorporation of business enterprises, marriages, and taxes — as through any dramatic nationalistic indoctrination.

In a surprisingly short time, settlers on both sides lost the sense of regional unity so pronounced during the preceding quarter-century. They remained good neighbors, but their economic and social contacts were increasingly casual.

To be sure, the two peoples continued to follow parallel courses in their development. These parallels were often so close that eastern Canadians continued to fear the "Americanization" of their West. But these were born of similar geographic, climatic, cultural, and economic environments, not of conscious imitation or adaptation.[1]

313

Both communities became marginal agricultural regions, prospering when it rained, suffering during periods of drought. Both remained debtor economies, relying upon the largess of outside metropolitan centers and resentful of their colonial dependence. Both confidently expected an immediate rush of settlement by farmers whose 160-acre homesteads would create economic stability as well as prosperity. Both waited another twenty years before this wave of farmers came, and then the prosperity they brought lasted only a few years.

These experiences were within the framework of a national life; few thought of themselves as fellow-plainsmen, sharing common problems and seeking similar solutions. The sense of "area-kinship" that spanned the unmarked boundary during the Whoop-Up era was gone.

Railways destroyed the commercial empires built around the Missouri River traffic and reduced Fort Benton and Fort Macleod to merchandising centers serving limited agricultural communities. Regional leadership in the "High Line" country of Montana passed to Great Falls, while in "Sunny Southern Alberta" it moved to Calgary.

Fort Benton's wealthy merchants resisted these changes as long as possible. As we have seen, they planned railroads to link their river town to Montana's population centers, but steamboating was now an economic anachronism and the transcontinental railway systems refused to build spur lines to the declining town.

For a brief moment, Benton's merchants continued their prosperity by shipping cargoes on the Canadian Pacific Railway. During 1883 and 1884, numerous bonded shipments passed to northern Montana via Winnipeg, Maple Creek, and Medicine Hat. Ironically, the builders of the Canadian Pacific briefly seized the economic hegemony on the northern plains that St. Paul railway planners coveted.

This was only a temporary reprieve. The foundations of Benton's economic life were gone, and the little town slowly withered away. With the Northern Pacific and Union Pacific railways serving the centers of Montana's growth and with the Canadian Pacific carrying the commerce north of the boundary, the town's markets were limited to the immediate area. As the Helena *Independent* pointed out, "Benton will lose its prestige and will rely for its life on the Teton, Highwood and limited surroundings." By 1885, this prophecy was fulfilled and Fort Benton was "quiet, and at least for the present, is doomed to a lull from her former growth." [2]

This lull lasted for nearly two decades. American agriculture was in the grip of one of its longest depressions and farmers retreated from the plains during the eighties and nineties. Rising prices after 1896 encouraged agricultural expansion and higher land values in the Middle West stimulated thousands of farmers to turn to the Northwest for "fat black land, cheap or even free." The completion of the Great Northern Railway through the "High Line" country opened the way for the granger invasion.

Across the boundary, a similar delay in settlement keenly disappointed Canadians. The acquisition of Rupert's Land and the building of the transcontinental railway opened the plains for Canadian enterprise. The government prepared the West for settlement by creating stable political institutions. But mass homesteading waited for nearly twenty years.

Several forces explain the slow development of the plains country. The depression that paralyzed American agriculture also affected Canadian farming. Then too, the Saskatchewan Rebellion of 1886 frightened away many land-seekers and discouraged western investors. The Great American Desert seemed to others to prevent successful farming along the Canadian Pacific route since the railway chose the shorter southern way to the mountains through the heart of Palliser's famous Triangle.

Dominion land policy excited considerable resentment. With nearly one half of the western lands reserved for the Hudson's Bay Company, for the Canadian Pacific railway, and for education, free land seemed difficult to claim. "We who are south of the Canadian Pacific railway have been handed over to the tender mercies of that company," complained the Fort Macleod

Gazette.[3] Land policy was less liberal than in the United States and as long as cheap land remained south of the boundary, fear of frost and drought continued to turn westward-moving farmers to more congenial lands.

Led by Mormons from Utah, a sprinkling of farmers moved into southern Alberta during the eighties. But they were only a vanguard for the thousands who invaded the subhumid plains at the turn of the century.

Their experiences, however, are not part of this story. By the time they arrived, the Whoop-Up Trail was gone. But the spirit of friendship it symbolized remained a living heritage in a frontier neighbor-ground where peace parks, not military garrisons, guard the international boundary that divides them.

Notes and Index

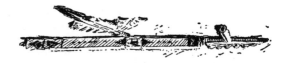

NOTES

Chapter 1

[1] Fort Macleod *Gazette*, July 1, 1882.
[2] Canada, *Sessional Papers*, No. 23, Pt. III, 1883, p. 22. See also Gerald L. Berry, *The Whoop-Up Trail: Early Days in Alberta-Montana* (Edmonton, 1953) and Charles M. MacInnes, *In the Shadow of the Rockies* (London, 1930).
[3] H. V. A. Ferguson, "Fort Benton Memories," manuscript in Historical Society of Montana Library, Helena.
[4] Fort Benton *Record*, February 1, 1875.
[5] *Ibid.*, December 12, 1879.
[6] Fort Macleod *Gazette*, November 14, 1882.

Chapter 2

[1] Oliver E. Baker, "Agricultural Regions of North America," *Economic Geography* (Worchester, Mass.), VII (October 1931), 336; J. Sullivan Gibson, "Agriculture of the Southern High Plains," *Economic Geography*, VIII (July 1932), 249; George A. Rogler and Leon C. Hurtt, "Where Elbowroom Is Ample," in United States Department of Agriculture, *Grass: The Yearbook of Agriculture, 1948* (Washington, D.C., 1948), 477.
[2] John Macoun, *Manitoba and the Great North-West: The Field for Investment, The Home of the Emigrant, Being a Full and Complete History of the Country* (Guelph, Ontario, 1882), 153.
[3] William F. Butler, *The Great Lone Land: A Narrative of Travel and Adventure in the North-West of America* (London, 1873), 199.
[4] Reuben Gold Thwaites (editor), *Original Journals of the Lewis and Clark Expedition, 1804–1806* (New York, 1904–5), V, 205.
[5] Joseph B. Tyrrell (editor), *David Thompson's Narrative of His Explorations in Western America, 1784–1812* (Toronto, Champlain Society, 1916), 189.
[6] United States Department of Interior, Geological Survey, *Fort Benton Folio*; A.G.O. records, National Archives, Annual Report, Chief Engineer, Department of Dakota, to A.A.G., September 24, 1880; Jesse Perry Rowe and Roy Arthur Wilson, *Geology and Economic Deposits of a Portion of Eastern Montana*, University of Montana, Series No. 1 (Missoula, 1916); Gerald L. Berry, *Whoop-Up Trail: Early Days in Alberta-Montana* (Edmonton, Alberta, 1953). Throughout this study I have used the American term "plains" rather than the

confusing and imprecise Canadian expression "prairies." Professor Henry Youle Hind regretted the universal acceptance in Canada of the word "prairie" to describe a region in which short grasses rather than long-stemmed grasses were the climax vegetation. "The plains and prairies of America," he wrote in 1860, "occupy regions differing widely from one another in physical characteristics. The phraseology of the half-breeds tends to mislead a traveler not familiar with the precise application of the words they use . . ." (*Narrative of the Canadian Red River Exploring Expedition of 1857 and of the Assiniboine and Saskatchewan Exploring Expedition of 1858* (London, 1860) I, 348.)

[7] Thwaites, *Journals of Lewis and Clark*, II, 100–1.

[8] A.G.O. records, National Archives, Chief Engineer, Department of Dakota, to A.A.G., September 24, 1880.

[9] United States Senate Document No. 78, 33rd Congress, 2nd Session, *Reports of Explorations and Surveys to Ascertain the Most Practicable and Economical Route for a Railroad from the Mississippi to the Pacific Ocean, 1853–1856* (Washington, D.C., 1857).

[10] John Palliser, *et al. Journals, Detailed Reports and Observations relative to Captain Palliser's Exploration of a Portion of British North America during the Years 1857, 1858, 1859, and 1860* (London, 1863), 7, 139–45.

[11] Alexander J. Russell, *The Red River Colony, Hudson's Bay and Northwest Territories, Considered in Relation to Canada* (Montreal, 1870), 66. See also George M. Grant, *Ocean to Ocean, Sanford Fleming's Expedition through Canada in 1872* (Toronto, 1872), 201–2.

[12] Hind, *Narrative*, II, 356.

[13] James C. Malin, "Soil, Animal and Plant Relations of the Grassland, Historically Reconsidered," *Scientific Monthly*, LXXVI (April 1953), 210. Professor Malin's voluminous writings on the Great Plains have suggested many interpretations to which I am deeply indebted throughout this study.

[14] Thwaites, *Journals of Lewis and Clark*, II, 131.

[15] A.G.O. records, National Archives, Annual Report, Chief Engineer, Department of Dakota, to A.A.G., September 24, 1880.

[16] William A. Bell, *New Tracks in North America* (London, 1870), 23.

[17] Thwaites, *Journals of Lewis and Clark*, II, 188–200.

[18] James Carnegie Southesk, *Saskatchewan and the Rocky Mountains: A Diary and Narrative of Travel in 1859 and 1860* (Edinburgh, 1860), 183.

[19] Hind, *Narrative*, II, 382.

[20] Donald C. Peattie, *Natural History of Western Trees* (New York, 1953), xii.

[21] Macoun, *Manitoba and the Great North-West*, 244.

[22] Seller G. Archer and Clarence E. Bunch, *The American Grass Book* (Norman, Oklahoma, 1953), 207, 276ff; H. E. Morris, W. E. Booth, G. F. Payne, and R. E. Stitt, *Important Grasses on Montana Ranges*, Montana State College, Agricultural Experiment Station, Bulletin 470 (Bozeman, Montana).

[23] Southesk, *Saskatchewan and the Rocky Mountains*, 109.

[24] Thwaites, *Journals of Lewis and Clark*, V, 208.

[25] Bell, *New Tracks in North America*, 38.

[26] Frank Gilbert Roe, *The North American Buffalo: A Critical Study of the Species in Its Wild State* (Toronto, 1951). This excellent study replaces William T. Hornaday's *Extermination of the American Bison* and Joel Allen's *The American Bisons: Living and Extinct*. Though Mr. Roe is at times unduly harsh with previous writers on this subject, his exhaustive treatment of the buffalo is indispensable to an understanding of the physical environment of the plains.

NOTES

[27] John C. Ewers, *The Story of the Blackfeet*, United States Indian Service, Indian Life and Customs Pamphlet No. 6 (Lawrence, Kansas, 1944).

[28] Tyrrell, *David Thompson's Narrative*, 348.

[29] Walter McClintock, *Old North Trail: or Life, Legends and Religion of the Blackfeet Indians* (London, 1910), 434–37.

[30] John McDougall, *Saddle, Sled and Snowshoe* (Toronto, 1896), 261.

[31] Tyrrell, *David Thompson's Narrative*, 364.

[32] Palliser, *Journals*, 199.

[33] Butler, *Great Lone Land*, 242.

[34] Hartley B. Alexander, *The World's Rim: Great Mysteries of the North American Indians* (Lincoln, Nebraska, 1953), 8–9.

[35] Tyrrell, *David Thompson's Narrative*, 334.

[36] *Ibid.*, 328–31; Arthur S. Morton, *Under Western Skies* (Toronto, 1937).

[37] Tyrrell, *David Thompson's Narrative*, 336.

[38] L. V. Kelly, *The Rangemen* (Toronto, 1913), 85; Berry, *Whoop-Up Trail*.

[39] Tyrrell, *David Thompson's Narrative*, 345.

[40] A. P. Nasatir, "Formation of the Missouri Company," *Missouri Historical Review*, XXV (October 1930), 18; Nasatir, *Before Lewis and Clark: Documents Illustrating the History of the Missouri, 1785–1804* (St. Louis, 1952), II, 392–93.

[41] Thwaites, *Journals of Lewis and Clark*, II, 131.

[42] Palliser, *Journals*, 135–40.

Chapter 3

[1] William F. Butler, *The Great Lone Land: A Narrative of Travel and Adventure in the North-West of America* (London, 1873), 281.

[2] W. S. Gladestone to Katherine Hughes, August 11, 1910, in Gladestone File, Alberta Provincial Library.

[3] James C. Southesk, *Saskatchewan and the Rocky Mountains: A Diary and Narrative of Travel in 1859 and 1860* (Edinburgh, 1875), 327.

[4] John Palliser, *Journals* (London, 1863), 117.

[5] Robert E. Fisk to Elizabeth Chester Fisk, October 20, 1866, in Fisk Papers, Historical Society of Montana Library.

[6] Horace Greeley, "The Plains: As I Crossed Them Ten Years Ago," *Harper's Magazine*, XXXVIII, No. 228 (May 1869), 789–95.

[7] Helena *Daily Herald*, June 15, 1870.

[8] Butler, *Great Lone Land*, 212–13.

[9] See Chapter 10 for a more complete study of the I. G. Baker and T. C. Power companies.

[10] Alexander Staveley Hill, *From Home to Home: Autumn Wanderings in the Northwest in the Years 1881, 1882, 1883, 1884* (London, 1885), 215.

[11] John Jerome Healy, "Frontier Sketches," *Fort Benton Record*, November 15, 1878.

[12] Cecil Denny, *Riders of the Plains: A Reminiscence of the Early and Exciting Days in the Northwest* (Calgary, 1905), 54.

[13] Wyndam-Quin (Earl of Dunraven), "Wapiti Running," *Nineteenth Century*, October 1880, 596.

[14] Al. Noyes, "Story as Told by S. C. Ashby," manuscript in Historical Society of Montana Library.

[15] Charles M. MacInnes, *In the Shadow of the Rockies* (London, 1930); Joseph K. Howard, *Strange Empire* (New York, 1952), 263.

[16] Denny, *Riders of the Plains*, 8–9.

¹⁷ Who was in the party is impossible to determine. Joseph Kipp, John Wren, Fred Wachter, Howell Harris, and others claimed to be builders of Standoff. Accounts of this and other incidents are related in MacInnes, *In the Shadow of the Rockies*; John P. Turner, *North-West Mounted Police*; Denny, *Riders of the Plains*; Berry, *Whoop-Up Trail*. Most reliable studies thus far are the articles of the able local historian Hugh A. Dempsey. See, for example, his "Amazing Death of Calf Shirt," *Montana Magazine of History*, III, No. 1 (January 1953), 65–73; and "Howell Harris and the Whisky Trade," *Montana Magazine of History*, III, No. 2 (Spring 1953), 1–8.

¹⁸ James W. Schultz, "An Appreciation of a Friend," manuscript in Historical Society of Montana Library.

¹⁹ Pincher Creek *Echo*, March 31, 1910.

²⁰ John Jerome Healy, as told to E. T. Adney, manuscript in Historical Society of Montana Library.

²¹ Quoted in John Macoun, *Manitoba and the Great North-West* (Guelph, Ontario, 1882), 570.

²² Hill, *From Home to Home*, 160.

²³ *Spitzee* is a corruption of the Blackfoot word *ipitsi*, meaning high. Spitzee or High River was the center of their activities.

²⁴ This account is based on Healy's letter in E. T. Adney's "The Spitzee Cavalry," manuscript in Historical Society of Montana Library.

²⁵ George Shepherd, "North of the Border — Up Canada Way," Fort Benton *River Press*, Centennial Edition, 1946.

²⁶ Public Archives of Canada, Department of Interior, Dominion Lands Branch, File 14, Edward McKay to Lieutenant Governor Alexander Morris, May 21, 1873, and Memorandum, A. Campbell to Privy Council, June 14, 1873.

Chapter 4

¹ This is the only phase of the entire incident above dispute. Major sources for this aspect of the story are the eyewitness accounts of the participants, including John C. Duval, "Cypress Hills Massacre, A True Account," Helena *Independent*, November 18, 1886; Donald Graham's account as reprinted in Hugh Dempsey, "Cypress Hills Massacre," *Montana Magazine of History*, III, No. 4 (Autumn 1953), 1–9; testimony in the extradition trial in Helena *Weekly Herald*, July 8, 1875; and testimony in the Winnipeg trial, Winnipeg *Standard*, June 24, 1876, and Winnipeg *Free Press*, June 24, 1876; a "true account" in the Fort Benton *Record*, June 26, 1875; and the first newspaper account of the fight in the Helena *Daily Herald*, June 11, 1873.

² P. M. Abel, "The Cypress Hills Massacre," *Country Guide* (Winnipeg), May 1951.

³ Fort Benton *Record*, June 26, 1875; Bozeman *Times*, July 6, 1875.

⁴ John Peter Turner, *The North-West Mounted Police, 1873–1893* (Ottawa, 1950), I, 79.

⁵ Farwell's testimony is found in several scattered sources. The chief source used throughout this account is in Consular Dispatch 219, James Wickes Taylor to J. L. Cadwalader, September 22, 1875, General Records of the State Department, National Archives. Other accounts are in the Helena *Weekly Herald*, July 8, 15, 22, 1875; Winnipeg *Standard*, June 24, 1876; Winnipeg *Free Press*, June 26, 1876.

⁶ Fort Benton *Record*, June 26, 1875.

⁷ Consular Dispatch 219, Taylor to Cadwalader, September 22, 1875.

NOTES

[8] *Ibid.*

[9] Winnipeg *Standard*, June 24, 1876.

[10] Farwell's reputation as a whisky trader was widely known in Fort Benton. The evidence of Baptiste Champagne is particularly damaging to his case. (Consular Dispatch 219.)

[11] Duval, "Cypress Hills Massacre."

[12] Contemporary estimates of the number of Indians slain in the fight range from fifteen to thirty-six. Later estimates reaching two hundred are greatly exaggerated.

[13] Dempsey, "Cypress Hills Massacre," 9.

[14] Winnipeg *Standard*, June 24, 1876.

[15] Winnipeg *Free Press*, June 24, 1876.

[16] *Ibid.*

[17] Royal Canadian Mounted Police, File 516-4, Statement of John Wells, May 26, 1874.

[18] R.C.M.P., File 516-4, Edward McKay to William Urquhart, August 24, 1873; Statement of Narcisse Lacerte, September 18, 1873. This testimony, based on hearsay evidence from a half-breed witness, Baptiste Morin, is probably the origin of the "massacre" version. "These Americans at first gave the Indians drink, and having made them drunk, murdered them in cold blood, firing on them with rifles and other firearms."

[19] General Records of the State Department, National Archives, Hamilton Fish to Sir Edward Thornton, August 15, 1873.

[20] Turner, *North-West Mounted Police*, I, 84–85, 101–2, 217–34.

[21] For a vigorous statement of this argument see the letter to the editor from Jack Blount, Fort Benton *Record*, May 15, 1875.

[22] Bozeman *Times*, July 6, 1875.

[23] Fort Benton *Record*, June 26, 1875, December 21, 1877.

[24] Helena *Weekly Herald*, July 29, 1875.

[25] Quoted in Turner, *North-West Mounted Police*, I, 35. See also James T. Stanford's eyewitness account in *Hill County Democrat* (Havre, Montana), August 20, 1926.

[26] Fort Benton *Record*, August 7, 1875.

[27] *Ibid.*, September 4, 11, 1875, November 13, 1875.

[28] Taylor to William Pound, March 20, 1876; Taylor to N. P. Langford, February 28, 1876, in Taylor Letterbooks, Minnesota Historical Society; N. P. Langford to Martin Maginnis, March 11, 1876, Maginnis Papers, Historical Society of Montana Library.

[29] "Report of a Committee of the Privy Council," approved by the governor general of Canada, December 17, 1875.

[30] Consular Dispatch 239, State Department to Taylor, April 25, 1876. "The trial should not take place without giving the prisoners the benefit of the testimony which is ready to be produced."

[31] Consular Dispatch 239, Taylor to State Department, June 8, 1876.

[32] Taylor to McKay, May 23, 1876. Taylor Letterbooks, Minnesota Historical Society; Winnipeg *Free Press*, June 24, 1876.

[33] Telegram in Dispatch 241, Taylor to Cadwalader, August 1, 1876.

[34] Consular Dispatch 241, Taylor to Fish, August 1, 1876.

[35] Telegram in Dispatch 241, Taylor to Cadwalader, August 1, 1876.

[36] J. W. Horan, *West No'West, A History of Alberta* (Edmonton, 1945), 24.

[37] Taylor to J. H. Evans, March 20, 1882, Taylor Letterbooks, Minnesota Historical Society.

WHOOP-UP COUNTRY

Chapter 5

[1] William F. Butler, *Great Lone Land*, 378–79. John P. Turner, *North-West Mounted Police, 1873–1893*, Vol. I, provides a detailed background for much of the material in this chapter. Unfortunately, Mr. Turner's failure to cite his authority for many statements and his absence of sources in American archives renders his study of limited value to the serious student.

[2] Royal Canadian Mounted Police, File 516-4, A. Campbell to Lieutenant Governor Morris, August 12, 1873.

[3] Quoted in Cecil Denny, *Law Marches West*, 4.

[4] R.C.M.P., Files, Orders in Council, Vol. I, Department of Justice Memorandum, May 11, 1875: ". . . but it was otherwise in respect of some portion of the stores, in consequence of which the start of the Mounted Police expedition to the Rocky Mountains was much delayed." Among other things, 330 Adams revolvers were found to be "practically useless." Officials concluded that these "never belonged to the Imperial stores."

[5] R.C.M.P., File 51-75, A. G. French to Minister of Justice, February 15, 1875.

[6] Denny, *Law Marches West*, 12.

[7] Denny, *Riders of the Plains*, 16, 34.

[8] *Report of the Commissioner*, Northwest Mounted Police, 1874, 15ff.

[9] *Ibid.*

[10] John McDougall, *On Western Trails*, 222–23.

[11] Denny, *Law Marches West*, 52.

[12] R.C.M.P., File 115-75, J. F. Macleod to A. G. French, February 2, 1875.

[13] *Fort Benton Record*, February 15, 1875.

[14] *Ibid.*, March 15, 1875.

[15] R.C.M.P., File 94-75, January 22, 1875.

[16] Canada, *Sessional Papers*, No. 10, 1878 (Ottawa, 1879), Special Appendix E, xiii.

[17] R.C.M.P., File 51-75. A. G. French to Minister of Justice, February 15, 1875.

[18] Alexander Sutherland, *A Summer in Prairie Land*, 52.

[19] R.C.M.P., File 516-4.

[20] R.C.M.P., File, Diary of Constable R. N. Wilson, July 25, 1883.

[21] *Fort Benton Record*, June 1, 1875.

[22] Toronto *Mail*, July 22, 1877, quoted in *Fort Benton Record*, September 7, 1877.

[23] Louis Riel to J. W. Taylor, October 1, 1884, Taylor Papers, Minnesota Historical Society.

[24] Walter P. Webb, *The Great Plains* (New York, 1931), 8.

[25] *Fort Benton Record*, November 23, 1877.

[26] R. Burton Deane, *Mounted Police Life in Canada* (New York, 1916), 2.

[27] Frederick White to John A. Macdonald, August 19, 1881, Macdonald Papers, Public Archives of Canada.

[28] Richard Knötel, *Handbuch der Uniformkunde; die militärische Tracht in ihrer Entwicklung bis zur Gegenwart* (Hamburg, 1937), 2.

[29] R.C.M.P., File 51-75, Memorandum, no date.

[30] *Fort Benton Record*, June 8, 1877.

[31] A. L. Haydon, *Riders of the Plains: Adventures and Romance with the North-West Mounted Police* (Chicago, 1910), 85.

[32] Canada, *Sessional Papers*, No. 18, Pt. III, 1882, 10.

NOTES

[33] E. B. Dewdney to Macdonald, February 24, 1883, "Memorandum Re: Colonel Norman Macleod" (italics are Dewdney's), Macdonald Papers, Public Archives of Canada.

[34] Canada, *Sessional Papers*, No. 3, Pt. II, 1881, 6.

[35] *Ibid.*, No. 28, 1888, 9.

[36] Fort Benton *Record*, April 13, 1877.

Chapter 6

[1] William Shepherd, *Prairie Experiences in Handling Cattle and Sheep* (New York, 1885), 181.

[2] Montague Davenport, *Under the Gridiron, A Summer in the United States and the Far West, Including a Run through Canada* (London, 1876), 53.

[3] Fort Macleod *Gazette*, November 4, 1882.

[4] Fort Benton *River Press*, August 17, 1881.

[5] Bernard De Voto, *Across the Wide Missouri* (New York, 1947), 300.

[6] James F. Macleod to W. F. Sanders, August 10, 1877, in W. F. Sanders Papers, Historical Society of Montana Library.

[7] Fort Benton *Record*, June 22, 1877.

[8] A.G.O. records, National Archives, Annual Report, District of Montana, to A.A.G., August 26, 1875; Fort Benton *Record*, May 1, 1875.

[9] H. V. A. Ferguson, "Fort Benton Memories," manuscript in Montana Historical Society Library; Helena *Weekly Herald*, August 27, 1868; Montana *Post*, August 28, 1868.

[10] Charles M. MacInnes, *In the Shadow of the Rockies* (London, 1930).

[11] Fort Macleod *Gazette*, October 14, 1882.

[12] Fort Benton *River Press*, November 30, 1881; Fort Benton *Record*, June 22, 1877.

[13] H. V. A. Ferguson, "Fort Benton Memories."

[14] Fort Benton *Record*, May 1, 1875.

[15] John J. Healy to Martin Maginnis, August 4, 1876, in Maginnis Papers, Historical Society of Montana Library.

[16] Alexander Staveley Hill, *From Home to Home: Autumn Wanderings in the Northwest in the Years 1881, 1882, 1883, 1884* (London, 1885), 264.

[17] A.G.O. records, Capt. O. B. Read to A.A.G., Department of Dakota, March 12, 1882; Fort Benton *River Press*, May 14, 1881.

[18] Fort Benton *River Press*, November 9, 1881.

[19] *Ibid.*, June 2, 1881.

[20] *Ibid.*, April 27, 1881.

[21] Justice Court Dockets, Sunriver Crossing, Vol. I, 1870–76; Vol. II, 1876–85.

[22] A. K. McClure, "Life of John X. Beidler," Beidler Papers, Historical Society of Montana Library.

[23] W. F. Wheeler to J. X. Beidler, July 18, 1877, Beidler Papers.

[24] F. C. Deimling to W. F. Sanders, January 28, 1879, in Beidler Papers.

[25] McClure, "Life of John X. Beidler."

[26] Beidler Diary, January 25, 1889, in Beidler Papers.

[27] Beidler Diary, October 23, 1889.

[28] W. T. Sherman to Secretary of War, August 19, 1877, in New York *Herald*, October 13, 1877.

[29] New York *Herald*, May 10, 1878.

[30] Detailed studies of military policy in this region are in Merrill G. Burlingame, *The Montana Frontier* (Helena, 1942); Ray H. Mattison, "The Army

Post on the Northern Plains, 1865–1885," *Nebraska History*, XXXV, No. 1 (March 1954), 1–27; Harold L. McElroy, "Mercurial Military: A Study of the Central Montana Frontier Army Policy," *Montana Magazine of History*, IV, No. 4 (Autumn 1954), 9–23; Robert G. Athearn, "Frontier Critics of the Western Army," *Montana Magazine of History*, V, No. 2 (Spring 1955), 16–28.

[31] A.G.O. records, Annual Report, Colonel John Gibbon to A.A.G., Department of Dakota, August 3, 1874; Major Guido Ilges to A.A.G., August 6, 1874.

[32] A.G.O. records, Annual Report, General A. N. Terry to A.A.G., November 12, 1875.

[33] Through the courtesy of Lewis Brachman of Helena, Montana, a limited collection of McNight papers was made available to me. They comprise an interesting picture of the activities of this trader at Fort Shaw and his financial relations with T. C. Power.

[34] Thomas J. Bogy to J. H. McNight, January 16, 1878, McNight Papers.

[35] Major Upham to McNight, April 7, 1873, McNight Papers.

[36] Frances M. A. Roe, *Army Letters from an Officer's Wife* (New York, 1909), 280–81.

[37] A.G.O. records, U.S.A. commands, Department of Dakota, Letters Received, December 19, 1874.

[38] *Ibid.*, Annual Report, A.A.G. District of Montana to A.G., Department of Dakota, 1882, 1883, 1884.

Chapter 7

[1] Canada, *Sessional Papers*, No. 10, 1878 (Ottawa, 1879), Special Appendix E, lxvii.

[2] George F. G. Stanley, *The Birth of Western Canada: A History of the Riel Rebellion* (London, 1936), vii.

[3] "Piegan Indians," House of Representatives, Executive Document No. 269, 41st Congress, 2nd Session (Washington, D.C., 1870), 10, Serial 1426.

[4] John Macoun, *Manitoba and the Great North-West* (Guelph, 1882), 551.

[5] Public Archives of Canada, Macdonald Papers, "Confidential Report on Industrial Schools for Indians," March 14, 1879, 9.

[6] William F. Butler, *Great Lone Land* (London, 1873), 242.

[7] William Black, *Green Pastures and Piccadilly* (New York, 1878), 365.

[8] Hiram M. Chittenden and Alfred T. Richardson, *Life, Letters and Travels of Father Pierre-Jean De Smet, S.J., 1801–1873*, 4 vols. (New York, 1905), I, 125; L. B. Palladino, *Indian and White in the Northwest: A History of Catholicity* (Baltimore, 1894), 331–34.

[9] John Palliser, *Journals*, 117; James Carnegie Southesk, *Saskatchewan and the Rocky Mountains* (Edinburgh, 1875), 154.

[10] Southesk, *Saskatchewan and the Rocky Mountains*, 167.

[11] John McDougall, *On Western Trails in the Early Seventies: Frontier Life in the Canadian North-West* (Toronto, 1911), 219. Much of the material on Protestant missions also comes from McDougall's other books: *In the Days of the Red River Settlement* (Toronto, 1903); *Forest, Lake and Prairie* (Toronto, 1895); *Pathfinding on Plain and Prairie* (Toronto, 1898); *Saddle, Sled and Snowshoe* (Cincinnati, 1896). John Maclean, *McDougall of Alberta* (Toronto, 1927), is a brief biography.

[12] Fort Benton *Record*, May 15, 1875, letter to the editor from Jack Blount.

[13] McDougall, *On Western Trails*, 11, 199, 212–13, 223.

NOTES

[14] William Newton, *Twenty Years on the Saskatchewan* (London, 1897), 16, 42.

[15] McDougall, *On Western Trails*, 171, 38.

[16] Minutes of the Rocky Mountain Conference of the Methodist Episcopal Church, 1873–86, Historical Society of Montana Library; *Area Messenger*, January 15, 1920, 5. Brief biographies of William Wesley Van Orsdel are Stella W. Brummitt, *Brother Van* (New York, 1919); George Mecklenburg, *The Last of the Old West*, Chapters XIV–XV; Alson Jesse Smith, *Brother Van: A Biography of the Reverend William Wesley Van Orsdel* (Nashville, 1943).

[17] Butler, *Great Lone Land*, 360–61. See also Southesk, *Saskatchewan and the Rocky Mountains*, 331; Macoun, *Manitoba and the Great North-West*, 532; Edward Laird Mills, *Plains, Peaks and Pioneers* (Portland, Oregon, 1947), 211.

[18] Southesk, *Saskatchewan and the Rocky Mountains*, 328; Fort Benton *River Press*, August 17, 1881.

[19] Palliser, *Journals*, 203.

[20] Report of the Secretary of Interior, House Executive Documents, 37th Congress, 3rd Session (Washington, D.C., 1863), 10–11, Serial 1157.

[21] Report of Agent Henry W. Reed, House Executive Documents, 37th Congress, 3rd Session (Washington, D.C., 1863), 324–25, Serial 1157.

[22] Report of Agent Gad E. Upson, House Executive Documents, 38th Congress, 2nd Session (Washington, D.C., 1865), 437–42, Serial 1220.

[23] Report of Commissioner of Indian Affairs, House Executive Documents, 38th Congress, 1st Session (Washington, D.C., 1864), 129–30, Serial 1182.

[24] Report of Agent Gad E. Upson, House Executive Documents, 38th Congress, 2nd Session (Washington, D.C., 1865), 437, Serial 1220.

[25] Robert G. Athearn, "Early Territorial Montana, A Problem in Colonial Administration," *Montana Magazine of History*, I, No. 3 (July 1951), 15–22; Athearn, "General Sherman and the Montana Frontier," *Montana Magazine of History*, III, No. 1 (January 1953), 55–64; Athearn, *Thomas Francis Meagher: An Irish Revolutionary in America* (Boulder, Colorado, 1949), 156–64.

[26] "Piegan Indians," House Executive Document No. 269, 41st Congress, 2nd Session (Washington, D.C., 1870), 23–24, 64–65, Serial 1426.

[27] T. F. Meagher to Commissioner of Indian Affairs, House Executive Documents, 39th Congress, 2nd Session (Washington, D.C., 1867), 196, Serial 1284.

[28] "Piegan Indians," House Executive Documents, No. 269, 41st Congress, 2nd Session (Washington, D.C., 1870), 24, Serial 1426.

[29] *Ibid.*, 28.

[30] *Ibid.*, 29, 40.

[31] *Ibid.*, 7.

[32] *Ibid.*, 28, 47.

[33] Butler, *Great Lone Land*, 268–69.

[34] *The New North West* (Deer Lodge, Montana), September 21, 1877.

[35] Summaries of American Indian policy are George W. Manypenny, *Our Indian Wards* (Cincinnati, 1880); L. F. Schmeckebier, *The Office of Indian Affairs, Its History, Activities and Organization* (Baltimore, 1927); Richard M. Utley, "The Celebrated Peace Policy of General Grant," *North Dakota History*, XX, No. 3 (July 1953), 121–42.

[36] Report of the Commissioner of Indian Affairs, House Executive Documents, 41st Congress, 2nd Session (Washington, D.C., 1870), 445–47, Serial 1414.

[37] McDougall, *On Western Trails*, 143.

[38] Fort Benton *Record*, February 1, 1875. See also Report of Commissioner of

Indian Affairs, House Executive Documents, 39th Congress, 2nd Session (Washington, D.C., 1866), 16, Serial 1284.

[39] A.G.O. records, National Archives, Annual Report, Department of Dakota to A.A.G., October 4, 1878.

[40] Minutes of Rocky Mountain Conference of Methodist Episcopal Church, 1876, 17.

[41] J. H. D. Street to Martin Maginnis, February 5, 1875, Maginnis Papers, Montana Historical Society Library, Helena.

[42] Fort Benton Record, February 1, 1875.

[43] Ibid., April 12, 1878.

[44] R. F. May to Maginnis, May 25, 1874, Maginnis Papers.

[45] C. A. Broadwater to Maginnis, December 6, 1881, Maginnis Papers.

[46] Fort Benton Record, March 1, 1878.

[47] Ibid., July 19, 1878.

[48] A.G.O. records, National Archives, Annual Report, District of Montana to A.A.G., September 21, 1881; P.A.C., Macdonald Papers, E. T. Galt to D. L. MacPherson, July 14, 1881.

[49] P.A.C., G 21 series, No. 2001, V. 4, Frelinghuysen to Sackville West, March 29, 1882.

[50] Ibid., Dewdney to MacPherson, July 4, 1881; Dewdney to Macdonald, October 3, 1880.

[51] Ibid., Frelinghuysen to Sackville West, April 17, 1883.

Chapter 8

[1] Fort Benton Record, December 15, 1876.

[2] U.S. War Department, Surgeon General's Office, Circular No. 4, "Report on Barracks and Hospitals with Descriptions of Military Posts" (Washington, D.C., 1870); Fort Benton Record, February 1, 1875.

[3] Fort Benton Record, May 1, 1875.

[4] Ibid., September 24, 1880.

[5] Montana and the Northwest Territory (Chicago, 1879), 45.

[6] H. V. A. Ferguson, "Fort Benton Memories," manuscript in Historical Society of Montana Library.

[7] Fort Benton Record, January 26, 1877.

[8] S. T. Hauser to Martin Maginnis, March 19, 1882, in Maginnis Papers, Historical Society of Montana Library.

[9] Fort Benton Record, August 10, 1882.

[10] Warranty Deeds, Books F and G, Fort Benton, 1883, 1884.

[11] Fort Benton Record, November 3, 1876.

[12] Montana Christian Advocate (Helena and Butte), March 1884.

[13] Al. Noyes, "Story as Told by S. C. Ashby," manuscript in Historical Society of Montana Library, Helena.

[14] Flora Gardner to D. M. Vinsonhaler, June 11, 1879, Historical Society of Montana Library.

[15] Bozeman, Avant Courier, July 24, 1874.

[16] Alexander Sutherland, A Summer in Prairie-Land, Notes of a Tour Throughout the North-West Territory (Toronto, 1881).

[17] Fort Benton Record, July 28, 1876.

[18] Ibid., July 24, 1875.

[19] John D. Higinbotham, When the West Was Young (Toronto, 1933), 89.

NOTES

[20] Mrs. Robert Fisk to Mrs. Isaac Chester, July 1867, Fisk Papers, Historical Society of Montana Library.

[21] John R. Craig, *Ranching with Lords and Commons* (Toronto, 1903), 71; C. E. D. Wood in Fort Macleod *Gazette*, May 4, 1883.

[22] William Shepherd, *Prairie Experiences in Handling Cattle and Sheep* (London, 1884), 78.

[23] *Ibid.*, 77.

[24] William H. Russell, *Hesperothen: Notes from the West, A Record of a Ramble in the United States and Canada in the Spring and Summer of 1881* (London, 1882), 168.

[25] John M. Murphy, *Rambles in North-Western America* (London, 1879), 208.

[26] *The Good Templar*, April 5, 1873.

[27] Craig, *Ranching with Lords and Commons*, 75.

[28] Fort Benton *River Press*, December 28, 1881.

[29] *Ibid.*, November 10, 1877.

[30] Chester McArthur Destler (editor), "Diary of a Journey into the Valleys of the Red River of the North and the Upper Missouri," *Mississippi Valley Historical Review*, XXXIII, No. 3 (December 1946), 425–42.

[31] Fort Benton *River Press*, October 27, 1886.

[32] Peter O'Leary, *Travels and Experiences in Canada, the Red River Territory and the United States* (London, 1875), 154.

Chapter 9

[1] Fort Benton *Record*, August 21, 1875.

[2] John D. Higinbotham, *When the West Was Young: Historical Reminiscences of the Early Canadian West* (Toronto, 1933), 73.

[3] Horace Greeley, "The Plains as I Crossed Them Ten Years Ago," *Harper's Magazine*, XXXVIII, No. 228 (May 1869), 195.

[4] Calgary *Daily Herald*, October 13, 1923. Quoted in Charles M. MacInnes, *In the Shadow of the Rockies*, 179.

[5] Fort Macleod *Gazette*, July 29, 1882.

[6] Manton Marble, "Red River and Beyond," *Harper's Magazine*, XXI, No. 112 (August 1860), 298.

[7] Fort Macleod *Gazette*, July 29, 1882.

[8] John Mortimer Murphy, *Rambles in North-Western America from the Pacific Ocean to the Rocky Mountains* (London, 1879), 197.

[9] Higinbotham, *When the West Was Young*, 209–10.

[10] *Yellowstone Journal* (Miles City, Montana) November 26, 1881.

[11] Fort Benton *Record*, June 16, 1876.

[12] Higinbotham, *When the West Was Young*, 197.

[13] Alexander Sutherland, *A Summer in Prairie-Land: Notes of a Tour Throughout the North-West Territory* (Toronto, 1881).

[14] Alexander Staveley Hill, *From Home to Home: Autumn Wanderings in the Northwest in the Years 1881, 1882, 1883, 1884* (London, 1885), 214.

[15] Canada, *Sessional Papers*, No. 4, 1880, "Report of Superintendent Winder" (Ottawa, 1881), 9.

[16] Fort Macleod *Gazette*, November 14, 1882.

[17] William Pearce, "Whiskey and Fur Traders in Southern Alberta," manuscript in Provincial Library of Alberta.

[18] Fort Macleod *Gazette*, June 4, 1883.

[19] Fort Benton *Record*, October 5, 1877.

Chapter 10

[1] Montague Davenport, *Under the Gridiron* (London, 1876), 138.

[2] *Ibid.*

[3] William Shepherd, *Prairie Experiences in Handling Cattle and Sheep* (London, 1884), 93.

[4] William F. Butler, *Great Lone Land* (London, 1873), 16, 380.

[5] William G. Conrad, "Business of Early Days at Fort Benton," Great Falls *Tribune*, December 16, 1906.

[6] Robert Vaughn, *Then and Now, or Thirty-Six Years in the Rockies* (Minneapolis, 1900), 242.

[7] Fort Benton *Record*, June 1, 1875.

[8] *Ibid.*, March 6, 1878.

[9] Harrison A. Trexler, *Missouri-Montana Highways* (Columbia, Missouri, 1918), 8.

[10] William Miller, *Men in Business* (Cambridge, 1952). See Chapter 7, Gregory and Neu, "American Industrial Elite in the 1870's, Their Social Origins," 193–211.

[11] H. A. Kennerly to Martin Maginnis, March 3, 1874, Maginnis Papers, Montana State Historical Society Library, Helena.

[12] Fort Benton *Record*, September 8, 1876.

[13] Through the generosity of the late Everett E. Edwards I have in my possession a limited collection of business records and government documents of the Baker and Power companies. Mr. Edwards, whose wide range of interests was matched by his unfailing generosity to fellow historians, collected the papers over a period of years. In this collection are several permits from the Office of Indian Affairs for Indian trading, including arms and ammunition.

[14] John J. Healy to Maginnis, August 4, 1876, Maginnis Papers, Historical Society of Montana Library.

[15] Fort Benton *Record*, May 12, 1876.

[16] Senate Executive Document No. 8, 41st Congress, 3rd Session, "Army Posts, Dept. Of Dakota," 7, Serial 1440.

[17] Fort Benton *Record*, May 5, 1876.

[18] T. C. Power to Maginnis, no date, but apparently written early in 1875, Maginnis Papers.

[19] John J. Healy to Maginnis, February 16, 1875, Maginnis Papers.

[20] I. G. Baker to Maginnis, February 7, 1874; J. J. Healy to Maginnis, February 16, 1875; T. C. Power to Maginnis, October 10, 1877, in Maginnis Papers.

[21] Power to Maginnis, October 10, 1877, Maginnis Papers.

[22] *Ibid.*, C. A. Broadwater to Maginnis, August 23, 1880.

[23] W. G. Conrad to S. T. Hauser, February 12, 1882; February 20, 1882, in S. T. Hauser Papers, Historical Society of Montana Library.

[24] Canada, Parliament, *Sessional Papers*, No. 70, 1880, 4.

[25] *Ibid.*, No. 188, 1879, 32, 130; *ibid.*, No. 1, 1881, "Comparative Statement of Receipts and Expenditures of Canada."

[26] Al. Noyes, "Story as Told by S. C. Ashby," manuscript in Historical Society of Montana Library.

[27] Canada, Parliament, *Sessional Papers*, No. 18, Part III, 1882, 13.

[28] "The Canadian element of this community [Fort Macleod] can't convince themselves that I. G. Baker & Co. have got the contracts. They think it can't be possible" (J. J. Healy in Fort Benton *Record*, April 13, 1882).

NOTES

²⁹ Petition to Congress, 1868, James W. Taylor Papers, Minnesota Historical Society.

³⁰ George M. Grant, *Ocean to Ocean: Sanford Fleming's Expedition through Canada in 1872* (Toronto, 1873), 181.

³¹ The Fort Benton *Record* and *River Press* published weekly summaries of shipments to British North America.

³² Public Archives of Canada, Macdonald Papers, A. T. Galt to Macdonald, July 18, 1883; August 10, 1883.

³³ Fort Benton *Record*, November 20, 1875.

³⁴ *Ibid.*, November 9, 1882.

³⁵ *Ibid.*, March 30, 1882.

³⁶ A. M. Woolfolk, *Helena and Benton Railroad* (Helena, 1876), 46–48; Fort Benton *Record*, October 6, 1876.

³⁷ Northern Pacific Railway, *Report of the President, 1882,* 27.

³⁸ Fort Benton *Record*, April 6, 1882.

³⁹ W. G. Conrad to S. T. Hauser, May 12, 1881, S. T. Hauser Papers, Historical Society of Montana Library.

⁴⁰ William Laurie, *Battle River Valley* (Battleford, Saskatchewan, 1883), 20.

⁴¹ T. C. Power business records in my possession.

⁴² Fort Benton *Record*, February 26, 1876.

⁴³ W. G. Conrad to S. T. Hauser, August 11, 1882, S. T. Hauser Papers.

⁴⁴ Fort Macleod *Gazette*, August 14, 1882; Fort Benton *Record*, December 22, 1881.

⁴⁵ John D. Higinbotham, *When the West Was Young* (Toronto, 1933), 83.

⁴⁶ W. G. Conrad, "Business of Early Days."

Chapter 11

¹ Robert Vaughn, *Then and Now, or Thirty-Six Years in the Rockies* (Minneapolis, 1900), 66; *Rocky Mountain Husbandman*, March 2, 16, 1882; Helena Weekly *Herald*, June 12, 1873; J. Choate to J. H. McNight, April 27, 1876. The McNight Papers are in the possession of Lewis Brachman, Helena.

² Flora Gardner to Mr. and Mrs. D. M. Vinsonhaler, June 11, 1879, Historical Society of Montana Library.

³ Fort Benton *River Press*, November 17, 1880.

⁴ John Hunsberger to J. H. McNight, February 6, 1876, McNight Papers.

⁵ David Hilger, "Early Wool History," Lewiston *Democrat*, August 15, 1902; *Rocky Mountain Husbandman*, March 2, 1882; *Montana Stock and Mining Journal*, September 1884, 82; *ibid.*, October 1884, 88.

⁶ Hilger, "Early Wool History."

⁷ Carston Conrad Kohrs, "Autobiography," typed manuscript in Historical Society of Montana Library.

⁸ Ernest S. Osgood, *Day of the Cattleman* (Minneapolis, 1929), is the standard account of this era of Montana's development. L. V. Kelly, *The Range Men: The Story of the Ranchers and Indians of Alberta* (Toronto, 1913), is an inadequate survey of the Canadian industry.

⁹ Fort Benton *Record*, June 14, 1878.

¹⁰ *Ibid.*, April 27, 1882.

¹¹ *Montana Stock and Mining Journal*, December 1884, 128.

¹² *Ibid.*, November 1884, 110.

¹³ *Ibid.*, December 1884, 128.

¹⁴ W. G. Conrad, "Business of Early Days at Fort Benton," Great Falls

Tribune, December 16, 1906; "Re-incorporating the Circle," Fort Benton *River Press*, June 2, 1943.

[15] Granville Stuart to Stuart, Kohrs and Co., December 31, 1883, S. T. Hauser Papers, Historical Society of Montana Library.

[16] Kohrs, "Autobiography"; Fort Benton *Record*, July 13, 1882, June 16, 1883; Fort Benton *River Press*, December 28, 1881; *Montana Livestock Journal*, July 1885.

[17] John R. Craig, *Ranching with Lords and Commons: or Twenty Years on the Range* (Toronto, 1903), 88.

[18] Alexander Staveley Hill, *From Home to Home: Autumn Wanderings in the Northwest in the Years 1881, 1882, 1883, 1884* (London, 1885), 23.

[19] Canada, *Sessional Papers*, No. 153, 1885 (Ottawa, 1886), "Report of Commissioner of North West Mounted Police to J. A. Macdonald," 15.

[20] John Macoun, *Manitoba and the Great North-West* (Guelph, 1882), 269-72, 281.

[21] Fort Macleod *Gazette*, August 14, 1882.

[22] *Ibid.*, September 23, 1882.

[23] Public Archives of Canada, Macdonald Papers, Note on letter E. B. Dewdney to Macdonald, June 28, 1883.

[24] *Ibid.*, William Carter to Macdonald, March 2, 1886.

[25] Fort Macleod *Gazette*, September 4, 1882.

[26] Kohrs, "Autobiography."

[27] Canada, *Sessional Papers*, No. 15, 1898 (Ottawa, 1899), 4; L. G. Thomas, "The Ranching Period in Southern Alberta" (M.A. Thesis, University of Alberta, 1935), 27-28.

[28] Thomas, "Ranching Period in Southern Alberta," 171, 137.

[29] John D. Higinbotham, *When the West Was Young: Historical Reminiscences of the Early Canadian West* (Toronto, 1933), 203.

[30] P.A.C., Macdonald Papers, Dewdney to Macdonald, September 15, 1879.

[31] Fort Benton *Record*, July 20, 1882.

[32] Canada, *Sessional Papers*, No. 18, Part III, 1882 (Ottawa, 1883), 14.

[33] P.A.C., Macdonald Papers, Dewdney to MacPherson, July 4, 1881.

[34] Fort Benton *Record*, February 2, 1882.

[35] Fort Macleod *Gazette*, May 14, 1883; July 14, 1883; June 23, 1883.

[36] Fort Benton *Record*, August 4, 18, 1881, September 15, 1881; Fort Benton *River Press*, October 5, 1881, November 30, 1881.

[37] Fort Macleod *Gazette*, April 24, 1883, May 24, 1883.

[38] Macoun, *Manitoba and the Great North-West*, 144.

[39] A.G.O. records, National Archives, Annual Report, Department of Dakota to A.A.G., General John Gibbon to General Philip Sheridan, October 4, 1878.

Chapter 12

[1] A.G.O. records, National Archives, Annual Report, Department of Dakota to Assistant Adjutant General, November 12, 1877.

[2] Public Archives of Canada, G 21 series, No. 2001, v. 3, H. Richardson to A. G. Irvine, May 26, 1876; Irvine to Richardson, July 1, 1876.

[3] Fort Benton *Record*, October 13, 1876.

[4] P.A.C., G 21 series, No. 2001, v. 3. "Affidavit of Gabriel Solomon," August 18, 1876.

[5] P.A.C., G 21 series, No. 2001, v. 3, J. M. Walsh to R. W. Scott, September 29, 1876.

NOTES

⁶ A.G.O. records, National Archives, Annual Report, Department of Dakota to A.A.G., November 21, 1876.

⁷ P.A.C., G 21 series, No. 2001, v. 3, Walsh to Macleod, December 31, 1876.

⁸ *Ibid.*, Walsh to Irvine, March 15, 1876.

⁹ *Ibid.*, Irvine to Scott, June 6, 1877.

¹⁰ *Ibid.*, Irvine to Scott, June 6, 1877.

¹¹ *Ibid.*, "Verbatim report of council with Sitting Bull on afternoon 2 June 1877."

¹² *Ibid.*, Irvine to Scott, June 6, 1877; John Peter Turner, *North-West Mounted Police,* I, 329.

¹³ P.A.C., G 21 series, No. 2001, v. 3, Macleod to Laird, March 19, 1877.

¹⁴ *Ibid.*, Laird to Minister of Interior, March 22, 1877.

¹⁵ *Ibid.*, Macleod to Alexander Mackenzie, May 30, 1877.

¹⁶ *Ibid.*, "Report of Privy Council, June 1, 1877"; Earl of Dufferin to H. M., Chargé d'Affaires, June 2, 1877; Plunkett to Dufferin, June 7, 1877.

¹⁷ *Ibid.*, Plunkett to Earl of Derby (secret), July 24, 1877.

¹⁸ *Ibid.*, Copies of W. T. Sherman to G. W. McCrary, July 16, 1872. Seward handed this note to Plunkett on August 14, 1877.

¹⁹ Consular Dispatch 258, J. W. Taylor to F. W. Seward, July 24, 1877, General Records of the State Department, National Archives. See also Dispatch 250, Taylor to State Department.

²⁰ P.A.C., G 21 series, No. 2001, v. 3, Evarts to Plunkett, July 31, 1877. See also Governor B. F. Potts to Martin Maginnis, December 16, 1877, Maginnis Papers, Historical Society of Montana Library.

²¹ Quoted in Fort Benton *Record*, September 28, 1877.

²² P.A.C., G 21 series, No. 2001, v. 3, David Mills to Privy Council, August 23, 1877; Plunkett to Earl of Derby, August 14, 1877.

²³ *Ibid.*, Plunkett to W. B. Richards, August 11, 1877.

²⁴ *Ibid.*, Carnarvon to Dufferin, September 6, 1877.

²⁵ *Ibid.*, Report of Privy Council, October 8, 1877.

²⁶ John S. Galbraith, *The Establishment of Canadian Diplomatic Status at Washington* (Berkeley, 1951), 9–17; Lester B. Shippee, *Canadian-American Relations, 1849–1874* (New Haven, 1939).

²⁷ Confidential Memorandum [n.d. but December 1879], John A. Macdonald Papers, v. 216, P.A.C.

²⁸ Canada, *Sessional Papers*, No. 10, 1878, "Report of the Dept. of Interior, 1877" (Ottawa, 1878).

²⁹ P.A.C., G 21 series, No. 2001, v. 3, Mills to Macleod, August 20, 1877.

Chapter 13

¹ Washington *National Republican*, August 15, 1877.

² Public Archives of Canada, G 21 series, No. 2001, v. 3, Plunkett to Richards, August 25, 1877.

³ *Ibid.* (Telegram), Scott to Macleod, August 16, 1877; Mills to Macleod, August 24, 1877.

⁴ *Ibid.*, Mills to Macleod, August 24, 1877; Mills to Macleod, August 28, 1877.

⁵ *Ibid.*, Plunkett to Richards, August 25, 1877.

⁶ Washington *National Republican*, August 24, 1877.

⁷ P.A.C., G 21 series, No. 2001, v. 3, Plunkett to Richards, August 30, 1877.

⁸ *Ibid.*, Washington *National Republican*, August 30, 1877.

⁹ *Report of the Commission appointed by Direction of the President of the*

WHOOP-UP COUNTRY

United States under Instructions of the Honorables the Secretary of War and the Secretary of the Interior, to meet the Sioux Chief, Sitting Bull (Washington, D.C., 1877). Hereafter cited as *Report of Sitting Bull Commission.*

[10] New York *Herald*, October 17, 1877.

[11] A.G.O. records, National Archives, Annual Report, Department of Dakota to A.A.G., November 12, 1877; Miles to Terry, October 3, 1877.

[12] P.A.C., G 21 series, No. 2001, v. 3, Macleod to Mills, October 27, 1877.

[13] New York *Herald*, October 22, 1877.

[14] Verbatim reports of the conference can be found in both Canadian and American sources. They are in substantial agreement save for minor stenographic differences. *Report of Sitting Bull Commission*; P.A.C., G 21 series, No. 2001, v. 3, "Sitting Bull Commission," October 17, 1877.

[15] P.A.C., G 21 series, No. 2001, v. 3, "Memorandum of Interview with Sitting Bull and other Sioux Chiefs," October 17, 1877.

[16] *Ibid.*, Macleod to Mills, October 27, 1877.

[17] Robert Vaughn, *Then and Now, or Thirty-Six Years in the Rockies* (Minneapolis, 1900), 375.

[18] New York *Herald*, October 23, 1877.

[19] P.A.C., G 21 series, No. 2001, v. 3, Mills to Macleod, December 6, 1877.

[20] *Ibid.*, Thornton to Earl of Derby, December 17, 1877.

[21] *Ibid.*, Derby to Thornton, November 30, 1877.

[22] *Ibid.*, Documents on the Corporal Ryan case are filed with Evarts to Thornton, December 1, 1877.

[23] *Ibid.*, Macleod to Scott, January 22, 1878; Macleod to Scott, January 29, 1878; James H. Mills to Martin Maginnis, January 26, 1878, in Maginnis Papers, Historical Society of Montana Library, Helena.

[24] A.G.O. records, National Archives, Annual Report, Department of Dakota to A.A.G., October 1, 1879, Terry to Miles, June 5, 1879.

[25] Fort Benton *Record*, November 29, 1878.

[26] A.G.O. records, National Archives, Annual Report, Department of Dakota to A.A.G., October 1, 1879; Miles to Terry, July 28, 1879.

[27] John Peter Turner, *North-West Mounted Police* (Ottawa, 1950), I, 459–62.

[28] P.A.C., G 21 series, No. 2001, v. 3, Walsh to Irvine, January 25, 1879.

[29] *Ibid.*, Macdonald to Lorne, February 28, 1879.

[30] *Ibid.*, Thornton to Salisbury, March 15, 1879; Lorne to Irvine, March 28, 1879.

[31] *Ibid.*, Thornton to Salisbury, March 28, 1879.

[32] *Congressional Record*, 46th Congress, 1st Session, IX (Washington, D.C., 1879), 164.

[33] P.A.C., G 21 series, No. 2001, v. 3, Evarts to Thornton, May 27, 1879.

[34] *Ibid.*, Lorne to Hicks-Beach, April 10, 1879.

[35] *Ibid.*, "Memorandum, Sir John A, Macdonald to Privy Council of Canada," June 21, 1879.

[36] *Ibid.*, "Memorandum, A. Campbell to Governor General in Council," August 13, 1879; Abbe Martin Marty to J. S. Dennis, October 31, 1879.

[37] *Ibid.* (Confidential), Foreign Office to Colonial Office, September 29, 1879.

[38] J. B. Hubbell to Martin Maginnis, January 12, 1881, Maginnis Papers, Historical Society of Montana Library, Helena.

[39] Fort Benton *Record*, August 18, 1881.

[40] A.G.O. records, Annual Report, Department of Dakota to A.A.G., October 9, 1881; Miles to Terry, October 27, 1880.

[41] *Ibid.*, Miles to Terry, November 9, 1880.

NOTES

[42] P.A.C., Macdonald Papers, Dewdney to Macdonald, October 23, 1880.

[43] Canada, *Sessional Papers*, No. 3, Pt. II, 1881, "Report of Superintendent Walsh."

[44] P.A.C., Macdonald Papers, Dewdney to Macdonald, June 19, 1881; July 4, 1881.

[45] J. L. Legare to A. G. B. Banntyne, July 20, 1881, J. W. Taylor Papers, Minnesota Historical Society.

[46] Fort Benton *Record*, July 28, 1881.

Chapter 14

[1] St. Paul *Advertiser*, February 21, 1857.

[2] James W. Taylor to Thomas D'Arcy McGee, June 25, 1862, Taylor Papers, Minnesota Historical Society.

[3] *Congressional Globe*, 40th Congress, 2nd Session, July 1, 1868, 3660.

[4] *Ibid.*, 41st Congress, 2nd Session, April 22, 1870, 2888.

[5] St. Paul *Pioneer and Democrat*, July 19, 1859.

[6] John L. Scripps, *The Undeveloped Northern Portion of the American Continent* (Chicago, 1856), 17, 19.

[7] *Ibid.*, 19.

[8] Chicago *Daily Democratic Press*, March 17, 1856.

[9] James M. Callahan, "Americo-Canadian Relations Concerning Annexation, 1846–1871," *Indiana University Studies*, 66–68 (June, September, and December 1925), II, 185–234; Alvin C. Gluek, "The Struggle for the British Northwest: A Study in Canadian-American Relations" (Ph.D. dissertation, University of Minnesota, 1953); P. F. Sharp, "The Northern Great Plains: A Study in Canadian-American Regionalism," *Mississippi Valley Historical Review*, XXXIX, No. 1 (June 1952), 61–76; Donald F. Warner, "Drang Nach Norden: The United States and the Riel Rebellion," *ibid.*, XXXIX, No. 4 (March 1953), 693–712.

[10] St. Paul *Advertiser*, March 20, 1858.

[11] *Congressional Globe*, 41st Congress, 2nd Session, April 22, 1870, 2889.

[12] Undated clipping from the *London Spectator* in Taylor Papers, Minnesota Historical Society.

[13] *Congressional Globe*, 41st Congress, 2nd Session, April 22, 1870, 2888.

[14] J. W. Taylor to Hugh McCulloch, November 13, 1868, Taylor Papers.

[15] Joe Patterson Smith, *The Republican Expansionists of the Early Reconstruction Era* (Chicago, 1933).

[16] *Congressional Globe*, 40th Congress, 3rd Session, Appendix, 5.

[17] "Commercial Relations with British America," House Executive Documents, No. 128, 39th Congress, 1st Session (Washington, D.C., 1866), Serial 1263. See also Theodore C. Blegen, "A Plan for the Union of British North America and the United States, 1866," *Mississippi Valley Historical Review*, IV, No. 4 (March 1918), 470–483.

[18] J. W. Taylor to W. K. Rogers, May 14, 1877, Taylor Papers.

[19] *Congressional Globe*, 40th Congress, 2nd Session, 79; *ibid.*, 80.

[20] *Ibid.*, 3659.

[21] *Ibid.*, 3660.

[22] Montreal *Gazette*, March 7, 1867. Quoted by Lester B. Shippee, *Canadian-American Relations, 1849–1874* (New Haven, 1939), 196.

[23] Canada, Senate, *Parliamentary Debates*, December 17, 1867.

[24] Canada, House of Commons, *Parliamentary Debates*, December 4, 1867.

[25] Toronto *Globe*, January 25, 1858. Quoted by John Lewis, *George Brown* (Toronto, 1906), 219.

[26] Canada, House of Commons, *Parliamentary Debates*, June 8, 1866, November 8, 1867.

[27] *Ibid.*, November 7, 1867.

[28] Alexander J. Russell, *The Red River Country, Hudson's Bay and the North West Territories Considered in Relation to Canada* (Montreal, 1870), 98–99.

[29] Canada, Legislative Assembly, *Parliamentary Debates*, June 26, 1866; Edward William Watkin, *Canada and the States, Recollections, 1851–1886* (London, 1887), xi.

[30] Canada, *Sessional Papers*, No. 19, 1867–68 (Ottawa, 1869), Despatch No. 95, Secretary of State for the Colonies to the Governor General, June 17, 1865.

[31] *Ibid.*, No. 7, 1867–68 (Ottawa, 1869), "Report of a Committee of the Honorable the Executive Council, approved by H. E. the Governor General in Council, 22nd June, 1866," 13.

[32] *Ibid.*, No. 19, 1867–68 (Ottawa, 1869), Sir Edmund Head to Sir Frederic Rogers, July 17, 1866, 14.

[33] Oscar Malmros to Alexander Ramsey, January 14, 1870, Alexander Ramsey Papers, Minnesota Historical Society.

[34] Accounts of the Manitoba Rebellion are in Joseph Kinsey Howard, *Strange Empire: A Narrative of the Northwest* (New York, 1952); George F. G. Stanley, *The Birth of Western Canada: A History of the Riel Rebellion* (London, 1936).

[35] George L. Becker to J. W. Taylor, December 18, 1869, Taylor Papers, Minnesota Historical Society.

[36] A. B. Nettleton to J. W. Taylor, October 21, 1871, Taylor Papers.

[37] St. Paul *Advertiser*, February 28, 1857. Taylor's railway plans are revealed in numerous letters and articles including Taylor to Donald A. Smith, March 26, 1892; manuscript for New York *Times*, June 18, 1870; manuscript for Toronto *Globe*, May 18, 1870; Taylor to E. D. Litchfield, September 18, 1869, Taylor Papers.

[38] A. G. Archibald to J. W. Taylor, January 3, 1871, Taylor Papers.

[39] John A. Stevens, Jr., *Report of a Special Committee on the Northern Pacific Railroad*, 4–5, 12.

[40] A. B. Nettleton to J. W. Taylor, July 7, 1871, Taylor Papers.

[41] J. W. Taylor to A. B. Nettleton, November 24, 1870, Taylor Papers.

[42] Public Archives of Canada, Macdonald Papers, Alexander T. Galt to John A. Macdonald, Confidential Memorandum, January 23, 1879.

[43] Canada, *Sessional Papers*, No. 18, Pt. III, 1882 (Ottawa, 1883), 13.

[44] Fort Benton *River Press*, September 7, 1881.

[45] John Macoun, *Manitoba and the Great North-West* (Guelph, 1882), 588.

[46] Fort Benton *Record*, August 25, 1881.

[47] William R. Stewart, "The Americanization of the Canadian West," *Cosmopolitan*, XXXIV (April 1903), 603; P. F. Sharp, "When Our West Moved North," *American Historical Review*, LV, No. 2 (January 1950), 286–300.

Chapter 15

[1] Paul F. Sharp, *Agrarian Revolt in Western Canada: A Survey Showing American Parallels* (Minneapolis, 1948), 18–20, 57–60.

[2] Fort Benton *Record*, July 20, 1882; *Montana Christian Advocate*, III (June 25, 1885), 6.

[3] Fort Macleod *Gazette*, July 4, 1883.

INDEX

Big Alkali Flat, 201
Big Hole battle, 272
Biggs, S. C., 74
Billings, 226
Black, John, 228
Black, William, quoted on Indian character, 135
Black Hills, 223
Black Moon, 251
Blackfeet, 34, 127, 163, 214: origins, 22; religion, 24–25; acquire horses, 25–27; demoralized by traders, 50; effect of white settlement, 133; Christian missions among, 136; slow to accept Christianity, 141; sign treaty of *1855*, 142; depredations in *1860s*, 144; depredations investigated, 146; fate under Grant's "Peace Policy," 152; indefinite reservation boundaries, 153; starvation period of *1879*, 155
Blackfoot Agency, 143, 169
Blackfoot Crossing Treaty (Treaty Seven), 155, 222, 242
Blackfoot Sioux, 250
Blackfoot Treaty of *1855*, 142
Blackfoot Treaty of *1865*, 145
"Blackfoot War," 145
Blizzards, 18, 197
"Block P" Line, 223, 232
Blood Indians, 214: origins, 22; starvation period, *1879–81*, 241
Boulder, Montana, 114
Bow River valley cattle ranges, 235
Bozeman, John, 146
Bozeman *Avant Courier*, criticizes Sheriff John J. Healy, 118, 119
Branding, 243
British imperialism, 302
"British justice," 302
Broadwater, C. A., 129, 154
Brooke, Lionel, 241
Bross, William, 180
"Brother Van" (William Wesley Van Orsdel), 140, 141
Brown, George, 302
Brown, John, 123
Bruce, John P., 169
Buck, W. H., 132
Buffalo, 21–22, 128
Buffalo grass (*buchloe dactyloides*), 20
Buffalo hunters, 38
Buffalo Indians, 23

Buffalo robe trade, 41, 214
Building on frontier, community, 166
Bull, Charles, 230
Bulltrains, 184, 188
Bullwhackers, 189, 191, 195
Bunch grasses, 20
Butler, William F.: quoted on Great Plains environment, 11; on Indian society, 24; on Rocky Mountain House, 35; on free trader philosophy, 40; urges mounted police for Canadian West, 79; quoted on Indian character, 135; on rivalry of Christian missionaries, 141; relates false version of Baker massacre, 149–50; quoted on American business philosophy, 209
Butte, 223

Calgary, 103, 220, 224, 314
Calumet, 25
Cameron, J. H., 75
Camp Disappointment, 31
"Canada First," 302
Canadian-American boundary line, 310
Canadian Pacific Railway, 188, 227, 238, 310, 313, 314, 315
Capital requirements on frontier, 226
Carnarvon, Henry Howard Molyneux Herbert, 4th Earl of, 264
Carroll, Matthew, 168
Carroll, Steell Company, 213
Carter, William, 239
Cattle rustling, 112, 232, 244, 245
Centennial Hotel, 172
Chandler, Zachariah, 296, 298
Chesterfield House, 34
Chicago, 313
Chicago *Daily Democratic Press*, 294
Chicago *Tribune*, 298
Chief Joseph, 154, 216, 272, 273
Chinooks, 17, 165, 198
Chivington massacre, 150
Chouteau, Pierre, Jr., 213
Chouteau and Meagher County Protective Association, 244
Chouteau Club, 178, 180
Chouteau County, 227
Chouteau House, 172
Christian missions in Whoop-Up country: Catholic, 137; Protestant, 138; Methodist, 138; Presbyterian, 140; ri-

INDEX

valry of Christian sects, 141; Black-
foot apathy to, 141
Clark, George Rogers, 28
Clark, William, 18, 28, 30
Clarke, Malcolm, 146, 148
Climate of Whoop-Up country, 17ff
Clingan, E. R., 178
Coal Banks, 166, 185
Cochrane Ranch, 238
Cocking, Matthew, 27
Colonial economy of West, 210, 314
Community building on frontier, 166
Concord stagecoaches, 185, 186
Confederate raids from Canada, 296
Confederation of British North Ameri-
can provinces, 301
Conrad, Charles, 68, 88, 213
Conrad, John, 213
Conrad, William G., 68, 213: quoted on
Fort Benton's decline as a commercial
center, 228
Conrad Circle Cattle Company (Benton
and St. Louis Cattle Company), 235,
238, 240
Continentalism, 293
Cooke, Jay, 298, 307, 309
Cooper, James Fenimore, 135
Cottonwood trees, 19
Coulson, S. B., 225
County attorney, role in western law
enforcement, 112
Cow Island, 165
Cowboys, 112, 236–37, 240
Craig, John R., quoted on cowboys, 237
Crazy Horse, 248
Crees, 26, 127
Cretaceous period, 12
Crow (chief), 275
Crow Indians, 127, 136, 163
Crowfoot, 255
Crozier, L. N. F., 129, 290: undermines
Sitting Bull's authority, 291
Culbertson, Alexander, 34
Culbertson, Miss Fannie, 177
Cullen, W. E., 69, 71
Cultural life on frontier, 176ff
Custer, George A., 254
Custer's massacre, 247
Cypress Hills, 20, 245
Cypress Hills massacre, 55, 217: map, 59;
causes, 60; account of fight, 64; effects
on Canadian public opinion, 67; ar-
rests, 69; extradition hearings in Hele-
na, 69–70; Fort Benton greets wolfers,
72; trial in Winnipeg, 74; tradition in
Canada, 77; Northwest Mounted Po-
lice policy, 97

Dairy products, 230
Davenport, Montague, quoted on law-
lessness in American West, 108
Davin, Nicholas, 135
Davis, D. W., 89, 215
Dawson, Andrew, 34
"Dawson route," 304
Dearborn River, 229
Deer Lodge valley cattle ranges, 233
De Mores, Marquis, quoted on capital-
ization of cattle companies, 234
Denny, Cecil, 41, 180: describes Indian
traders, 42; describes Sioux, 83
Depression of 1857, 295
Depression of 1873, 211
Desert Land Act, 236
De Smet, Pierre-Jean, 136, 138
De Trobriand, P. R., 146, 148
Devereaux, Jeff, 58, 72
De Voto, Bernard, 109
Dewdney, Edgar B., 221, 280, 290:
quoted on presence of Canadian In-
dians south of boundary, 104; encour-
ages Canadian Indians to hunt in
United States, 155; quoted on Indian
depredations, 242; quoted on Canadian
Indian policy, 242
Diamond R Transportation Company,
184, 190, 224, 232
Donnelly, Ignatius, 293, 301
Donnelly, John J., 70, 73, 154, 168, 169,
306, 312
Droughts, 229
Dufferin, Earl of, 261, 280
Dunraven, Windham Thomas
Wyndham-Quin, 4th Earl of, 42
Duval, John, 62

Eastern Montana Stock Growers' Asso-
ciation, 245
Economic regionalism, 3, 227, 311: dis-
rupted by Canadian Pacific Railway,
313
Economy of West, colonial, 210, 314
Education on frontier, 132, 177, 205
Eighteen Mile Coulee, 201

339

INDEX

INDEX

347